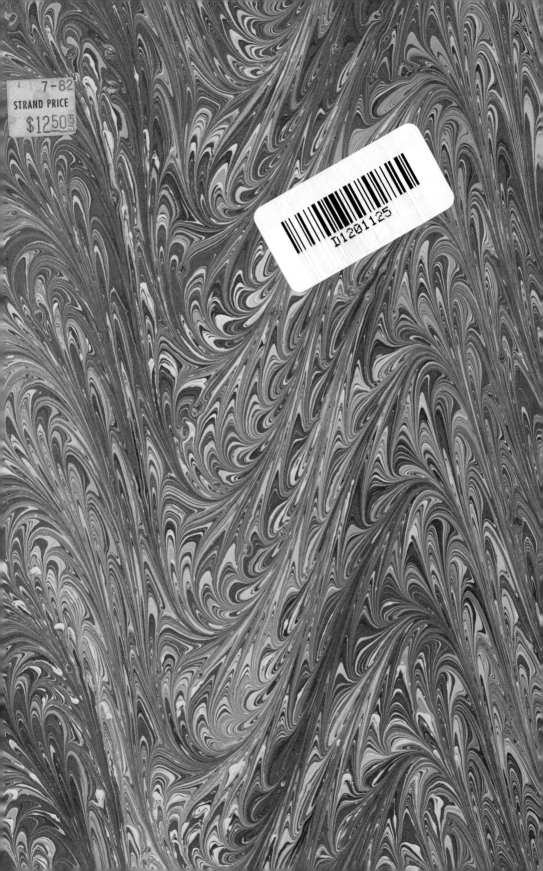

D1201125

Anton Chekhov
GREATEST PLAYS

Anton Chekhov

GREATEST PLAYS

Translated by Elisaveta Fen

ILLUSTRATED BY STAN HUNTER

THE FRANKLIN LIBRARY
Franklin Center, Pennsylvania

CONTENTS

THE CHERRY ORCHARD

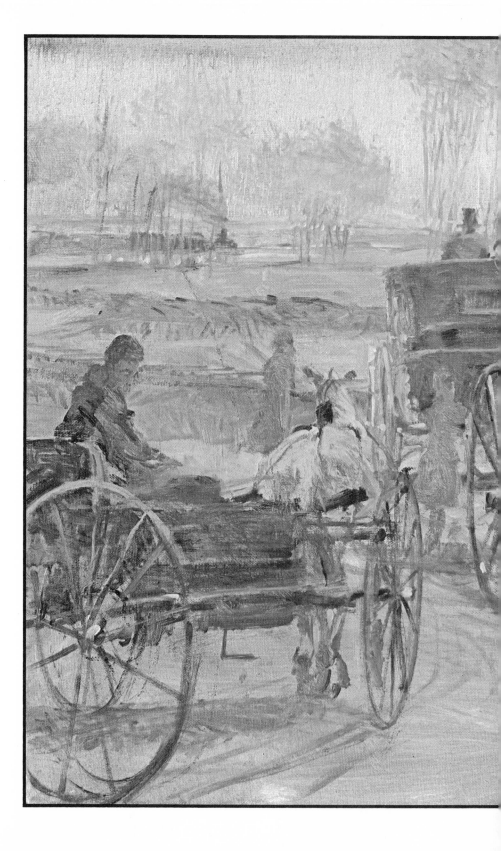

CHARACTERS

RANEVSKAYA, Lyubov Andreyevna (*Lyuba*), a landowner
ANYA (*Anichka*), her daughter, aged seventeen
VARYA (*Varvara Mikhailovna*), her adopted daughter, aged twenty-four
GAYEV, Leonid Andreyevich (*Lenya*), brother of Madame Ranevskaya
LOPAKHIN, Yermolai Alekseevich, a businessman
TROFIMOV, Pëtr Sergeevich (*Petya*), a student
SIMEONOV-PISHCHIK, Boris Borisovich, a landowner
CHARLOTTA IVANOVNA, a German governess
YEPIKHODOV, Semën Panteleyevich, a clerk on Ranevskaya's estate
DUNYASHA (*Avdotya Fëdorovna*), a parlormaid
FIRS (*Firs Nikolaevich*), a manservant, aged eighty-seven
YASHA, a young manservant
A TRAMP
STATIONMASTER
POST OFFICE CLERK
GUESTS, SERVANTS

The action takes place on the estate
of Madame Ranevskaya

ACT ONE

*A room, which used to be the children's bedroom and is still re-
ferred to as the nursery. There are several doors: one of them leads
into Anya's room. It is early morning: the sun is just coming up.
The windows of the room are shut, but through them the cherry
trees can be seen in blossom. It is May, but in the orchard there is
morning frost.*

*Enter Dunyasha, carrying a candle, and Lopakhin with a book
in his hand.*

LOPAKHIN   The train's arrived, thank God. What time is it?

DUNYASHA   It's nearly two. [*blows out the candle*] It's light already.

LOPAKHIN   How late was the train then? Two hours at least.
[*yawns and stretches*] How stupid I am! What a fool I've
made of myself! Came here on purpose to go to the station and
meet them—and then overslept! Dropped off to sleep in the
chair. Annoying. . . . I wish you'd woken me up.

DUNYASHA   I thought you'd gone. [*listens*] Sounds as if they're
coming.

LOPAKHIN   [*Also listens*] No. They'll have to get their luggage
out and all that. [*pause*] Lyubov Andreyevna has been abroad
for five years; I don't know what she's like now. She used to be
a good soul. An easygoing, simple kind of person. I remember
when I was a boy of about fifteen, my father—he had a small
shop in the village then—hit me in the face and made my nose

7

bleed. We had come to the manor for something or other, and he'd been drinking. I remember it as if it happened yesterday: Lyubov Andreyevna—she was still young and slender then—brought me in and took me to the washstand in this very room, the nursery it was then. "Don't cry, little peasant," she said, "it'll be better before you're old enough to get married." [*pause*] "Little peasant." She was right enough; my father was a peasant. Yet here I am—all dressed up in a white waistcoat and brown shoes. But you can't make a silk purse out of a sow's ear. I am rich; I've got a lot of money. But anyone can see I'm just a peasant, anyone who takes the trouble to think about me and look under my skin. [*turning over pages in the book*] I've been reading this book, and I haven't understood a word of it. I fell asleep reading it.

DUNYASHA   The dogs didn't sleep all night; they know their masters are coming.

LOPAKHIN   What's the matter, Dunyasha?

DUNYASHA   My hands are trembling. I feel as if I'm going to faint.

LOPAKHIN   You're too refined and sensitive, Dunyasha. You dress yourself up like a lady, and you do your hair like one too. That won't do you know. You must remember your place.

Enter Yepikhodov with a bunch of flowers. He wears a jacket and brightly polished high boots that squeak loudly. As he comes in, he drops the flowers

YEPIKHODOV   [*Picks up the flowers*] The gardener sent these. He says they're to go in the dining room. [*hands the flowers to Dunyasha*]

LOPAKHIN   And bring me some kvass.

DUNYASHA   Very well.

YEPIKHODOV   Outside it's about three degrees below freezing, and the cherry trees are covered with bloom. I can't approve of this climate of ours, you know. [*sighs*] No, I can't. It doesn't contribute to—to things, I mean. And do you know, Yermolai Alekseevich, I bought myself a pair of boots the day before yesterday, and they squeak so terribly. Well, I mean to say, it's utterly impossible you know. What can I put on them?

LOPAKHIN   Oh, leave me alone. You make me tired.

YEPIKHODOV   Every day something or other unpleasant happens to me. But I don't complain. I'm accustomed to it; I even laugh at it.

Enter Dunyasha; she serves Lopakhin kvass

I'll leave you now. [*bumps into a chair, which falls over*] You see! [*triumphantly*] You can see for yourself what it is, I mean to say. . . . So to speak. It's simply extraordinary! [*goes out*]

DUNYASHA   I want to tell you a secret, Yermolai Alekseevich. Yepikhodov proposed to me.

LOPAKHIN   Ah!

DUNYASHA   I don't know what to do. He's a quiet man, but sometimes he gets talking, and then you can't understand anything he says. It sounds nice; it sounds very moving, but you just can't understand it. I think I like him a little, and he's madly in love with me. He's an unlucky sort of person; something unpleasant seems to happen to him every day. That's why they tease him and call him "twenty-two misfortunes."

LOPAKHIN   [*Listens*] I think I can hear them coming.

DUNYASHA   Coming! Oh, dear! I don't know what's the matter with me. I feel cold all over.

LOPAKHIN   Yes, they really are coming! Let's go and meet them at the door. I wonder if she'll recognize me. We haven't met for five years.

DUNYASHA   [*Agitated*] I'm going to faint. . . . Oh, I'm fainting!

The sound of two coaches driving up to the house is heard. Lopakhin and Dunyasha go out quickly. The stage is empty. Then there are sounds of people arriving in the adjoining room. Firs, leaning on a stick, crosses the stage hurriedly: he has been to the station to meet Lyubov Andreyevna. He is dressed in an old-fashioned livery coat and a top hat and is muttering to himself, though it is impossible to make out what he is saying. The noises offstage become louder. A voice says, "Let's go through here." Enter Lyubov Andreyevna, Anya, and Charlotta Ivanovna leading a small dog—all in traveling clothes; Varya, wearing an overcoat and a kerchief over her head; Gayev; Simeonov-Pishchik; Lopakhin; Dunyasha, carrying a bundle and an umbrella; and other servants with luggage

ANYA   Let's go through here. You remember what room this is, Mamma?

LYUBOV ANDREYEVNA   [*Joyfully, through her tears*] The nursery!

VARYA   How cold it is! My hands are quite numb. [*to Lyubov Andreyevna*] Your rooms are just as you left them, Mamma dear, the white one and the mauve one.

LYUBOV ANDREYEVNA   The nursery, my dear, my beautiful room! I used to sleep here when I was little. [*cries*] And now I feel as if I were little again. [*she kisses her brother, then Varya, then her brother again*] And Varya is just the same as ever, looking like a nun. I recognized Dunyasha too. [*kisses Dunyasha*]

GAYEV   The train was two hours late. Just think of it! What efficiency!

CHARLOTTA   [*To Pishchik*] My dog actually eats nuts.

PISHCHIK   [*Astonished*] Fancy that!

They all go out except Anya and Dunyasha

DUNYASHA   We've waited and waited for you. [*helps Anya to take off her hat and coat*]

ANYA   I haven't slept for four nights. I'm frozen.

DUNYASHA   You went away during Lent and it was snowing and freezing then, but now it's springtime. Darling! [*she laughs and kisses her*] I could hardly bear waiting for you, my pet, my precious. But I must tell you at once, I can't wait a minute longer.

ANYA   [*Without enthusiasm*] What is it this time?

DUNYASHA   Yepikhodov, the clerk, proposed to me just after Easter.

ANYA   You never talk about anything else. [*tidies her hair*] I've lost all my hairpins. [*she is very tired and can hardly keep on her feet*]

DUNYASHA   I really don't know what to think. He loves me. He does love me so!

ANYA [*Looking through the door into her room, tenderly*] My own room, my own windows, just as if I had never been away! I'm home again! Tomorrow I'm going to get up and run straight into the garden! Oh, if only I could go to bed and sleep now! I couldn't sleep all the way back, I was so worried.

DUNYASHA Pëtr Sergeevich arrived the day before yesterday.

ANYA [*Joyfully*] Petya!

DUNYASHA He's sleeping in the bathhouse and living there too. "I wouldn't like to inconvenience them," he said. [*looks at her watch*] I ought to wake him up, but Varvara Mikhailovna told me not to. "Don't you wake him," she said.

Enter Varya with a bunch of keys at her waist

VARYA Dunyasha, make some coffee, quick! Mamma is asking for coffee.

DUNYASHA It'll be ready in a moment. [*goes out*]

VARYA Thank God you've arrived. You're home again. [*embracing her*] My darling's come back! My precious!

ANYA If you only knew the things I had to put up with!

VARYA I can just imagine it.

ANYA I left just before Easter: it was cold then. Charlotta never stopped talking, never quit doing her silly magic tricks all the way. Why did you make me take Charlotta?

VARYA But how could you go alone, darling? At seventeen!

ANYA When we arrived in Paris it was cold and snowing. My French was awful. Mamma was living on the fifth floor, and when I got there she had visitors. There were some French ladies there and an old priest with a little book; and the room was full of cigarette smoke, so untidy and uncomfortable. Suddenly I felt so sorry for Mamma, so sorry, that I took her head between my hands and just couldn't let it go. Afterward Mamma cried and was very sweet to me.

VARYA [*Tearfully*] I can hardly bear listening to you.

ANYA She had already sold her villa near Menton and she had nothing left, positively nothing. And I hadn't any money left either, not a kopeck; I had hardly enough to get to Paris. And Mamma couldn't grasp that! In station restaurants she would order the most expensive dishes and tip the waiters a ruble each. Charlotta was just the same. And Yasha expected a full-course dinner for himself: it was simply dreadful. You know, Yasha is Mamma's valet; we brought him with us.

VARYA Yes, I've seen the wretch.

ANYA Well, how are things going? Have we paid the interest?

VARYA Far from it.

ANYA Oh, dear! Oh, dear!

VARYA The estate will be up for sale in August.

ANYA Oh, dear!

LOPAKHIN [*Puts his head through the door and bleats*] Me-e-e. [*disappears*]

VARYA [*Tearfully*] I'd like to give him this. [*clenches her fist*]

ANYA [*Her arms around Varya, dropping her voice*] Varya, has he proposed to you?

Varya shakes her head

But he loves you. Why don't you talk it over with him? What are you waiting for?

VARYA I don't believe anything will come of it. He's too busy; he has no time to think of me. He pays no attention to me at all. I'd rather he didn't come; it makes me miserable to see him. Everyone's talking of our wedding. Everyone's congratulating me, but in fact there's nothing in it—it's all a kind of dream. [*in a changed tone of voice*] You've got a new brooch —a bee, isn't it?

ANYA [*Sadly*] Mamma bought it for me. [*she goes into her room and now speaks gaily, like a child*] You know, I went up in a balloon in Paris!

VARYA My darling's home again! My precious girl!

Dunyasha returns with a coffeepot and prepares coffee

[*standing by Anya's door*] You know, dearest, as I go about the house doing my odd jobs, I'm always dreaming and dreaming. If only we could marry you to some rich man, I feel my mind would be at ease. I'd go away then, first to a hermitage, then on to Kiev, to Moscow . . . walking from one holy place to another. I'd go on and on. Oh, what a beautiful life!

ANYA The birds are singing in the garden. What time is it?

VARYA   It must be past two. Time you went to bed, darling. [*goes into Anya's room*] A beautiful life!

Enter Yasha, carrying a traveling blanket and a small bag

YASHA   [*Crossing the stage, in an affectedly genteel voice*] May I go through here?

DUNYASHA   I can hardly recognize you, Yasha. You've changed so abroad.

YASHA   Hm! And who are you?

DUNYASHA   When you left here, I was no bigger than this. [*shows her height from the floor with her hand*] I'm Dunyasha, Fëdor Kozoyedov's daughter. You can't remember!

YASHA   Hm! Quite a little peach! [*looks around, puts his arms around her. She cries out and drops a saucer. Yasha goes out quickly*]

VARYA   [*In the doorway, angrily*] What's going on here?

DUNYASHA   [*Tearfully*] I've broken a saucer.

VARYA   That's a good omen.

ANYA   [*Coming out of her room*] We ought to warn Mamma that Petya is here.

VARYA   I gave orders not to wake him.

ANYA   [*Pensively*] It was six years ago that Father died, and then, only a month after that, little brother Grisha was drowned in the river. He was only seven, such a pretty little boy! Mamma couldn't bear it and went away. She never looked back. [*shivers*] How well I understand her! If she only knew how I understand her! [*pause*] And, of course, Petya Trofimov was Grisha's tutor; he might remind her . . .

Enter Firs, wearing a jacket and a white waistcoat

FIRS   [*Goes to the coffeepot, preoccupied*] Madam will have her coffee here. [*puts on white gloves*] Is the coffee ready? [*to Dunyasha, severely*] What about the cream?

DUNYASHA   Oh, my goodness! [*goes out quickly*]

FIRS   [*Fussing around the coffeepot*] The girl's daft. [*mutters*] From Paris . . . The master used to go to Paris years ago. . . . Used to go by coach. [*laughs*]

VARYA Firs, what are you laughing at?

FIRS What can I get you, madam? [*happily*] The mistress is home again! Home at last! I don't mind if I die now. [*weeps with joy*]

Enter Lyubov Andreyevna, Lopakhin, Gayev, and Simeonov-Pishchik, the last wearing a long peasant coat of finely woven cloth and wide trousers tucked inside high boots. Gayev, as he comes in, moves his arms and body as if he were playing billiards

LYUBOV ANDREYEVNA How does it go now? Let me think. . . . I sink the red. I go in off into the middle pocket!

GAYEV I put mine into the corner pocket! . . . Years ago you and I slept in this room, little brother and sister together; and now I'm fifty-one, strange as it may seem.

LOPAKHIN Yes, time flies.

GAYEV What?

LOPAKHIN Time flies, I say.

GAYEV This place smells of patchouli.

ANYA I think I'll go to bed. Good night, Mamma. [*kisses her*]

LYUBOV ANDREYEVNA My precious child! [*kisses her hands*] You're glad to be home, aren't you? I still feel dazed.

ANYA Good night, Uncle.

GAYEV [*Kisses her face and hands*] God bless you. How like your mother you are! [*to his sister*] You looked exactly like her at her age, Lyuba.

Anya shakes hands with Lopakhin and Pishchik, goes out and shuts the door after her

LYUBOV ANDREYEVNA She's very tired.

PISHCHIK It's a long journey.

VARYA [*To Lopakhin and Pishchik*] Well, gentlemen? It's past two; time to break up the party.

LYUBOV ANDREYEVNA [*Laughs*] You're just the same, Varya. [*draws Varya to her and kisses her*] Let me have some coffee; then we'll all go.

Firs places a cushion under her feet

Thank you, my dear. I've gotten into the habit of drinking coffee. I drink it day and night. Thank you, my dear old friend. [*kisses Firs*]

VARYA I'd better see if all the luggage is there. [*goes out*]

LYUBOV ANDREYEVNA Is it really me sitting here? [*laughs*] I feel like dancing and flinging my arms around. [*hides her face in her hands*] What if I'm just dreaming? God, how I love my own country! I love it so much. I could hardly see it from the train; I was crying all the time. [*through tears*] However, I must drink my coffee. Thank you, Firs, thank you, my dear old friend. I am so glad I found you still alive.

FIRS The day before yesterday.

GAYEV He doesn't hear very well.

LOPAKHIN I've got to leave for Kharkov soon after four. What a nuisance! I'd like to have a good look at you, to have a talk. You look as lovely as ever.

PISHCHIK [*Breathing heavily*] She looks prettier. In her Parisian clothes . . . enough to turn anybody's head!

LOPAKHIN Your brother here, Leonid Andreyevich, says that I'm a country bumpkin, a tightfisted peasant, but I don't pay any attention to that. Let him say what he likes. The only thing I want is for you to have faith in me as you did before. Merciful God! My father was your father's serf and your grandfather's too, but you did so much for me in the past that I forget everything and love you as if you were my own sister . . . more than my own sister.

LYUBOV ANDREYEVNA I just can't sit still! I simply can't! [*she jumps up and walks around the room in great agitation*] This happiness is too much for me. You can laugh at me; I'm foolish. My dear bookcase! [*kisses bookcase*] My own little table!

GAYEV You know, old Nanny died while you were away.

LYUBOV ANDREYEVNA [*Sits down and drinks coffee*] Yes, I know. May the Kingdom of Heaven be hers. They wrote to tell me.

GAYEV Anastasi died too. Petrushka Kosoi has left me and is working for the police in town. [*takes a box of boiled sweets from his pocket and puts one in his mouth*]

PISHCHIK   My daughter, Dashenka, sends her greetings to you.

LOPAKHIN   I feel I'd like to tell you something nice, something jolly. [*glances at his watch*] I'll have to go in a moment; there's no time to talk. However, I could tell you in a few words. You know, of course, that your cherry orchard is going to be sold to pay your debts. The auction is to take place on the twenty-second of August, but there's no need for you to worry. You can sleep in peace, my dear; there's a way out. This is my plan. Please listen carefully. Your estate is only twenty miles from town, and the railway line is not far away. Now if your cherry orchard and the land along the river are divided into plots and leased out for summer residences, you'll have a yearly income of at least twenty-five thousand rubles.

GAYEV   But what nonsense!

LYUBOV ANDREYEVNA   I don't quite understand you, Yermolai Alekseevich.

LOPAKHIN   You'll charge the tenants at least twenty-five rubles a year for a plot of one acre, and if you advertise now, I'm prepared to stake any amount you like that you won't have a spot of land unoccupied by the autumn; it will be snatched up. In fact I really feel I must congratulate you; you're saved after all! It's a marvelous location and the river's deep enough for bathing. But, of course, the place will have to be cleaned up, put in order. For instance all the old outbuildings will have to be pulled down, as well as this house, which is no good to anybody. The old cherry orchard would be cut down too.

LYUBOV ANDREYEVNA   Cut down? My dear man, forgive me, you don't seem to understand. If there's one thing interesting, one thing really outstanding, in the whole county, it's our cherry orchard.

LOPAKHIN   The only outstanding thing about this orchard is that it's very large. It only produces a crop every other year, and then there's nobody to buy it.

GAYEV   This orchard is actually mentioned in the encyclopedia.

LOPAKHIN   [*Glancing at his watch*] If you can't think clearly about it or come to a decision, the cherry orchard and the whole estate as well will be sold by auction. You must decide! There's no other way out, I assure you. There's no other way.

FIRS   In the old days, forty or fifty years ago, the cherries were dried, preserved, marinated, made into jam, and sometimes . . .

GAYEV Be quiet, Firs.

FIRS And sometimes whole cartloads of dried cherries were sent to Moscow and Kharkov. The money they brought in! And the dried cherries in those days were soft, juicy, sweet, tasty. They knew how to do it then. They had a recipe.

LYUBOV ANDREYEVNA And where is that recipe now?

FIRS Forgotten. No one can remember it.

PISHCHIK [*To Lyubov Andreyevna*] What was it like in Paris? Did you eat frogs?

LYUBOV ANDREYEVNA I ate crocodiles.

PISHCHIK Fancy that!

LOPAKHIN Up to just recently there were only gentry and peasants living in the country, but now there are all these summer residents. All the towns, even quite small ones, are surrounded with villas. And probably in the course of the next twenty years or so, these people will multiply tremendously. At present they merely drink tea on the veranda, but they might start cultivating their plots of land, and then your cherry orchard would be gay with life and wealth and luxury.

GAYEV [*Indignantly*] What nonsense!

Enter Varya and Yasha

VARYA Here are two telegrams for you, Mamma dear. [*picks out a key and unlocks an old bookcase with a jingling noise*] Here they are.

LYUBOV ANDREYEVNA They are from Paris. [*tears them up without reading them*] I've finished with Paris.

GAYEV Do you know, Lyuba, how old this bookcase is? A week ago I pulled out the bottom drawer, and I found some figures burned in the wood. It was made exactly a hundred years ago. What do you think of that, eh? We ought to celebrate its anniversary. An inanimate object, true, but still—a bookcase!

PISHCHIK [*Astonished*] A hundred years! Fancy that!

GAYEV Yes. This is a valuable piece of furniture. [*feeling around the bookcase with his hands*] My dear, venerable bookcase! I salute you! For more than a hundred years you have devoted yourself to the highest ideals of goodness and justice. For a hundred years you have never failed to fill us with an urge to useful work. Several generations of our family have had their courage sustained and their faith in a better future fortified by your silent call. You have fostered in us the ideal of public good and social consciousness. . . .

LOPAKHIN [*After a pause*] Yes.

LYUBOV ANDREYEVNA You're just the same, Lenya.

GAYEV [*Slightly embarrassed*] I put it into the corner pocket! I drop it into the middle pocket!

LOPAKHIN [*Glances at his watch*] Well, it's time for me to be going.

YASHA [*Brings medicine to Lyubov Andreyevna*] Would you care to take your pills now?

PISHCHIK Don't take medicines, my dear. They don't do you any good . . . or harm either. Let me have them. [*takes the box from her, pours the pills into the palm of his hand, blows on them, puts them all into his mouth, and takes a drink of kvass*] There!

LYUBOV ANDREYEVNA [*Alarmed*] But you're mad!

PISHCHIK I've taken all the pills.

LOPAKHIN What a digestion!

All laugh

FIRS His Honor came to see us in Holy Week and ate half a bucketful of salt cucumbers. [*mutters*]

LYUBOV ANDREYEVNA What is it he's saying?

VARYA He's been muttering for the last three years. We're accustomed to it.

YASHA It's his age.

Charlotta Ivanovna, very thin and tightly laced in a white dress, with a lorgnette at her waist, passes across the stage

LOPAKHIN Forgive me, Charlotta Ivanovna, I haven't yet had time to say how d'you do to you. [*tries to kiss her hand*]

CHARLOTTA [*Withdrawing her hand*] If you were permitted to kiss a lady's hand, you'd want to kiss her elbow next and then her shoulder.

LOPAKHIN I'm unlucky today.

All laugh

Charlotta Ivanovna, do a trick for us.

CHARLOTTA There's no need to now. I want to go to bed. [*goes out*]

LOPAKHIN I'll see you in three weeks' time. [*kisses Lyubov Andreyevna's hand*] Meanwhile, good-bye. Time to go. [*to Gayev*] Au revoir. [*embraces Pishchik*] Au revoir. [*shakes hands with Varya, then with Firs and Yasha*] I don't want to go really. [*to Lyubov Andreyevna*] If you think over this question of country villas and come to a decision, let me know, and I'll get you a loan of fifty thousand or more. Think it over seriously.

VARYA [*Angrily*] Will you ever go away?

LOPAKHIN I'm going, I'm going. [*goes out*]

GAYEV What a boor! I beg your pardon. Varya's going to marry him. He's Varya's precious fiancé.

VARYA Please don't say anything uncalled for, Uncle dear.

LYUBOV ANDREYEVNA Well, Varya, I will be very glad. He's a good man.

PISHCHIK He's a man—let's admit it—a most admirable fellow. . . . My Dashenka says so too. . . . She says all sorts of things. [*he drops asleep and snores but wakes up again at once*] Incidentally, my dear, will you lend me two hundred and forty rubles? I've got to pay the interest on the mortgage tomorrow.

VARYA [*In alarm*] We haven't got it; we really haven't!

LYUBOV ANDREYEVNA It's quite true. I have nothing.

PISHCHIK It'll turn up. [*laughs*] I never lose hope. Sometimes I think everything's lost, I'm ruined, and then—lo and behold! —a railway line is built through my land, and they pay me for it! Something or other is sure to happen tomorrow if not today. Perhaps Dashenka will win two hundred thousand rubles. She's got a lottery ticket.

LYUBOV ANDREYEVNA   I've finished my coffee; now I can go and rest.

FIRS   [*Brushing Gayev's clothes, admonishing him*] You've put on the wrong pair of trousers again! What am I to do with you?

VARYA   [*In a low voice*] Anya's asleep. [*quietly opens a window*] The sun has risen; it's warmer already. Look, Mamma dear, how wonderful the trees are! Heavens, what lovely air! The starlings are singing!

GAYEV   [*Opens another window*] The orchard is all white. You haven't forgotten, Lyuba? How straight this long avenue is— quite straight, just like a ribbon that's been stretched taut. It glitters on moonlit nights. Do you remember? You haven't forgotten?

LYUBOV ANDREYEVNA   [*Looks through the window at the orchard*] Oh, my childhood, my innocent childhood! I used to sleep in this nursery. I used to look at the orchard from here, and I woke up happy every morning. In those days the orchard was just as it is now; nothing has changed. [*laughs happily*] All, all white! Oh, my orchard! After the dark, stormy autumn and the cold winter, you are young and joyous again; the angels have not forsaken you! If only this burden could be taken from me. If only I could forget my past!

GAYEV   Yes, and now the orchard is going to be sold to pay our debts, strange as it seems.

LYUBOV ANDREYEVNA   Look, there's Mother walking through the orchard . . . in a white dress! [*laughs happily*] It is her!

GAYEV   Where?

VARYA   Bless you, Mamma dear!

LYUBOV ANDREYEVNA   It's no one; I only imagined it. Over there, you see, on the right, as you turn to the summer house there's a small white tree and it's bending over. It looks like a woman.

Enter Trofimov. He is dressed in a shabby student's uniform and wears glasses

What a wonderful orchard! Masses of white blossom, the blue sky . . .

TROFIMOV   Lyubov Andreyevna! [*she turns to him*] I'll just make my bow and go at once. [*kisses her hand warmly*] I was told to wait until the morning, but it was too much for my patience.

Lyubov Andreyevna looks at him, puzzled

VARYA   [*Through tears*] This is Petya Trofimov.
TROFIMOV   Petya Trofimov, I used to be tutor to your Grisha. Have I really changed so much?

Lyubov Andreyevna puts her arms around him and weeps quietly

GAYEV   [*Embarrassed*] Now, now, Lyuba . . .
VARYA   [*Weeps*] Didn't I tell you to wait until tomorrow, Petya?
LYUBOV ANDREYEVNA   My Grisha . . . my little boy . . . Grisha . . . my son . . .
VARYA   There's nothing we can do about it, Mamma darling. It was God's will.
TROFIMOV   [*Gently, with emotion*] Don't, don't . . .
LYUBOV ANDREYEVNA   [*Quietly weeping*] My little boy was lost . . . drowned. What for? What for, my friend? [*more quietly*] Anya's asleep there, and here I am, shouting and making a scene. Well, Petya? How is it you've lost your good looks? Why have you aged so?
TROFIMOV   A peasant woman in the train called me "that moth-eaten gent."
LYUBOV ANDREYEVNA   In those days you were quite a boy, a nice young student, and now your hair is thin, you wear glasses. Are you still a student? [*walks to the door*]
TROFIMOV   I expect I will be a student to the end of my days.
LYUBOV ANDREYEVNA   [*Kisses her brother, then Varya*] Well, go to bed now. You have aged too, Leonid.
PISHCHIK   [*Following her*] So you're going to bed now? Ouch, my gout! I'd better stay the night here. And tomorrow morning, Lyubov Andreyevna, my dear, I'd like to borrow those two hundred and forty rubles.
GAYEV   How the fellow keeps at it!
PISHCHIK   Two hundred and forty rubles. You see, I've got to pay the interest on the mortgage.

LYUBOV ANDREYEVNA   I have no money, my dear.

PISHCHIK   I'll pay you back, my dear lady. It's a trifling amount after all.

LYUBOV ANDREYEVNA   Very well then. Leonid will give you the money. You give him the money, Leonid.

GAYEV   I'll be delighted; anything he wants, of course!

LYUBOV ANDREYEVNA   What else can we do? He needs it. He'll pay it back.

Lyubov Andreyevna, Trofimov, Pishchik, and Firs go out. Gayev, Varya, and Yasha remain

GAYEV   My sister hasn't lost her habit of throwing money away. [*to Yasha*] Out of the way, my man, you smell of the kitchen.

YASHA   [*With a sneer*] I see you're just the same as you used to be, Leonid Andreyevich.

GAYEV   What's that? [*to Varya*] What did he say?

VARYA   [*To Yasha*] Your mother's come from the village. She's been sitting in the servants' hall since yesterday, wanting to see you.

YASHA   I wish she'd leave me alone!

VARYA   You . . . aren't you ashamed of yourself?

YASHA   It's quite unnecessary. She could have come tomorrow. [*goes out*]

VARYA   Dear Mamma is just the same as she used to be; she hasn't changed a bit. If she had her own way, she'd give away everything.

GAYEV   Yes. You know, if a lot of cures are suggested for a disease, it means that the disease is incurable. I've been thinking and puzzling my brains, and I've thought of plenty of ways out, plenty—which means there aren't any. It would be a good thing if somebody left us some money, or if we married off our Anya to some very rich man, or if one of us went to Yaroslavl and tried our luck with the old aunt, the countess. You know she's very rich.

VARYA   [*Weeping*] If only God would help us.

GAYEV   Do stop blubbering! The countess is very rich, but she doesn't like us. First because my sister married a lawyer and not a nobleman.

Anya appears in the doorway

She married a man who wasn't of noble birth; and then you can't say her behavior's been exactly virtuous. She's a good, kind, lovable person, and I'm very fond of her, but whatever extenuating circumstances you may think of, you must admit that she's a bit easygoing morally. You can sense it in every movement.

VARYA [*In a whisper*] Anya's standing in the doorway.

GAYEV What? [*pause*] Funny thing, something's gotten into my right eye. I can't see properly. And on Thursday, when I was at the District Court . . .

Anya comes in

VARYA Well, why aren't you asleep, Anya?

ANYA I can't get to sleep. I just can't.

GAYEV My dear little girl! [*kisses Anya's face and hands*] My dear child! [*through tears*] You're not just a niece to me, you're an angel, you're everything to me. Please believe me, believe . . .

ANYA I believe you, Uncle. Everyone loves you, respects you. But, dear Uncle, you shouldn't talk; you should try to keep quiet. What was that you were saying just now about my mother, about your own sister? Why were you saying it?

GAYEV Yes, yes! [*he takes her hand and puts it over his face*] You're quite right; it's dreadful! My God! My God! And the speech I made today in front of the bookcase . . . so foolish! And it was only after I'd finished that I realized it was foolish.

VARYA It's true, Uncle dear; you ought to try to keep quiet. Just keep quiet, that's all.

ANYA If you keep quiet, you'll be happier inside.

GAYEV I'll be quiet. [*kisses Anya's and Varya's hands*] I'll be quiet. But I must tell you something important. Last Thursday I went to the District Court, and I got talking with some friends, and from what they said it looks as if it might be possible to get a loan on promissory notes in order to pay the interest to the bank.

VARYA If only God would help us!

GAYEV I'll go there again on Tuesday and have another talk. [*to Varya*] Don't keep crying. [*to Anya*] Your mother's going to have a talk with Lopakhin; he won't refuse her of course. And after you've had a rest, you will go to Yaroslavl to see the countess, your grandmother. And so we'll approach the matter from three angles, and—the thing's done! We'll pay the interest, I'm sure of it. [*he puts a sweet into his mouth*] I swear on my honor, on anything you like, that the estate will not be sold! [*excited*] I'll stake my happiness! Here's my hand, you can call me a good-for-nothing liar if I allow the auction to take place. I swear on my soul!

ANYA [*Calmer, with an air of happiness*] How good you are, Uncle, and how sensible! [*puts her arms around him*] I feel calmer now. I feel so calm and happy.

Enter Firs

FIRS [*Reproachfully*] Leonid Andreyevich, aren't you ashamed of yourself? When are you going to bed?

GAYEV Presently, presently. You go away, Firs. I don't need your help. Well, children dear, bye-bye now. All the news tomorrow; you must go to bed now. [*kisses Anya and Varya*] You know, I'm a man of the eighties. People don't think much of that period, but all the same, I can say that I've suffered quite a lot in the course of my life for my convictions. It's not for nothing that the peasants love me. You have to know the peasants! You have to know from which side . . .

ANYA You're starting it again, Uncle!

VARYA You'd better keep quiet, Uncle dear.

FIRS [*Sternly*] Leonid Andreyevich!

GAYEV Coming, coming! Go to bed! In off the cushion! I sink the white! [*goes out. Firs hobbles after him*]

ANYA My mind is at rest now. I don't really feel like going to Yaroslavl; I don't like Grandmamma. But still, I'm not worrying. I'm grateful to Uncle. [*she sits down*]

VARYA I must get some sleep. I'm going. Oh, by the way, while you were away something unpleasant happened here. You know, there are only a few old servants living in the servants' quarters: just Yefimyushka, Polya, Yevstignei, and Karp. Well, they let some tramps sleep there, and I didn't say anything about it. But some time afterward I heard some gossip; people said I had ordered them to be fed on nothing but dried peas. Because I was mean, you see. Yevstignei was at the bottom of it all. "Well," I said to myself, "if that's how the matter stands, just you wait!" So I sent for Yevstignei. [*yawns*] In he comes. "What's all this, Yevstignei," I said to him, "idiot that you are." [*she walks up to Anya*] Anichka! [*pause*] She's asleep! [*takes her arm*] Come to bed! Come! [*leads her away*] My darling's fallen asleep! Come. [*they go toward the door*]

The sound of a shepherd's pipe is heard from far away, beyond the orchard. Trofimov crosses the stage, but, seeing Varya and Anya, stops

Sh-sh! She's asleep. . . . Asleep. Come, my dear.

ANYA   [*Softly, half-asleep*] I'm so tired. I can hear bells tinkling all the time. Uncle . . . dear. . . . Mamma and Uncle.

VARYA   Come, darling, come. [*they go into Anya's room*]

TROFIMOV   [*Deeply moved*] Anya, my one bright star! My spring flower!

CURTAIN

ACT TWO

An old wayside shrine in the open country; it leans slightly to one side and has evidently been long abandoned. Beside it there are a well, an old seat, and a number of large stones, which apparently served as gravestones in the past. A road leads to Gayev's estate. On one side and some distance away is a row of dark poplars, and it is there that the cherry orchard begins. Farther away is seen a line of telegraph poles, and beyond them, on the horizon, the vague outlines of a large town, visible only in very good, clear weather.

The sun is about to set. Charlotta, Yasha, and Dunyasha are sitting on the seat. Yepikhodov is standing nearby, playing a guitar. All look pensive. Charlotta is wearing a man's old peaked cap; she has taken a shotgun off her shoulder and is adjusting a buckle on the strap.

CHARLOTTA [*Thoughtfully*] I don't know how old I am. I haven't got a proper identity card, you see. And I keep on imagining I'm still quite young. When I was little Father and Mother used to tour the fairs and give performances—very good ones they were too. And I used to jump the *salto mortale* and do all sorts of other tricks. When Papa and Mamma died a German lady took me into her house and began to give me lessons. So then I grew up and became a governess. But where I come from and who I am, I don't know. Who my parents were —perhaps they weren't properly married—I don't know. [*she*

26

takes a cucumber from her pocket and begins to eat it] I don't know anything. [*pause*] I'm longing to talk to someone, but there isn't anyone. I haven't anyone.

YEPIKHODOV [*Plays the guitar and sings*] "What care I for the noisy world? What are friends and foes to me?" How pleasant it is to play the mandolin!

DUNYASHA That's a guitar, not a mandolin. [*she looks at herself in a hand mirror and powders her face*]

YEPIKHODOV To a man that's crazy with love this is a mandolin. [*sings quietly*] "If only my heart might be warmed by the ardor of love requited."

Yasha joins in

CHARLOTTA How dreadful their singing is! *Ach!* It is like the jackals.

DUNYASHA [*To Yasha*] You are lucky to have been abroad!

YASHA Of course I am. I'm bound to agree with you there. [*yawns, then lights a cigar*]

YEPIKHODOV Stands to reason. Abroad everything's been in full swing. I mean to say, everything's been going on for ever so long.

YASHA Obviously.

YEPIKHODOV Personally, I'm a cultured sort of fellow. I read all sorts of extraordinary books, you know, but somehow I can't seem to make out where I'm going, what it is I really want, I mean to say—to live or to shoot myself, so to speak. All the same I always carry a revolver on me. Here it is. [*shows the revolver*]

CHARLOTTA I have finished. Now I'm going. [*slips the strap of the gun over her shoulder*] Yes, you are a very clever man, Yepikhodov, and rather frightening too; the women must fall madly in love with you! Brrr! [*walks off*] All these clever people are so stupid. I have no one to talk to. I am so lonely, always so lonely. No one belongs to me, and . . . and who I am, what I exist for, nobody knows. [*goes out leisurely*]

YEPIKHODOV Candidly speaking—and I do want to keep strictly to the point, by the way—I feel I simply must explain that fate, so to speak, treats me absolutely without mercy, just like a storm treats a small ship, as it were. I mean to say, supposing I'm wrong, for instance, then why should I wake up this morning and suddenly see a simply colossal spider sitting on my chest like this? [*makes a gesture with both hands*] Or supposing I pick up a jug to have a drink of kvass, there's sure to be something frightful inside it, like a cockroach. [*pause*] Have you read Buckle? [*pause*] May I trouble you for a word, Avdotya Fëdorovna?

DUNYASHA   All right, go on.

YEPIKHODOV   I'd very much like to speak to you alone. [*sighs*]

DUNYASHA   [*Embarrassed*] Very well then. Only will you bring me my little cape first? It's hanging beside the wardrobe. It's rather chilly here.

YEPIKHODOV   Very well, I'll bring it. Now I know what to do with my revolver. [*picks up his guitar and goes, twanging it*]

YASHA   Twenty-two misfortunes! He's a stupid fellow, between you and me. [*yawns*]

DUNYASHA   I hope to God he won't shoot himself. [*pause*] I've gotten sort of anxious, worrying all the time. I came to live here with the master and mistress when I was still a little girl, you see. Now I've lost the habit of living a simple life, and my hands are as white . . . as white as a young lady's. I've grown sensitive and delicate, just as if I were one of the nobility. I'm afraid of everything. . . . Just afraid. If you deceive me, Yasha, I don't know what will happen to my nerves.

YASHA   [*Kisses her*] Little peach! Mind you, a girl ought to keep herself in hand, you know. Personally I dislike it more than anything if a girl doesn't behave herself.

DUNYASHA   I love you so much, so much! You're educated; you can reason about everything. . . .

YASHA   [*After a pause, yawns*] Y-yes. To my way of thinking, it's like this: if a girl loves somebody, it means she's immoral. [*pause*] It's nice to smoke a cigar in the open air. [*listens*] Someone's coming this way. Our ladies and gentlemen.

Dunyasha impulsively puts her arms around him

Go home now, as if you'd been down to the river bathing. Go by this path or you'll meet them, and they might think I've been keeping company with you. I couldn't stand that.

DUNYASHA [*Coughing softly*] My head's aching from that cigar. [*goes out*]

Yasha remains sitting by the shrine. Enter Lyubov Andreyevna, Gayev, and Lopakhin

LOPAKHIN We must decide once and for all; time won't wait. After all, my question's quite a simple one. Do you consent to lease your land for villas or don't you? You can answer in one word: yes or no? Just one word!

LYUBOV ANDREYEVNA Who's been smoking such abominable cigars here? [*sits down*]

GAYEV How very convenient it is having a railway here. [*sits down*] Here we are—we've been up to town for lunch and we're back home already. I sink the red into the middle pocket! I'd like to go indoors now and have just one game.

LYUBOV ANDREYEVNA You've plenty of time.

LOPAKHIN Just one word! [*beseechingly*] Do give me an answer!

GAYEV [*Yawns*] What do you say?

LYUBOV ANDREYEVNA [*Looking into her purse*] Yesterday I had a lot of money, but today there's hardly any left. My poor Varya is feeding everyone on milk soups to economize, the old servants in the kitchen get nothing but dried peas to eat, and here I am spending money senselessly. I don't know why. [*she drops the purse, scattering gold coins*] Now I've scattered it all over the place. [*annoyed*]

YASHA Allow me, madam; I'll pick them up in a minute. [*gathers up the money*]

LYUBOV ANDREYEVNA Thank you, Yasha. Why did I go out to lunch? It was quite vile, that restaurant of yours, with its beastly music; and the tablecloths smelt of soap too. Do you have to drink so much, Lenya? Do you have to eat so much? And talk so much? Today at the restaurant you talked too much again, and it was all so pointless. About the seventies, about the decadents. And to whom? Imagine talking about the decadents to the restaurant waiters!

LOPAKHIN Yes, imagine.

GAYEV [*Waving his hand*] I'm hopeless, I know. [*to Yasha, with irritation*] Why are you always buzzing around in front of me?

YASHA [*Laughs*] I can never hear you talk without laughing.

GAYEV [*To his sister*] Either he goes or I do.

LYUBOV ANDREYEVNA Go away, Yasha, go along.

YASHA [*Hands the purse to Lyubov Andreyevna*] I'll go now. [*he can hardly restrain his laughter*] This very minute. [*goes out*]

LOPAKHIN You know, that wealthy fellow Deriganov, he's intending to buy your estate. They say he's coming to the auction himself.

LYUBOV ANDREYEVNA Where did you hear that?

LOPAKHIN They were saying so in town.

GAYEV Our aunt in Yaroslavl promised to send us money, but when and how much it will be we don't know.

LOPAKHIN How much will she send you? A hundred thousand? Two hundred?

LYUBOV ANDREYEVNA Well, hardly. Ten or twelve thousand perhaps. We'll be thankful for that much.

LOPAKHIN You must forgive me for saying it, but really I've never met such irresponsible, unbusinesslike, queer people as you are. You are told in plain language that your estate is up for sale, and you simply don't seem to understand it.

LYUBOV ANDREYEVNA But what are we to do? Tell us: what?

LOPAKHIN I keep on telling you. Every day I tell you the same thing. You must lease the cherry orchard and the land for villas, and you must do it now, as soon as possible. The auction is going to be held almost at once. Please try to understand! Once you definitely decide to have the villas, you'll be able to borrow as much money as you like, and then you'll be out of the woods.

LYUBOV ANDREYEVNA Villas and summer visitors! Forgive me, but it's so vulgar.

GAYEV I absolutely agree with you.

LOPAKHIN Honestly, I feel I'll burst into tears or shriek or fall down and faint. I simply can't stand it. You've literally worn me out. [*to Gayev*] An old woman, that's what you are!

GAYEV What's that?

LOPAKHIN An old woman!

LYUBOV ANDREYEVNA [*Alarmed*] No, don't go. Do stay, my dear. Please stay! Perhaps we could think of something.

LOPAKHIN It hardly seems worth trying.

LYUBOV ANDREYEVNA Don't go, please! Somehow it's more

cheerful with you here. [*pause*] I keep expecting something dreadful to happen, as if the house were going to fall down on us.

GAYEV [*In deep thought*] Carom off the cushions! I sink it into the middle pocket.

LYUBOV ANDREYEVNA We've sinned too much.

LOPAKHIN Sinned, indeed! What were your sins?

GAYEV [*Puts a sweet into his mouth*] They say I've eaten up my whole fortune in sweets. [*laughs*]

LYUBOV ANDREYEVNA Oh, my sins! Look at the way I've always squandered money continually. It was sheer madness. And then I got married to a man who only knew how to get into debt. Champagne killed him—he was a terrific drinker—and then, worse luck, I fell in love with someone else. We had an affair, and just at that very time—it was my first punishment, a blow straight to my heart—my little boy was drowned here, in this river . . . and then I went abroad. I went away for good and never meant to return; I never meant to see the river again. I just shut my eyes and ran away in a frenzy of grief, but *he* . . . he followed me. It was so cruel and brutal of him! I bought a villa near Menton because he became ill there, you see, and for three years I never had any rest, day or night. He was a sick man; he quite wore me out. My soul seemed to dry right up. Then last year when the villa had to be sold to pay the debts, I went to Paris, and there he robbed me and left me. He went away and lived with another woman. . . . I tried to poison myself. . . . It was all so foolish, so shameful! And then suddenly I felt an urge to come back to Russia, to my own country and my little girl. [*wipes away her tears*] Oh, Lord, Lord, be merciful; forgive me my sins! Don't punish me anymore! [*takes a telegram out of her pocket*] I had this from Paris today. He's asking my forgiveness, begging me to return. [*tears up the telegram*] Sounds like music somewhere. [*listens*]

GAYEV That's our famous Jewish band. Do you remember: four violins, a flute, and a contrabass?

LYUBOV ANDREYEVNA Is that still in existence? It would be nice to get them to come to the house one day, and we could have a little dance.

LOPAKHIN [*Listens*] I can't hear anything. [*sings quietly*] "And the Germans, if you pay, will turn Russian into Frenchman, so they say." [*laughs*] I saw such a good play at the theater yesterday. Very amusing.

LYUBOV ANDREYEVNA   I'm sure it wasn't at all amusing. Instead of going to see plays, you should take a good look at yourself. Just think what a drab kind of life you lead, what a lot of nonsense you talk!

LOPAKHIN   It's perfectly true. Yes, I admit it—we lead an idiotic existence. [*pause*] My dad was a peasant, a blockhead. He didn't understand anything, and he didn't teach me anything but just beat me when he was drunk, and always with a stick at that. As a matter of fact, I'm just as much of a fool and a half-wit myself. No one taught me anything. My writing is awful; I'm ashamed even to show it to people: it's just like a pig's.

LYUBOV ANDREYEVNA   You ought to get married, my friend.

LOPAKHIN   Yes. That's true.

LYUBOV ANDREYEVNA   You ought to marry our Varya. She's a nice girl.

LOPAKHIN   Yes.

LYUBOV ANDREYEVNA   She comes from the common folk, and she's a hardworking girl: she can work the whole day without stopping. But the main thing is that she loves you, and you've been attracted to her for a long time youself.

LOPAKHIN   Well, I'm quite willing. She's a nice girl. . . .

GAYEV   [*After a pause*] I've been offered a job at the bank. Six thousand a year. Have you heard?

LYUBOV ANDREYEVNA   Indeed I have. You'd better stay where you are.

Enter Firs with an overcoat

FIRS   [*To Gayev*] Will you please put it on, sir. It's so chilly.

GAYEV   [*Puts on the overcoat*] You *are* a nuisance.

FIRS   Tut, tut! You went off this morning and never told me you were going. [*looks him over*]

LYUBOV ANDREYEVNA   How you've aged, Firs!

FIRS   What can I get you, madam?

LOPAKHIN   They say that you've aged a lot.

FIRS   I've been alive a long time. They were going to marry me off before your dad was born. [*laughs*] And when freedom was granted to the people, I'd already been made a chief valet. I wouldn't take my freedom then; I stayed with the master and mistress. [*pause*] I remember everyone was glad at the time, but what they were glad about, no one knew.

LOPAKHIN   Oh, yes, it was a good life all right! At least people got flogged!

FIRS   [*Not hearing him*] Rather! The peasants belonged to the gentry, and the gentry belonged to the peasants; but now everything's separate, and you can't understand anything.

GAYEV   Be quiet, Firs. Tomorrow I must go to town. I was promised an introduction to some general or other who'll lend us some money on a promissory note.

LOPAKHIN   Nothing will come of that. And you won't be able to pay the interest anyway.

LYUBOV ANDREYEVNA   He's talking through his hat. There aren't any generals.

Enter Trofimov, Anya, and Varya

GAYEV   Here come the children.

ANYA   There's Mamma.

LYUBOV ANDREYEVNA   Come here, my dears. My dear children. [*embraces Anya and Varya*] If you both only knew how much I love you! Sit down beside me here.

All sit down

LOPAKHIN   Our "eternal student" is always with the young ladies.

TROFIMOV   It's none of your business anyway.

LOPAKHIN   He'll soon be fifty, yet he's still a student.

TROFIMOV   I wish you'd drop your idiotic jokes.

LOPAKHIN   But why are you getting annoyed? You *are* a queer fellow!

TROFIMOV   Why do you keep pestering me?

LOPAKHIN   [*Laughs*] Just let me ask you one question: what do you make of me?

TROFIMOV   My opinion of you, Yermolai Alekseevich, is simply this: you're a wealthy man, and before long you'll be a millionaire. And in so far as a wild beast is necessary because it devours everything in its path and so converts one kind of matter into another, you are necessary also.

Everybody laughs

VARYA   You'd better tell us about the planets, Petya.

LYUBOV ANDREYEVNA   No, let's continue what we were talking about yesterday.

TROFIMOV   What were we talking about?

GAYEV   About pride.

TROFIMOV   We talked a lot yesterday, but we didn't agree on anything. The proud man, in the sense you understand him, has something mystical about him. Maybe you're right in a way, but if we try to think it out simply, without being too farfetched about it, the question arises: why should he be proud? Where's the sense in being proud when you consider that man, as a species, is not very well constructed physiologically, and in the vast majority of cases is coarse, stupid, and profoundly unhappy too? We ought to stop all this self-admiration. We ought to—just work.

GAYEV   You'll die just the same whatever you do.

TROFIMOV   Who knows? And anyway what does it mean—to die? It may be that man possesses a hundred senses, and only the five that are known to us perish in death, while the remaining ninety-five live on afterward.

LYUBOV ANDREYEVNA   How clever you are, Petya!

LOPAKHIN   [*Ironically*] Oh, awfully clever!

TROFIMOV   Humanity is perpetually advancing, always seeking to perfect its own powers. One day all the things that are beyond our grasp at present are going to fall within our reach, only to achieve this we've got to work with all our might, to help the people who are seeking after truth. Here in Russia very few people have started to work so far. Nearly all the members of the intelligentsia that I know care for nothing, do nothing, and are still incapable of work. They call themselves "intelligentsia," but they still talk contemptuously to their servants, they treat the peasants as if they were animals, they study without achieving anything, they don't read anything serious, they just do nothing. As for science they only talk about it, and they don't understand much about art either. They all look very grave and go around with grim expressions on their faces, and they only discuss important matters and philosophize. Yet all the time anyone can see that our working people are abominably fed and have to sleep without proper beds, thirty to forty to a room, with bedbugs, bad smells, dampness, and immorality everywhere. It's perfectly obvious that all our nice-sounding talk is intended only to mislead ourselves and others. Tell me then, where are the day nurseries that we're always talking about, where are the reading rooms? We only write about them in novels, but actually there just aren't any. There's nothing but dirt, bestiality, Asiatic customs. I'm afraid of these deadly serious faces; I don't like them. I'm afraid of serious talk. It would be better for us just to keep quiet.

LOPAKHIN   Well, let me tell you that *I'm* up soon after four every morning, and I work from morning till night. I always have money in hand, my own and other people's, and I have plenty of opportunities to learn what the people around me are like. You only have to start on a project to realize how few honest, decent people there are around. Sometimes when I can't sleep, I start brooding over it. The Lord God has given us vast forests, immense fields, wide horizons; surely we ought to be giants, living in such a country as this.

LYUBOV ANDREYEVNA   Whatever do you want giants for? They're all right in fairy tales; otherwise they're just terrifying.

Yepikhodov crosses the stage in the background, playing his guitar

[*pensively*] There goes Yepikhodov.

ANYA   [*Pensively*] There goes Yepikhodov.

GAYEV   The sun's gone down, ladies and gentlemen.

TROFIMOV   Yes.

GAYEV   [*In a subdued voice, as if reciting a poem*] Oh, glorious nature, shining with eternal light, so beautiful, yet so indifferent to our fate . . . You, whom we call Mother, uniting in yourself both life and death, you live and you destroy.

VARYA   [*Imploringly*] Uncle, dear!

ANYA   You're starting again, Uncle!

TROFIMOV   You'd better screw back off the red into the middle pocket.

GAYEV   I'll keep quiet, I'll keep quiet.

They all sit deep in thought. The silence is only broken by the subdued muttering of Firs. Suddenly a distant sound is heard, coming as if out of the sky, like the sound of a string snapping, slowly and sadly dying away

LYUBOV ANDREYEVNA   What was that?

LOPAKHIN   I don't know. Somewhere a long way off a lift cable in one of the mines must have broken. But it must be somewhere very far away.

GAYEV   Or perhaps it was some bird. A heron perhaps.

TROFIMOV   Or an owl.

LYUBOV ANDREYEVNA   [*Shudders*] It sounded unpleasant, somehow. . . .

FIRS   [*After a pause*] It was the same before the misfortune; the owl hooted and the samovar kept singing.

GAYEV   What misfortune?

FIRS   Before they gave us freedom. . . .

LYUBOV ANDREYEVNA   [*After a pause*] Come along, my friends! Let us go home; it's getting dark. [*to Anya*] You've got tears in your eyes. What is it, my little one? [*embraces her*]

ANYA   Never mind, Mamma. It's nothing.

TROFIMOV   Someone's coming.

Enter a tramp in a white, battered peaked cap and an overcoat; he is slightly tipsy

THE TRAMP   Excuse me, can I get straight to the station through here?

GAYEV   You can. Follow the road.

THE TRAMP   I'm greatly obliged to you, sir. [*coughs*] Lovely weather today. [*recites*] "Oh, my brother, my suffering brother! Come to Mother Volga, whose groans . . ." [*to Varya*] Mademoiselle, may a starving Russian citizen trouble you for a few coppers?

Varya cries out, frightened

LOPAKHIN [*Angrily*] Really there's a limit to everything!

LYUBOV ANDREYEVNA [*At a loss what to do*] Take this. . . . Here you are. [*searches in her purse*] I have no silver. Never mind, here's a gold one.

THE TRAMP I'm deeply grateful to you! [*goes off*]

Laughter

VARYA [*Frightened*] I'm going. I'm going. Oh, Mamma dear, you know there's no food in the house, and you gave him all that!

LYUBOV ANDREYEVNA Well, what can you do with a fool like me? I'll give you all I've got when we get home. Yermolai Alekseevich, you'll lend me some more, won't you?

LOPAKHIN Certainly I will.

LYUBOV ANDREYEVNA Let's go on now; it's time. By the way, Varya, we almost fixed up your marriage just now. I congratulate you.

VARYA [*Through her tears*] It's no laughing matter, Mamma!

LOPAKHIN Get thee to a nunnery, Ophelia!

GAYEV Look how my hands are trembling: I haven't played billiards for a long time.

LOPAKHIN Ophelia, nymph, in thy orisons be all my sins remembered!

LYUBOV ANDREYEVNA Come along, everybody. It's almost suppertime.

VARYA That man scared me so. My heart keeps thumping.

LOPAKHIN My friends, just one word, please just one word: on the twenty-second of August the cherry orchard is going to be sold. Just consider that! Just think . . .

All go out, except Trofimov and Anya

ANYA [*Laughs*] Thank the tramp for this! He frightened Varya; now we are alone.

TROFIMOV Varya's afraid—afraid we might suddenly fall in love with each other—so she follows us around all day long.

She's so narrow-minded, she can't grasp that we are above falling in love. To rid ourselves of all that's petty and unreal, all that prevents us from being happy and free—that's the whole aim and meaning of our life. Forward! Let's march on irresistibly toward that bright star over there, shining in the distance! Forward! Don't fall behind, friends!

ANYA [*Raising her hands*] How well you talk! [*pause*] It's wonderful here today.

TROFIMOV Yes, the weather's marvelous.

ANYA What have you done to me, Petya? Why is it that I don't love the cherry orchard as I used to? I used to love it so dearly. It seemed to me that there wasn't a better place in all the world than our orchard.

TROFIMOV The whole of Russia is our orchard. The earth is great and beautiful and there are many, many wonderful places on it. [*pause*] Just think, Anya: your grandfather, your great-grandfather, and all your forefathers were serf owners—they owned living souls. Don't you see human beings gazing at you from every cherry tree in your orchard; from every leaf and every tree trunk, don't you hear voices? They owned living souls—and it has perverted you all, those who came before you, and you who are living now; so that your mother, your uncle, and even you yourself no longer realize that you're living in debt, at other people's expense, at the expense of people you don't admit farther than the kitchen. We are at least two hundred years behind the times; we still have no real background, no clear attitude to our past. We just philosophize and complain of depression or drink vodka. Yet it's perfectly clear that to begin to live in the present, we must first atone for our past and be finished with it, and we can only atone for it by suffering, by extraordinary, unceasing exertion. You must understand this, Anya.

ANYA The house we live in hasn't really been ours for a long time. I'll leave it; I give you my word.

TROFIMOV Leave it, and if you have any keys to it, throw them down a well. Be free like the wind.

ANYA [*In rapture*] How well you put it!

TROFIMOV You must believe me, Anya, you must. I'm not thirty yet, I'm young, and I'm still a student, but I've suffered so much already. As soon as the winter comes, I get half-starved and ill and worried, poor as a beggar, and there's hardly anywhere I haven't been where I haven't been driven by fate. And yet, always, every moment of the day and night my soul has been filled with such marvelous hopes and visions. I can see happiness, Anya; I can see it coming.

ANYA [*Pensively*] The moon's coming up.

Yepikhodov can be heard playing his guitar, the same melancholy tune as before. The moon rises. Somewhere in the vicinity of the poplars Varya is looking for Anya and calling, "Anya! Where are you?"

TROFIMOV Yes, the moon is rising. [*pause*] There it is—happiness—it's coming nearer and nearer. I seem to hear its footsteps. And if we don't see it, if we don't know when it comes, what does it matter? Other people will see it!

VARYA'S VOICE Anya! Where are you?

TROFIMOV That Varya again! [*angrily*] It's disgusting!

ANYA Well? Let us go to the river. It's nice there.

TROFIMOV Let's go.

Trofimov and Anya go out

VARYA'S VOICE Anya! Anya!

CURTAIN

ACT THREE

The drawing room of the Ranevskaya house. Adjoining the drawing room at the back, and connected to it by an archway, is the ballroom. A Jewish band, the same that was mentioned in Act Two, is heard playing in the hall. It is evening; the candles in a chandelier are lit. In the ballroom a party is dancing the grand rond. *Simeonov-Pishchik is heard calling out,* "Promenade à une paire!"; *then all come into the drawing room. Pishchik and Charlotta Ivanovna form the leading couple; then come Trofimov and Lyubov Andreyevna, Anya with a post office clerk, Varya with the stationmaster, and so on. Varya cries quietly and wipes away her tears as she dances. Dunyasha is in the last couple. They walk across the drawing room. Pishchik shouts,* "Grand rond balancez!" *and* "Les cavaliers à genoux et remerciez vos dames!"

Firs, wearing a tailcoat, crosses the room with soda water on a tray.

PISHCHIK   I've got this high blood pressure—I've had a stroke twice already, you know—and it makes dancing difficult; but if you're one of a pack, as the saying goes, you've got to wag your tail, whether you bark or not. Actually I'm as strong as a horse. My dear father—he liked his little joke, God bless him —he used to say that the ancient family of Simeonov-Pishchik was descended from the very same horse that Caligula sat in the Senate. [*sits down*] But the trouble is, we've no money. A hungry dog can only think about food. . . . [*falls asleep and snores but wakes up almost at once]* Just like myself— I can't think of anything but money.

TROFIMOV   It's quite true; there *is* something horsy about your build.

PISHCHIK   Oh, well, the horse is a good animal. You can sell a horse.

From the adjoining room comes the sound of someone playing billiards. Varya appears in the ballroom, under the arch

TROFIMOV   [*Teasing her*] Madame Lopakhin! Madame Lopakhin!

VARYA   [*Angrily*] The "moth-eaten gent"!

TROFIMOV   Yes, I am a moth-eaten gent, and I'm proud of it.

VARYA   [*Brooding bitterly*] So now we've hired a band—but how are we going to pay for it? [*goes out*]

TROFIMOV   [*To Pishchik*] If all the energy you've wasted in the course of a lifetime looking for money to pay interest on your debts—if all that energy had been used for something else, you'd probably have turned the world upside down by now.

PISHCHIK   The philosopher Nietzsche, the greatest, the most famous—a man of the highest intellect in fact—says it's justifiable to forge bank notes.

TROFIMOV   Have you read Nietzsche then?

PISHCHIK   Well, no. Dashenka told me. But just now I'm in such a frightful position that I wouldn't mind forging a few bank notes. The day after tomorrow I've got to pay three hundred and ten rubles. I've borrowed one hundred and thirty already. [*feels in his pockets with alarm*] The money's gone! I've lost the money. [*tearfully*] Where's the money? [*with an expression of joy*] Here it is, inside the lining! The shock's made me sweat!

Enter Lyubov Andreyevna and Charlotta

LYUBOV ANDREYEVNA   [*Singing "Lezginka," a popular dance tune, under her breath*] Why is Leonid so late? What's he doing in town? [*to Dunyasha*] Dunyasha, offer the musicians some tea.

TROFIMOV   I suppose the auction didn't take place.

LYUBOV ANDREYEVNA   The band came at the wrong time, and

the party started at the wrong time. Well, never mind. [*sits down and sings quietly*]

CHARLOTTA [*Hands a pack of cards to Pishchik*] Here's a pack of cards—think of any card now.

PISHCHIK I've thought of one.

CHARLOTTA Now shuffle the pack. That's right. Now give it to me, my good Monsieur Pishchik. *Eins, zwei, drei!* Now look for it. There it is, in your breast pocket.

PISHCHIK [*Takes the card out of his breast pocket*] The eight of spades, absolutely right! [*in astonishment*] Fancy that!

CHARLOTTA [*Holding the pack of cards on the palm of her hand, to Trofimov*] Tell me quickly, which card is on top?

TROFIMOV Well. Let us say the queen of spades.

CHARLOTTA Here it is! [*she claps her hand over the pack of cards, which disappears*] What fine weather we're having today!

A woman's voice, apparently coming from beneath the floor, answers her, "Oh, yes, madam, the weather's perfectly marvelous!"

[*addressing the voice*] How charming you are, quite delightful!

VOICE And I like you very much also, madam.

STATIONMASTER [*Applauding*] Madame ventriloquist, well done!

PISHCHIK [*Astonished*] Fancy that! Charlotta Ivanovna, how fascinating you are! I'm quite in love with you!

CHARLOTTA [*Shrugging her shoulders*] In love? Do you know how to love? *Guter Mensch, aber schlechter Musikant.*

TROFIMOV [*Slaps Pishchik on the shoulder*] A regular old horse!

CHARLOTTA Attention please! Here's just one more trick. [*she takes a blanket from a chair*] Now I'm offering this very nice blanket for sale. [*shakes it out*] Would anyone like to buy it?

PISHCHIK [*Astonished*] Just imagine!

CHARLOTTA *Eins, zwei, drei!* [*she lifts up the blanket and discloses Anya standing behind it*]

Anya drops a curtsy, runs to her mother, gives her a hug, then runs back into the ballroom. Everyone is delighted

LYUBOV ANDREYEVNA [*Clapping*] Bravo, bravo!

CHARLOTTA Just once more. *Eins, zwei, drei!* [*lifts the blanket; behind it stands Varya, who bows*]

PISHCHIK [*Astonished*] Fancy that!

CHARLOTTA Finished! [*she throws the blanket over Pishchik, curtsies, and runs off to the ballroom*]

PISHCHIK [*Hurries after her*] The little rascal! Have you ever seen anything like it? Have you ever . . . ? [*goes out*]

LYUBOV ANDREYEVNA Still no Leonid. I can't understand what he's doing all this time in town. In any case everything must be over by now; either the estate's been sold or the auction never took place. Why must he keep us in ignorance so long?

VARYA [*Trying to comfort her*] Uncle bought it; dear Uncle, I'm sure he did.

TROFIMOV [*Sarcastically*] Oh, yes?

VARYA Grandmamma sent him power of attorney to buy the estate in her name and transfer the mortgage to her. She's done it for Anya's sake. God will help us. I'm sure of it. Uncle will buy the estate.

LYUBOV ANDREYEVNA Grandmamma sent us fifteen thousand rubles to buy the estate in her name—she doesn't trust us, you see—but the money wouldn't even pay the interest. [*she covers her face with her hands*] Today my fate is being decided, my fate.

TROFIMOV [*To Varya, teasingly*] Madame Lopakhin!

VARYA [*Irritably*] The eternal student! Why, you've been thrown out of the university twice already!

LYUBOV ANDREYEVNA Why get so cross, Varya? He does tease you about Lopakhin, but what's the harm? If you feel inclined to, why don't you marry Lopakhin; he's a nice, interesting fellow. Of course, if you don't feel like it, don't. No one's trying to force you, darling.

VARYA I do take it very seriously, Mamma dear . . . and I want to be frank with you about it. He's a nice man and I like him.

LYUBOV ANDREYEVNA Then marry him. What are you waiting for? I can't understand you.

VARYA Mamma darling, I can't propose to him myself, can I? It's two years now since everyone started talking to me about him, and everyone is still doing it, but he either says nothing or else he just talks in a sort of teasing way. I understand what's the matter. He's getting rich, he's occupied with his business, and he has no time for me. If only I had some money, just a little, even a hundred rubles, then I'd have left everything and gone away, the farther the better. I'd have gone into a convent.

TROFIMOV   A beautiful life!

VARYA   [*To Trofimov*] Of course a student like you has to be clever! [*softly and tearfully*] How plain you've become, Petya. How much older you look! [*to Lyubov Andreyevna, her tearfulness gone*] The only thing I can't bear, Mamma dear, is to be without work. I must be doing something all the time.

Enter Yasha

YASHA   [*With difficulty restraining his laughter*] Yepikhodov's broken a billiard cue! [*goes out*]

VARYA   But why is Yepikhodov here? Who allowed him to play billiards? I can't understand these people. [*goes out*]

LYUBOV ANDREYEVNA   Don't tease her, Petya. Don't you see she's upset already?

TROFIMOV   She's too much of a busybody; she will poke her nose into other people's affairs. She wouldn't leave us alone the whole summer, neither Anya nor me. She was afraid we might fall in love with each other. Why should she mind? Besides, I didn't show any sign of it. I'm too far removed from such trivialities. We are above love!

LYUBOV ANDREYEVNA   And I suppose I'm below love. [*in great agitation*] Why isn't Leonid back? I only want to know whether the estate's sold or not. Such a calamity seems so incredible that somehow I don't even know what to think. I feel quite lost. Honestly I feel I could shriek out loud this very moment. I will be doing something silly. Help me, Petya. Say something, speak!

TROFIMOV   Isn't it all the same whether the estate's sold today or not? It's finished and done with long ago, there's no turning back, the bridges are burned. You must keep calm, my dear. You mustn't deceive yourself; for once in your life you must look the truth straight in the face.

LYUBOV ANDREYEVNA What truth? *You* can see where the truth is and where it isn't, but I seem to have lost my power of vision; I don't see anything. You're able to solve all your problems in a resolute way—but, tell me, my dear boy, isn't that because you're young, because you're not old enough yet to have suffered on account of your problems? You look ahead so boldly—but isn't that because life is still hidden from your young eyes, so that you're not able to foresee anything dreadful or expect it? You've a more courageous and honest and serious nature than we have, but do consider our position carefully; do be generous—even if only a little bit—and spare me. I was born here, you know. My father and mother lived here, and my grandfather too, and I love this house. I can't conceive of life without the cherry orchard, and if it really has to be sold, then sell me with it. [*embraces Trofimov and kisses him on the forehead*] You know, my son was drowned here. [*weeps*] Have pity on me, my dear, dear friend.

TROFIMOV You know that I sympathize with you with all my heart.

LYUBOV ANDREYEVNA But you must say it differently. . . . Differently. [*takes out a handkerchief; a telegram falls onto the floor*] There's such a weight on my mind today, you can't imagine. This place is too noisy, my very soul seems to shudder with every sound, and I'm trembling all over—yet I can't go to my room for fear of being alone and quiet. Don't blame me, Petya. I love you as if you were my own child. I would willingly let Anya marry you, honestly I would, but, my dear boy, you must study, you must finish your course. You don't do anything; fate seems to drive you from one place to another—such a strange thing. Isn't it? Isn't it? And you should do something about your beard; make it grow somehow. [*laughs*] You are a funny boy!

TROFIMOV [*Picks up the telegram*] I don't want to be a dandy.

LYUBOV ANDREYEVNA That telegram's from Paris. I get one every day. Yesterday and today. That savage is ill again, and things are going badly with him. He wants me to forgive him, implores me to return; and really I do feel I ought to go to Paris and stay near him for a bit. You're looking very stern, Petya, but what's to be done, my dear boy? What am I to do? He's ill and lonely and unhappy. And who's there to take care of him, to prevent him from making a fool of himself, and give him his medicine at the proper time? And anyway why should I hide it or keep quiet about it? I love him, of course I love him. I do, I do. It's a millstone around my neck, and I'm going to the bottom with it—but I love him and I can't live without him. [*she presses Trofimov's hand*] Don't think badly of me, Petya; don't speak, don't say anything.

TROFIMOV [*With strong emotion*] Please, please forgive my frankness, but that man's been robbing you!

LYUBOV ANDREYEVNA No, no, no, you mustn't talk like that. [*puts her hands over her ears*]

TROFIMOV He's a cad. You're the only one who doesn't know it! He's a petty cad, a worthless . . .

LYUBOV ANDREYEVNA [*Angry, but in control of herself*] You're twenty-six or twenty-seven years old but you're still like a schoolboy in a prep school!

TROFIMOV Never mind me!

LYUBOV ANDREYEVNA You ought to be a man. At your age you ought to understand people who are in love. And you ought to be able to love, to fall in love! [*angrily*] Yes, yes! And you're not "pure," but you just make a fad of purity. You're a ridiculous crank, a freak.

TROFIMOV [*Horrified*] What is she saying?

LYUBOV ANDREYEVNA "I'm above love!" You're not above love; you're daft, as our Firs would say. Not to have a mistress at your age!

TROFIMOV [*Horrified*] This is dreadful! What's she saying? [*walks quickly toward the ballroom, his head between his hands*] This is dreadful. I can't; I'm going. [*goes out but returns at once*] Everything's finished between us! [*goes out through the door into the hall*]

LYUBOV ANDREYEVNA [*Calls after him*] Petya, wait! You funny fellow, I was joking! Petya!

From the hall comes the sound of someone running quickly upstairs, then falling down with a crash. There are shrieks from Anya and Varya, followed by laughter

What's happened?

Anya runs in

ANYA [*Laughing*] Petya's fallen downstairs. [*runs out*]

LYUBOV ANDREYEVNA   What a queer fellow he is!

The stationmaster stands in the middle of the ballroom and begins to recite "The Sinner" by Aleksei Tolstoy. The others listen, but he has hardly had time to recite more than a few lines when the sound of a waltz reaches them from the hall, and the recitation breaks off. Everyone dances. Enter from the hall Trofimov, Anya, and Varya

LYUBOV ANDREYEVNA   Now, Petya. There, my dear boy. I ask your forgiveness. Let's dance. [*she dances with Petya*]

Anya and Varya dance. Enter Firs, then Yasha. Firs stands his walking stick by the side door. Yasha looks at the dancers from the drawing room

YASHA   How goes it, Grandad?

FIRS   I'm not too well. We used to have generals, barons, and admirals dancing at our balls, but now we send for the post office clerk and the stationmaster, and even they don't come too willingly. I seem to have grown so weak somehow. . . . My old master, that's the mistress's grandfather, used to give everyone powdered sealing wax for medicine, whatever the illness was. I've been taking it every day for the last twenty years or perhaps even longer. Maybe that's why I'm still alive.

YASHA   How you weary me, Grandad! [*yawns*] I wish you'd go away and die soon.

FIRS   Eh, you! You're daft. [*mutters*]

Trofimov and Lyubov Andreyevna dance in the ballroom, then in the drawing room

LYUBOV ANDREYEVNA   Thank you. I'd like to sit down for a bit. [*sits down*] I'm tired.

Enter Anya

ANYA [*Agitated*] A man in the kitchen was saying just now that the cherry orchard was sold today.

LYUBOV ANDREYEVNA Sold? Who to?

ANYA He didn't say. He's gone. [*she dances with Trofimov. Both go to the ballroom*]

YASHA There was some old man there gossiping away. A stranger.

FIRS And Leonid Andreyevich's not back yet; he's still not back. He's only got his light overcoat on—his "between seasons" coat—and he might easily catch a cold. These youngsters!

LYUBOV ANDREYEVNA I feel as though I'm going to die. Yasha, go and find out who bought it.

YASHA But the old man's been gone a long time. [*laughs*]

LYUBOV ANDREYEVNA [*With a touch of annoyance*] Well, what are you laughing at? What are you so happy about?

YASHA Yepikhodov's such a comic guy—a stupid fellow. Twenty-two misfortunes!

LYUBOV ANDREYEVNA Firs, if the estate is sold, where will you go?

FIRS I'll go wherever you order me to.

LYUBOV ANDREYEVNA Why are you looking like that? Are you ill? I would go to bed, you know.

FIRS Yes. [*with a faint smile*] If I went to bed, who'd wait on the guests? Who'd keep things going? There's no one in the house but me.

YASHA [*To Lyubov Andreyevna*] Lyubov Andreyevna! I want to ask you for something, please! If you go to Paris again, do me a favor and take me with you. It's quite impossible for me to stay here. [*looking around, in a subdued voice*] There's no need for me to say it. You can see it for yourself: the people are uneducated, and they're immoral too. Besides it's so boring, and the food they give you in the kitchen is abominable. Then this Firs keeps on walking around and muttering all sorts of silly things. Take me with you, please!

Enter Pishchik

PISHCHIK Allow me to ask you for a dance, beautiful lady.

Lyubov Andreyevna gets up to dance

I'll have that hundred and eighty rubles from you all the same, my charmer. Yes, I will. [*dances*] Just one hundred and eighty rubles, that's all. [*they go into the ballroom*]

YASHA [*Sings quietly*] "Will you understand the agitation of my soul?"

In the ballroom a woman in checked trousers and a gray top hat starts jumping in the air and throwing her arms around. There are shouts of "Bravo, Charlotta Ivanovna!"

DUNYASHA [*Stops to powder her face*] The young mistress ordered me to dance—there are so many gentlemen and only a few ladies—but I get so dizzy from dancing, and my heart beats too fast. Firs Nikolaevich, the post office clerk, told me something just now that quite took my breath away.

The music stops

FIRS What did he tell you?

DUNYASHA "You are like a flower," he said.

YASHA [*Yawns*] What ignorance! [*goes out*]

DUNYASHA Like a flower . . . I'm so sensitive. I love it when people say nice things to me.

FIRS You'll get your head turned all right.

Enter Yepikhodov

YEPIKHODOV Avdotya Fëdorovna, you don't seem to want to look at me, as if I were some sort of insect. [*sighs*] What a life!

DUNYASHA What is it you want?

YEPIKHODOV Perhaps you may be right, no doubt. [*sighs*] But, of course, if one looks at it from a certain point of view—if I may so express myself, forgive my frankness—you've driven me into such a state. I know what my fate is; every day some misfortune's sure to happen to me, but I've been so long accustomed to it, that I look at life with a smile. You gave me your word, and though I . . .

DUNYASHA Please, please, let's have a talk later, but now leave me alone. I feel in a kind of dream just now. [*plays with her fan*]

YEPIKHODOV Some misfortune or other happens to me every day, and yet—if I may so express myself—I only smile; I even laugh.

Varya enters from the ballroom

VARYA Haven't you gone yet, Semën? What an ill-mannered fellow you are really! [*to Dunyasha*] You'd better go, Dunyasha. [*to Yepikhodov*] First you go and play billiards and break a cue, and now you're walking around the drawing room like a visitor.

YEPIKHODOV Permit me to inform you that you can't start imposing penalties on me.

VARYA I'm not imposing penalties; I'm merely telling you. All you do is walk from one place to another, instead of getting on with your work. We keep a clerk, but what for no one knows.

YEPIKHODOV [*Offended*] Whether I work, walk around, eat, or play billiards, the only people who are entitled to judge my actions are those who are older than me and know what they're talking about.

VARYA You dare say that to me? [*flying into a temper*] You dare to say that? You're suggesting I don't know what I'm talking about? Get out of here! This very minute!

YEPIKHODOV [*Cowed*] I wish you'd express yourself more delicately.

VARYA [*Beside herself*] Get out this minute! Out!

He goes to the door. She follows him

Twenty-two misfortunes! I don't want any more of you here! I don't want ever to set eyes on you again!

Yepikhodov goes out. He is heard from outside the door saying, "I'll complain about you."

Ah, you're coming back, are you? [*she seizes the stick that Firs left by the door*] Come on, come on . . . I'll show you! Ah, you're coming back, are you? There, I'll give it to you. [*swings the stick, and at that moment Lopakhin enters*]

LOPAKHIN [*Whom the stick did not, in fact, touch*] Thank you very much!

VARYA [*Angry and sarcastic*] I beg your pardon!

LOPAKHIN Don't mention it. Thanks for a pleasant surprise.

VARYA It's not worth thanking me for. [*goes to the side, then looks around and says gently*] I haven't hurt you, have I?

LOPAKHIN No, not at all. There's a huge bump coming up though.

VOICES IN THE BALLROOM Lopakhin's arrived! Yermolai Alekseevich!

PISHCHIK Look here, you can see him, you can hear him! [*embraces Lopakhin*] You smell of cognac, my dear fellow, my fine boy! We're making merry here too.

Enter Lyubov Andreyevna

LYUBOV ANDREYEVNA It's you, Yermolai Alekseevich? Why have you been so long? Where is Leonid?

LOPAKHIN Leonid Andreyevich returned with me; he's coming along.

LYUBOV ANDREYEVNA [*Agitated*] Well, what happened? Was there an auction? Speak, tell me!

LOPAKHIN [*Embarrassed, fearing to betray his joy*] The auction was over by four o'clock. We missed our train and had to wait until half past nine. [*with a deep sigh*] Ugh! My head's going around.

Enter Gayev. He carries some parcels in his right hand and wipes away his tears with his left

LYUBOV ANDREYEVNA Lenya, what happened? Well, Lenya? [*impatiently, with tears*] Tell me quickly, for God's sake! . . .

GAYEV [*Does not reply but waves his hand at her. To Firs, weep-*

ing] Here, take this. It's some anchovies and Kerch herrings. I've had nothing to eat all day. What I've been through!

Through the open door leading to the billiard room comes the sound of billiard balls in play and Yasha's voice saying, "Seven and eighteen." Gayev's expression changes and he stops crying

I'm dreadfully tired. Come, Firs, I want to change. [*goes out through the ballroom, Firs following*]

PISHCHIK What happened at the auction? Come, tell us!

LYUBOV ANDREYEVNA Has the cherry orchard been sold?

LOPAKHIN It has.

LYUBOV ANDREYEVNA Who bought it?

LOPAKHIN I did.

A pause. Lyubov Andreyevna is overcome; only the fact that she is standing beside a table and a chair prevents her from falling. Varya takes a bundle of keys off her belt, throws them on the floor in the middle of the drawing room, and walks out

Yes, I bought it. Wait a moment, ladies and gentlemen, please. I don't feel quite clear in my head. I hardly know how to talk. [*laughs*] When we got to the auction, Deriganov was there already. Of course Leonid Andreyevich only had fifteen thousand rubles, and Deriganov at once bid thirty over and above the mortgage. I could see how things were going, so I muscled in and offered forty. He bid forty-five, I bid fifty-five; he kept on adding five thousand each time and I added ten thousand each time. Well, it finished at last. I bid ninety thousand over and above the mortgage, and I got the property. Yes, the cherry orchard's mine now! Mine! [*laughs*] My God! The cherry orchard's mine! Come on, tell me I'm drunk, tell me I'm out of my mind, say I've imagined all this. [*stamps his foot*] Don't laugh at me! If only my father and grandfather could rise from their graves and see everything that's happened—how their Yermolai, their much-beaten, half-literate Yermolai, the lad who used to run around with bare feet in the winter—how he's bought this estate, the most beautiful place on God's earth! Yes, I've bought the very estate where my father and grandfather were serfs, where they weren't even admitted to the kitchen! I must be asleep, I must be dreaming, I only think it's true. It's all just my imagination; my imagination's been wandering. [*picks up the keys, smiling tenderly*] She threw these down because she wanted to show she's not mistress here anymore. [*jingles the keys*] Well, never mind. [*the band is heard tuning up*] Hey, you musicians, come on now, play something! I want some music! Now then, all of you, just you wait and see Yermolai Lopakhin take an ax to the cherry orchard, just you see the trees come crashing down! We're going to build a whole lot of new villas, and our children and great-grandchildren are going to see a new living world growing up here. Come on there, let's have some music!

The band plays. Lyubov Andreyevna has sunk into a chair and is crying bitterly

[*reproachfully*] Why didn't you listen to me before, why didn't you? My poor, dear lady, you can't undo it now. [*with great emotion*] Oh, if only we could be done with all this, if only we could alter this distorted, unhappy life somehow!

PISHCHIK [*Taking his arm, in a subdued voice*] She's crying. Come into the ballroom; leave her alone. Come on. [*takes his arm and leads him away to the ballroom*]

LOPAKHIN Never mind! Come on, band, play, play! Everything must be just as *I* wish it now. [*ironically*] Here comes the new landowner! Here comes the owner of the cherry orchard! [*he pushes a small table accidentally and nearly knocks over some candlesticks*] Never mind, I can pay for everything! [*goes out with Pishchik*]

No one remains in the ballroom or drawing room except Lyubov Andreyevna, who sits hunched up in a chair, crying bitterly. The band continues playing quietly. Anya and Trofimov enter quickly. Anya goes up to her mother and kneels beside her. Trofimov remains standing by the entrance to the ballroom

ANYA Mamma! Mamma, you're crying? Dear, kind, sweet Mamma, my darling precious, how I love you! God bless you,

Mamma! The cherry orchard's sold, it's quite true; there isn't any cherry orchard anymore, it's true. But don't cry, Mamma —you still have your life ahead of you, you still have your dear, innocent heart. You must come away with me, darling; we must get away from here! We'll plant a new orchard, even more splendid than this one—and when you see it, you'll understand everything, your heart will be filled with happiness, like the sun in the evening. And then you'll smile again, Mamma! Come with me, darling, come!

CURTAIN

ACT FOUR

The same setting as for Act One. There are no pictures on the walls or curtains at the windows; only a few remaining pieces of furniture are piled up in a corner as if for sale. There is an oppressive sense of emptiness. At the back of the stage, beside the door, suitcases and other pieces of luggage have been piled together as if ready for a journey. The voices of Varya and Anya can be heard through the door on the left, which is open. Lopakhin stands waiting. Yasha is holding a tray laden with glasses of champagne. In the hall Yepikhodov is tying up a large box. From somewhere behind the scenes comes the low hum of voices: the peasants have called to say good-bye. Gayev's voice is heard saying, "Thank you, friends, thank you."

YASHA The villagers have come to say good-bye. In my view, Yermolai Alekseevich, they're kindhearted folk, but they haven't much understanding.

The hum subsides. Lyubov Andreyevna and Gayev enter from the hall. Lyubov Andreyevna is not crying but her face is pale and tremulous. She seems unable to speak

GAYEV You gave them your purse, Lyuba. You shouldn't have done that. You really shouldn't.
LYUBOV ANDREYEVNA I couldn't help myself, I couldn't help myself! [*both go out*]

LOPAKHIN [*Calls after them through the door*] Have some champagne, please do, please! Just one little glass before you go. I didn't think of bringing any from town, and I could only get one bottle at the station. Have some, please. [*pause*] Won't you have any, ladies and gentlemen? [*walks away from the door*] If I'd known, I wouldn't have brought any. Then I won't have any either.

Yasha carefully puts the tray on a chair

You have a drink, Yasha, if nobody else will.

YASHA Here's to the travelers! And here's to you staying behind. [*drinks*] This champagne isn't the real thing, I can tell you.

LOPAKHIN Eight rubles a bottle. [*pause*] It's devilishly cold here.

YASHA The stoves weren't lighted today. It doesn't matter since we're going. [*laughs*]

LOPAKHIN Why are you laughing?

YASHA Because I'm feeling glad.

LOPAKHIN October's here, but it's still sunny and calm, as if it were summer. Good building weather. [*looks at his watch, then at the door*] Ladies and gentlemen, don't forget there are only forty-six minutes before the train's due to leave. That means we must start in twenty minutes. Hurry up.

Trofimov, wearing an overcoat, comes in from outdoors

TROFIMOV I think it's time to start. The horses are at the door. God knows where my galoshes are; they've disappeared. [*calls through the door*] Anya, my galoshes aren't here; I can't find them.

LOPAKHIN And I must be off to Kharkov. I'll travel with you on the same train. I will stay the whole winter in Kharkov. I've hung around here too long, and it's torture having no work to do. I can't be without work. I just don't know what to do with my hands; they feel limp and strange, as if they didn't belong to me.

TROFIMOV We'll soon be gone; then you can start your useful labors again.

LOPAKHIN Have a little drink.

TROFIMOV   No, thanks.

LOPAKHIN   You're going to Moscow then?

TROFIMOV   Yes, I'll see them off to town, and then tomorrow I'm off to Moscow.

LOPAKHIN   Well, well. I expect the professors are holding up their lectures, waiting for your arrival!

TROFIMOV   That's none of your business.

LOPAKHIN   How many years have you been studying at the university?

TROFIMOV   I wish you'd think up something new; that's old and stale. [*looks for his galoshes*] Incidentally since we're not likely to meet again, I'd like to give you a bit of advice, by way of a farewell: stop throwing your arms around! Try to get rid of that habit of making wide, sweeping gestures. Yes, and all this talk too about building villas, these calculations about summer residents that are going to turn into small property owners, these forecasts—they're all sweeping gestures too. When all's said and done, I like you, despite everything. You've slender, delicate fingers, like an artist's; you've a fine, sensitive soul.

LOPAKHIN   [*Embraces him*] Good-bye, my friend. Thank you for everything. I can let you have some money for your journey if you need it.

TROFIMOV   Whatever for? I don't want it.

LOPAKHIN   But you haven't any!

TROFIMOV   Yes, I have, thank you. I've just gotten some for a translation. Here it is, in my pocket. [*anxiously*] But I can't see my galoshes anywhere.

VARYA   [*From the other room*] Take your beastly things! [*she throws a pair of rubber galoshes into the room*]

TROFIMOV   But why are you angry, Varya? Hm . . . but these aren't my galoshes!

LOPAKHIN   I had a thousand acres of poppies sown last spring, and now I've just made forty thousand net profit on it. And when they were in bloom, what a picture it was! What I want to say is that I've made the forty thousand, and now I'm offering to lend you money because I'm in a position to do it. Why are you so stuck up? I'm a peasant. I've no manners.

TROFIMOV   Your father was a peasant; mine had a chemist's shop. But there's nothing in that.

Lopakhin takes out his wallet

Leave it alone, leave it alone. Even if you offered me two hundred thousand, I wouldn't take it. I'm a free man. And all that you value so highly and hold so dear, you rich men—and beggars too for that matter—none of it has the slightest power over me. It's all just so much fluff blowing around in the air. I'm strong, I'm proud, I can do without you, I can pass you by. Humanity is advancing toward the highest truth, the greatest happiness that it is possible to achieve on earth, and I am in the vanguard!

LOPAKHIN   Will you get there?

TROFIMOV   Yes. [*pause*] I'll get there myself or show others the way to get there.

The sound of an ax striking a tree is heard in the distance

LOPAKHIN   Well, good-bye, my friend, it's time to go. We show off in front of one another, and in the meantime life is slipping by. When I work for long hours on end, without taking any time off, I feel happier in my mind and I even imagine I know why I exist. But how many people there are in Russia, my friend, who exist for no purpose whatever! Well, never mind, perhaps it doesn't matter. They say Leonid Andreyevich has taken a post at the bank, at six thousand a year. I don't expect he'll stick to it; he's too lazy.

ANYA   [*In the doorway*] Mamma asks you not to cut the orchard down until she's left.

TROFIMOV   I should say not! Haven't you got any tact? [*goes out through the hall*]

LOPAKHIN   All right, all right. These people! [*follows Trofimov*]

ANYA   Has Firs been taken to the hospital?

YASHA   I told them to take him this morning. He's gone, I think.

ANYA   [*To Yepikhodov, who passes through the ballroom*] Semën Panteleyevich, will you please find out whether Firs has been taken to the hospital?

YASHA   [*Offended*] I told Yegor this morning. Do you have to ask ten times?

YEPIKHODOV   This superannuated Firs—candidly speaking, I mean—he's beyond repair; he ought to go and join his ancestors. As for me, I can only envy him. [*he places a suitcase on top of a cardboard hatbox and squashes it*] There you are, you see! I might have known it! [*goes out*]

YASHA   [*Sardonically*] Twenty-two misfortunes!

VARYA   [*From behind the door*] Has Firs been taken to the hospital?

ANYA   Yes.

VARYA   Why haven't they taken the letter to the doctor then?

ANYA   I'll send someone after them with it. [*goes out*]

VARYA   [*From the adjoining room*] Where's Yasha? Tell him his mother is here and wants to say good-bye to him.

YASHA   [*Waves his hand*] She makes me lose patience with her.

While the foregoing action has been taking place, Dunyasha has been fussing with the luggage. Now that Yasha is alone, she comes up to him

DUNYASHA   If only you'd look at me once, Yasha! You're going. You're leaving me behind! [*she cries and throws her arms around his neck*]

YASHA   What's the point of crying? [*drinks champagne*] In a week's time I'll be in Paris again. Tomorrow we'll get into an express train— and off we'll go. We will just disappear! I can hardly believe it. *Vive la France!* This place doesn't suit me; I can't live here—there's nothing going on. I've seen enough of all this ignorance. I've had enough of it. [*drinks*] What are you crying for? Behave like a respectable girl, then there won't be any need to cry.

DUNYASHA   [*Looking into a hand mirror and powdering her nose*] Write to me from Paris, won't you? You know that I've loved you, Yasha. I've loved you so much! I've got a soft heart, Yasha!

YASHA   Someone's coming. [*pretends to be busy with a suitcase, singing quietly to himself*]

Enter Lyubov Andreyevna, Gayev, Anya, and Charlotta Ivanovna

GAYEV   We ought to be going. There isn't much time left. [*looks at Yasha*] Who smells of herring here?

LYUBOV ANDREYEVNA   In ten minutes we ought to be getting into the carriage. [*glances around the room*] Good-bye, dear house, old Grandfather house. Winter will pass, spring will come again, and then you won't be here anymore; you'll be pulled down. How much these walls have seen! [*kisses her daughter ardently*] My little treasure, you look simply radiant; your eyes are shining like diamonds. Are you glad? Very glad?

ANYA   Yes, very. Our new life is just beginning, Mamma!

GAYEV   [*Brightly*] So it is indeed. Everything's all right now. Before the cherry orchard was sold everybody was worried and upset, but as soon as it was all settled finally and once and for all, everybody calmed down and felt quite cheerful in fact. I'm an employee of a bank now, a financier. . . . I sink the red. . . . And you, Lyuba, you're looking better too when all's said and done. There's no doubt about it.

LYUBOV ANDREYEVNA   Yes, my nerves are better, it's true.

Someone helps her on with her hat and coat

I'm sleeping better too. Take my things out, Yasha; it's time. [*to Anya*] My little girl, we'll soon be seeing each other again. I'm going to Paris—I will live there on the money that your grandmamma in Yaroslavl sent us to buy the estate—God bless Grandmamma!—and that money won't last long either.

ANYA   You'll come back soon, Mamma—quite soon, won't you? I will study and pass my exams at the high school and then I'll work and help you. We'll read all sorts of books together, Mamma, won't we? [*she kisses her mother's hands*] We'll read during the long autumn evenings; we'll read lots of books, and a new, wonderful world will open up before us. [*dreamily*] Mamma, come back.

LYUBOV ANDREYEVNA   I'll come back, my precious. [*embraces her*]

Enter Lopakhin. Charlotta quietly sings to herself

GAYEV   Happy Charlotta! She's singing.

CHARLOTTA   [*Picks up a bundle that looks like a baby in swaddling clothes*] Bye-bye, little baby. [*a sound like a baby crying is heard*] Be quiet, my sweet, be a good little boy. [*the crying continues*] My heart goes out to you, baby! [*throws the bundle down*] Are you going to find me another job, please? I can't do without one.

LOPAKHÍN We'll find you one, Charlotta Ivanovna, don't worry.

GAYEV Everybody's leaving us. Varya's going away. We've suddenly become unwanted.

CHARLOTTA I haven't got anywhere to live in town. I'll have to go. [*hums*] Oh, well, never mind.

Enter Pishchik

LOPAKHIN What a phenomenon!

PISHCHIK [*Out of breath*] Ouch, let me get my breath. . . . I'm worn out. My good friends. Give me some water.

GAYEV I suppose you've come to borrow money? I'd better go. Excuse me. [*goes out*]

PISHCHIK I've not been to see you for a long time, my beautiful lady. [*to Lopakhin*] So you're here. I'm glad to see you; you're a man of great intelligence. Here . . . take this. [*hands money to Lopakhin*] Four hundred rubles. I still owe you eight hundred and forty.

LOPAKHIN [*Shrugs his shoulders, bewildered*] It's like a dream. Where did you get it from?

PISHCHIK Wait a moment. . . . I'm so hot. A most extraordinary thing happened. Some English people came to see me and discovered a sort of white clay on my land. [*to Lyubov Andreyevna*] Here's four hundred for you also, my dear enchantress. [*hands her the money*] You'll get the rest later on. [*takes a drink of water*] Just now a young fellow in the train was telling me that some great philosopher or other advises people to jump off roofs. You just jump off, he says, and that settles the whole problem. [*as though astonished at what he has just said*] Fancy that! More water, please.

LOPAKHIN Who were these Englishmen?

PISHCHIK I leased the land with the clay to them for twenty-four years. And now you must excuse me; I'm in a hurry. I've got to get along as quickly as I can. I'm going to Znoykov's,

then to Kardamonov's. I owe money to all of them. [*drinks*]
Good health to you all. I'll call again on Thursday.

LYUBOV ANDREYEVNA   We're just on the point of moving to
town, and tomorrow I'm going abroad.

PISHCHIK   What's that? [*in agitation*] What are you going to
town for? I see now. This furniture and the suitcases . . . Well, never mind. [*tearfully*] Never mind. These
Englishmen, you know, they're men of the greatest intelligence. Never mind. I wish you every happiness. God be with
you. Never mind, everything comes to an end eventually.
[*kisses Lyubov Andreyevna's hand*] And when you hear that
my end has come, just think of—a horse and say, "There used
to be a fellow like that once. Simeonov-Pishchik his name was.
God be with him!" Wonderful weather we're having. Yes.
[*goes out, overcome with embarrassment, but returns at once
and stands in the doorway*] Dashenka sent greetings to you.
[*goes out*]

LYUBOV ANDREYEVNA   Well, we can go now. I'm leaving with
two worries on my mind. One is Firs—he's sick you know.
[*glances at her watch*] We have another five minutes or so.

ANYA   Mamma, Firs has been taken to the hospital already.
Yasha sent him this morning.

LYUBOV ANDREYEVNA   The other is Varya. She's been accustomed to getting up early and working, and now without work
she's like a fish out of water. She's gotten so thin and pale, and
she cries a lot, poor thing. [*pause*] You know very well, Yermolai Alekseevich, that I'd been hoping to get her married to
you, and everything seemed to show that you meant to marry
her too. [*whispers to Anya, who nods to Charlotta, and they
both go out*] She loves you, and you must be fond of her too.
And I just don't know, I just don't know why you seem to keep
away from each other. I don't understand it.

LOPAKHIN   Neither do I myself, I must confess. It's all so
strange somehow. If there's still time, I'm ready even now.
Let's settle it at once—and get it over! Without you here, I
don't feel I shall ever propose to her.

LYUBOV ANDREYEVNA   That's an excellent idea! You'll hardly
need more than a minute, that's all. I'll call her at once.

LOPAKHIN   There's champagne here too, quite suitable for the occasion. [*takes a look at the glasses*] But they're empty; someone's drunk it up.

Yasha coughs

I should have said lapped it up.

LYUBOV ANDREYEVNA   [*With animation*] I'm so glad. We'll go outside. Yasha, *allez!* I'll call her. [*through the door*] Varya, come here a moment; leave what you're doing for a minute! Varya! [*goes out with Yasha*]

LOPAKHIN   [*Glancing at his watch*] Yes.

Suppressed laughter and whispering is heard from behind the door, and finally Varya comes in and starts examining the luggage

VARYA   [*After some time*] It's strange, I just can't find . . .

LOPAKHIN   What are you looking for?

VARYA   I packed the things myself, yet I can't remember . . .

LOPAKHIN   [*After a pause*] Where are you going to now, Varvara Mikhailovna?

VARYA   I? To the Ragulins. I've agreed to look after the house for them—to be their housekeeper or something.

LOPAKHIN   That's at Yashnevo, isn't it? About seventy miles from here. [*pause*] So this is the end of life in this house.

VARYA   [*Examining the luggage*] But where could it be? Or perhaps I've packed it in the trunk? Yes, life in this house has come to an end; there won't be any more.

LOPAKHIN   And I'm going to Kharkov presently. On the next train. I've got a lot to do there. And I'm leaving Yepikhodov here. I've engaged him.

VARYA   Well!

LOPAKHIN   Do you remember, last year about this time it was snowing already, but now it's quite still and sunny. It's rather cold though. About three degrees below freezing.

VARYA   I haven't looked. [*pause*] Besides our thermometer's broken.

A voice is heard from outside the door: "Yermolai Alekse-evich!"

LOPAKHIN [*As if he had long been expecting it*] Coming this moment! [*goes out quickly*]

Varya, sitting on the floor, with her head on the bundle of clothes, sobs softly. The door opens; Lyubov Andreyevna enters quietly

LYUBOV ANDREYEVNA Well? [*pause*] We must go.

VARYA [*Stops crying and wipes her eyes*] Yes, it's time, Mamma dear. I'll just be able to get to the Ragulins today, if only we don't miss the train.

LYUBOV ANDREYEVNA [*Calls through the door*] Anya, put your coat on.

Enter Anya, followed by Gayev and Charlotta Ivanovna. Gayev wears a heavy overcoat with a hood. Servants and coachmen come into the room. Yepikhodov fusses with the luggage

Now we can start on our journey!

ANYA [*Joyfully*] Yes, our journey!

GAYEV My friends, my dear, kind friends! Now as I leave this house forever, how can I remain silent, how can I refrain from expressing to you, as a last farewell, the feelings that now overwhelm me?

ANYA [*Imploringly*] Uncle!

VARYA Uncle, dear, please don't!

GAYEV [*Downcast*] I sink the red and follow through. . . . I'll keep quiet.

Enter Trofimov, then Lopakhin

TROFIMOV Well, ladies and gentlemen, it's time to go.

LOPAKHIN Yepikhodov, my coat!

LYUBOV ANDREYEVNA   I'll just sit down for one little minute more. I feel as if I'd never seen the walls and ceilings of this house before, and now I look at them with such longing and affection.

GAYEV   I remember when I was six years old—it was Holy Trinity day—I was sitting on this windowsill, looking at Father. He was just going to church. . . .

LYUBOV ANDREYEVNA   Have they taken out all the luggage?

LOPAKHIN   It looks as if they have. [*to Yepikhodov, as he puts on his coat*] See that everything's all right, Yepikhodov.

YEPIKHODOV   [*In a husky voice*] Don't worry, Yermolai Alekseevich!

LOPAKHIN   What are you talking like that for?

YEPIKHODOV   I've just had a drink of water. I must have swallowed something.

YASHA   [*With contempt*] What ignorance!

LYUBOV ANDREYEVNA   When we leave here there won't be a soul in the place.

LOPAKHIN   Until the spring.

Varya pulls an umbrella from a bundle of clothes. Lopakhin pretends to be frightened that she is going to strike him

Now, why . . . why are you doing that? I never thought of . . .

TROFIMOV   Ladies and gentlemen, come, let's get into the carriage. It's high time. The train will be in soon.

VARYA   Petya, here they are, your galoshes, beside the suitcase. [*tearfully*] And how dirty and worn-out they are!

TROFIMOV   [*Puts them on*] Come along, ladies and gentlemen!

GAYEV   [*Greatly embarrassed, afraid of breaking into tears*] The train, the station . . . In off into the middle pocket.

LYUBOV ANDREYEVNA   Let us go!

LOPAKHIN   Is everyone here? No one left behind? [*locks the door on the left*] There are some things put away there; it had better be locked up. Come along!

ANYA   Good-bye, old house! Good-bye, old life!

TROFIMOV   Greetings to the new life! [*goes out with Anya*]

Varya glances around the room and goes out slowly. Yasha and Charlotta, with her little dog, follow

LOPAKHIN And so, until the spring. Come along, ladies and gentlemen. *Au revoir!* [*goes out*]

Lyubov Andreyevna and Gayev are left alone. They seem to have been waiting for this moment, and now they embrace each other and sob quietly, with restraint, so as not to be heard

GAYEV [*With despair in his voice*] Sister, my sister . . .
LYUBOV ANDREYEVNA Oh, my darling, my precious, my beautiful orchard! My life, my youth, my happiness . . . good-bye! . . . Good-bye!
ANYA'S VOICE [*Gaily*] Mamma!
TROFIMOV'S VOICE [*Gaily and excitedly*] Yoo-hoo!
LYUBOV ANDREYEVNA For the last time—to look at these walls, these windows. . . . Mother used to love walking up and down this room.
GAYEV Sister, my sister!
ANYA'S VOICE Mamma!
TROFIMOV'S VOICE Yoo-hoo!
LYUBOV ANDREYEVNA We're coming. [*both go out*]

The stage is empty. The sound of doors being locked is heard, then of carriages driving off. It grows quiet. The stillness is broken by the dull thuds of an ax on a tree. They sound forlorn and sad.

There is a sound of footsteps and from the door on the right Firs appears. He is dressed as usual in a coat and white waistcoat and is wearing slippers. He looks ill

FIRS [*Walks up to the middle door and tries the handle*] Locked. They've gone. [*sits down on a sofa*] They forgot about me. Never mind. . . . I'll sit here for a bit. I don't suppose Leonid Andreyevich put on his fur coat. I expect he's gone in his light one. [*sighs, preoccupied*] I didn't see to it. These youngsters! [*mutters something unintelligible*] My life's gone as if I'd never lived. [*lies down*] I'll lie down a bit. You haven't got any strength left, nothing's left, nothing. . . . Oh, you . . . you're daft! [*lies motionless*]

A distant sound is heard, coming as if out of the sky, like the sound of a string snapping, slowly and sadly dying away. Silence ensues, broken only by the sound of an ax striking a tree in the orchard far away

CURTAIN

THE SEA GULL

CHARACTERS

ARKADINA, Irina Nikolaevna (*Madame Trepleva by marriage*), an actress

TREPLEV, Konstantin Gavriilovich (*Kostya*), her son, a young man

SORIN, Pëtr Nikolaevich (*Petrusha*), her brother

ZARECHNAYA, Nina Mikhailovna, a young girl, the daughter of a wealthy landowner

SHAMRAYEV, Ilya Afanasievich, a retired army lieutenant and Sorin's steward

POLINA, Andreyevna, his wife

MASHA (*Marya Ilyinichna, Mashenka*), his daughter

TRIGORIN, Boris Alekseevich, a writer

MEDVEDENKO, Semën Semënovich, a schoolmaster

DORN, Yevgeni Sergeevich, a doctor

YAKOV, a workman

A CHEF

A HOUSEMAID

The action takes place in Sorin's house and garden.
Between the third and fourth acts there is
an interval of two years

ACT ONE

The park on Sorin's estate. A wide avenue leads toward a lake in the background. A rough stage erected for an amateur theatrical performance has been built across the avenue and conceals the view of the lake. There are bushes close to the stage, right and left, and in the foreground, a few chairs and a small table.

The sun has just gone down. Yakov and some other men are working on the stage behind the curtain; they can be heard hammering and coughing. Masha and Medvedenko, returning from a walk, enter from the left.

MEDVEDENKO   Why do you always wear black?

MASHA   I am in mourning for my life. I'm unhappy.

MEDVEDENKO   But why? [*meditatively*] I can't understand it. You're in good health. Your father isn't rich, but he's comfortably well-off. My life is much harder than yours. I only get twenty-three rubles a month, and from that my pension is deducted. Yet I don't wear mourning.

MASHA   It isn't money that matters. Even a pauper can be happy.

MEDVEDENKO   Yes, in theory he can, but in practice it works out like this: there's myself, my mother, two sisters, and a small brother; and there's my salary, twenty-three rubles in all. We all have to eat and drink, don't we? And then what about tea and sugar? What about tobacco? You've got to scrape and save.

MASHA [*Glancing back at the stage*] They'll be starting the show soon.

MEDVEDENKO Yes. Zarechnaya is going to act, and the play is by Konstantin Gavriilovich. They are in love with one another, and today their souls will be merged in an attempt to create a single work of art. But your soul and mine have no points of contact. I love you. I can't stay at home because of my longing for you, and I walk six miles here and six miles back every day; but I get nothing from you except indifference. Oh, it's quite understandable. I haven't any money we are a large family. . . . Who would want to marry a man who hasn't even got enough to eat?

MASHA Nonsense. [*takes snuff*] I feel touched by your love, but I can't return it, that's all. [*holds out the snuff box*] Have some snuff.

MEDVEDENKO I don't feel like it now. . . .

MASHA It's close. There'll be a thunderstorm tonight, I think. You're always philosophizing or else talking about money. You believe there is no greater misfortune than poverty, but in my opinion it's a thousand times better to go around in rags and be a beggar than . . . However, that's something you wouldn't understand.

Sorin and Treplev enter from the right

SORIN [*Leaning on a walking stick*] Somehow country life doesn't suit me, my boy. It's obvious that I will never get accustomed to it. Last night I went to bed at ten, and this morning I woke up at nine, feeling as though my brain was sticking to the inside of my skull from sleeping too long. [*laughs*] Then after dinner I fell asleep again by mistake, and now I feel sort of exhausted, as if I'd had a nightmare.

TREPLEV You're right; you ought to live in town. [*seeing Masha and Medvedenko*] Say there, you two, we'll be calling you as soon as we begin, but you shouldn't be here now. Please go away.

SORIN [*To Masha*] Marya Ilyinichna, I wish you'd ask your father to have the dog let off his chain. It keeps howling. My sister was kept awake again all night.

MASHA Why don't you speak to my father yourself? I won't. Please excuse me. [*to Medvedenko*] Come, let's go.

MEDVEDENKO You will send someone to tell us when you're going to begin, won't you?

Masha and Medvedenko go out

SORIN That means that the dog will be howling all night again. The strange thing is that I've never really lived in the country in the way I wanted to. I used to take a month's leave and come down here to have a rest, and all that sort of thing. But as soon as I got here, people started to plague me with all sorts of rubbish, and within a day I'd feel like running away again. [*laughs*] I was always pleased to leave this place. But there you are, I'm retired now; I've got nowhere to go. I've got to live here now, whether I want to or not.

YAKOV [*Appears from behind the curtain*] We're going to have a swim, Konstantin Gavriilovich.

TREPLEV Very well then, but you must be sure to be back in your places in ten minutes. [*looking at his watch*] We're going to start soon.

YAKOV Yes, sir. [*goes out*]

TREPLEV [*Looking over the stage*] There's a theater for you! Just the curtain and the two wings and beyond it—open space. No scenery. You have an unimpeded view of the lake and the horizon. We'll raise the curtain at half past nine when the moon comes up.

SORIN Splendid!

TREPLEV But if Zarechnaya is late, the whole effect will be lost, of course. It's time she were here now. Her father and stepmother always keep watch on her, and it's as hard for her to break out of the house as it would be if it were a prison. [*adjusting his uncle's tie*] Your hair and beard are all in a tangle. Shouldn't you have them cut or trimmed or something?

SORIN [*Combing his hair*] That's the tragedy of my life. My appearance. . . . Even in my young days I looked as if I were a secret drinker, and all that sort of thing. The women never loved me. [*sits down*] Why is my sister in such a bad mood today?

TREPLEV   Why? She's bored. [*sits down beside him*] Jealous too. She's down on me anyway, and she's down on this show and on my play because Zarechnaya, and not she, is acting in it. She hasn't read my play, but she hates it all the same.

SORIN   [*Laughing*] Well, really! What an idea!

TREPLEV   It makes her angry to think that it won't be she, but Zarechnaya, who's going to make a success of it on this tiny stage! [*glancing at his watch*] A psychological oddity—that's my mother. Oh, there is no doubt about her being very gifted and intelligent: she's capable of weeping bitterly over a book, of reciting the whole of Nekrasov by heart, of nursing the sick with the patience of an angel. But just try and give a word of praise to Duse! Oh-ho-ho! You mustn't praise anybody but her, you mustn't write about anybody but her, you must acclaim her and go into raptures over her wonderful acting in *The Lady with the Camellias* or *The Fumes of Life*. But we can't offer her such intoxicating praise here in the country; so she feels bored and in a bad mood. And we all seem like enemies; we are all to blame. And then she's superstitious: she's afraid of having three candles lit, she's afraid of the number thirteen. And she's tightfisted too. She has seventy thousand in the bank, in Odessa—that I know for certain. But you try to borrow money from her, and she'll just burst into tears.

SORIN   You've somehow got it into your head that your mother doesn't like your play, and so you're upset, and so on. Calm yourself; your mother adores you.

TREPLEV   [*Pulling off the petals of a flower, one by one*] She loves me . . . she loves me not . . . she loves me . . . loves me not . . . loves me . . . loves me not. [*laughing*] You see, my mother doesn't love me. And why should she indeed? She wants to live, to have love affairs, to wear light-colored blouses, and here I am, twenty-five years old already. I'm always reminding her that she isn't young any longer. When I'm not around she's thirty-two, but when I'm with her she's forty-three, and she hates me for it. Moreover, she knows that I have no use for the theater. She loves the theater; she imagines that she's serving humanity. Whereas in my opinion the theater of today is in a rut and full of prejudices and conventions. When I see the curtain rise on a room with three walls; when I watch these great and talented people, these high priests of a sacred art depicting the way people eat, drink, make love, walk around, and wear their clothes, in the artificial light of the stage; when I hear them trying to squeeze a moral out of the tritest words and emptiest scenes—some petty little moral that's easy to understand and suitable for use in the home; when I'm presented with a thousand variations of the same old thing, the same thing again and again—well, I just have to escape. I run away as Maupassant ran away from the Eiffel Tower, which so oppressed him with its vulgarity.

SORIN   We can't do without the theater.

TREPLEV   We need new art forms. New forms are wanted, and if they aren't available, we might as well have nothing at all. I'm fond of my mother, very fond of her, but she leads such a fatuous life, forever fussing around with this novelist of hers, her name always being bandied about in the papers. I find it all so fatiguing. And sometimes I simply regret, like the ordinary selfish mortal I am, that I have a famous actress for a mother. And I find myself imagining that if she were an ordinary woman I would have been happier. Uncle, can you imagine a sillier, a more hopeless situation? Often she'd have a roomful of visitors, all famous people—writers and actors; and there I'd be among them, alone—a nonentity, tolerated only because I was her son. Who am I? What am I? I left the university in my third year, owing to "circumstances over which we have no control," as the editors sometimes say. I have no special gifts, not a kopeck of my own, and in my passport I'm described as a member of the lower middle class, born in Kiev. Well, my father was a member of the petty bourgeoisie, as you know—although he was a well-known actor too—and his native town was Kiev. So when all these artists and writers who were gathered together in my mother's drawing room condescended to pay a little attention to me, I used to feel that they were sizing me up as they looked at me standing there in all my insignificance. I read their thoughts, and I suffered with the humiliation of it all.

SORIN   By the way, you might tell me, what sort of a person is this writer? He's hard to understand. Always so silent.

TREPLEV   He's intelligent, unaffected, a bit on the melancholy side, I think. Really a very decent fellow. He's still a long way from forty, but he's famous already and he's had his fill of the good things of life. As for his writing . . . Well, how shall I put it? It's very clever and charming, but . . . if you've been reading Tolstoy or Zola, you don't feel like reading Trigorin afterward.

SORIN   I must admit I am fond of writers, my boy. You know, years ago there were just two things I wanted passionately. One was to get married and the other was to be a novelist. I haven't managed to pull it off either way. Yes, even to be a minor writer must be rather nice, when all is said and done.

TREPLEV   [*Listening*] I can hear footsteps. [*throws his arms around his uncle*] I can't live without her. The very sound of her footsteps is beautiful. I feel insanely happy. [*quickly walking to meet Nina Zarechnaya, who comes in*] You . . . enchanting being . . . My dream.

NINA   [*Agitated*] I'm not late. Surely I'm not late.

TREPLEV   [*Kissing her hands*] No, no, no.

NINA   I've been worrying the whole day. I've been feeling so afraid! I was afraid Father wouldn't let me come . . . but he's just gone out with my stepmother. The sky was red, the moon was coming up, and I kept hurrying the horse, urging it on and on. [*laughs*] I'm glad, all the same! [*shakes Sorin warmly by the hand*]

SORIN   [*Laughing*] Your dear little eyes look as if they'd been crying. He-he! That isn't as it should be, you know.

NINA   It's nothing. . . . Look how out of breath I am! I'll have to leave in half an hour. We must hurry. I can't, I can't! Don't try to keep me, for heaven's sake! My father doesn't know I've come.

TREPLEV   It's time to begin, as a matter of fact. We must go and call everybody.

SORIN   I'll go and call them, and all that sort of thing. I'll go at once. [*walks left, singing "The Two Grenadiers," then glances back*] I remember I once burst into song like this and the assistant public prosecutor said to me, "My, Your Excellency, that's a powerful voice you've got." Then he thought a bit and added, "But a revolting one too." [*laughs and goes out*]

NINA   My father and stepmother won't let me come here. They say this place is bohemian. They're afraid of my going on the stage. And I am drawn to this place, to this lake, as if I were a sea gull.

TREPLEV   We are alone.

NINA   I believe there's someone there.

TREPLEV   There isn't anybody. [*they kiss*]

NINA   What sort of a tree is this?

TREPLEV   An elm.

NINA   Why is it so dark?

TREPLEV   It's late; everything's turning dark now. Don't go early, I implore you.

NINA   I can't stay.

TREPLEV   And what if I followed you home, Nina? I would stay in the garden all night, watching your window.

NINA   You can't do that; the watchman would notice you. And Tresor isn't used to you yet. He'd bark.

TREPLEV   I love you.

NINA   Sh-sh!

TREPLEV   [*Hearing footsteps*] Who's there? Is it you, Yakov?

YAKOV   [*Behind the stage*] Yes, sir.

TREPLEV   Take up your positions. It's time to begin. Is the moon coming up?

YAKOV   Yes, sir.

TREPLEV   Have you got the wood alcohol? Have you got the sulfur? There must be a smell of sulfur as soon as the red eyes are seen. [*to Nina*] You can go now; everything is ready for you there. Are you nervous?

NINA   Yes, very. Your mother—she's all right; I'm not afraid of her. But there's Trigorin. I'm so afraid and ashamed of acting in front of him . . . a famous writer. Is he young?

TREPLEV   Yes.

NINA   What marvelous stories he's written!

TREPLEV   [*Coldly*] I don't know about that. I haven't read them.

NINA   It's difficult to act in your play. There are no real living characters in it.

TREPLEV   Living characters! We don't have to depict life as it is or as it ought to be, but as we see it in our dreams.

NINA   But there's hardly any action in your play; there are only speeches. And then I do think there ought to be love in a play. [*both go behind the stage*]

Polina Andreyevna and Dorn come in

POLINA   It's getting damp out here. Please do go back and put on your galoshes.

DORN   I feel hot.

POLINA   You don't take care of yourself. It's just sheer obstinacy. You're a doctor, and you know perfectly well that the damp air is bad for you, but you just want to cause me pain and anxiety. Yesterday you stayed outside on the terrace the whole evening on purpose.

DORN   [*Hums*] "Say not your youth was ruined . . ."

POLINA   You were so absorbed in your conversation with Irina Nikolaevna that you simply weren't aware of the cold. Now own up, you do find her attractive.

DORN   I'm fifty-five.

POLINA   That's nothing. A man's not old at that age. You've kept your good looks and you're still attractive to women.

DORN   Well, what am I to do about it?

POLINA   You're so anxious to prostrate yourselves before an actress. Every single one of you!

DORN   [*Hums*] "Again I stand before you . . ." It's in the nature of things for people to admire artists and treat them differently from . . . well, let us say, tradesmen. It's a sort of idealism.

POLINA   Women always used to be falling in love with you and throwing themselves at you. Was that idealism too?

DORN   [*Shrugging his shoulders*] Well, what of it? There was a lot that was good in the feelings these women had for me. What they mostly loved in me was my skill as a doctor. Ten or fifteen years ago, you remember, I was the only good obstetrician in the whole district. Besides I've always been honorable.

POLINA   [*Seizing him by the hand*] You dear man!

DORN   Sh-sh! They're coming.

Enter Arkadina on Sorin's arm, accompanied by Trigorin, Shamrayev, Medvedenko, and Masha

SHAMRAYEV   I remember I saw her play marvelously at the Poltava Fair in '73! A sheer delight! Marvelous acting! [*to Arkadina*] I wonder if you happen to know where Chadin—Pavel

Semënych Chadin, the comedian—is at present? He was quite inimitable in the part of Raspliuyev, better than Sadovski himself. I'm willing to swear he was, my dear lady! But where is he now?

ARKADINA You're always inquiring about some old fossil or other. How should I know? [*sits down*]

SHAMRAYEV [*With a sigh*] Pashka Chadin! We don't have men like him nowadays! The theater is in a decline, Irina Nikolaevna. We used to have massive oak trees; now we see nothing but stumps.

DORN It's true enough, there aren't so many outstandingly gifted people nowadays. On the other hand, the average actor is much more competent.

SHAMRAYEV I can't agree at all with you there. However, it's a matter of taste. *De gustibus aut bene, aut nihil.*

Treplev enters from behind the stage

ARKADINA [*To her son*] When is it going to start, my dear?

TREPLEV In a minute. Please have patience.

ARKADINA [*Reciting from* Hamlet]
"Oh, Hamlet, speak no more!
    Thou turn'st mine eyes into my very soul;
    And there I see such black and grained spots
    As will not leave their tinct."

TREPLEV [*From* Hamlet]
"And let me wring thy heart, for so I shall,
    If it be made of penetrable stuff."

A horn is sounded behind the stage

Ladies and gentlemen, we are about to begin! Attention please! [*pause*] I'll start now. [*taps with a stick and recites in a loud voice*] O venerable shades of ancient days, you who float over this lake at night, lull us to sleep and bring us dreams of things as they will be two hundred thousand years from now.

SORIN Two hundred thousand years from now there will be just nothing.

TREPLEV   Well then, let them show us that nothing!

ARKADINA   Yes, let them. We are asleep already.

The curtain rises, revealing the view of the lake, with the moon above the horizon and its reflection in the water. Nina Zarech-naya, in white, is sitting on a rock

NINA   The men, the lions, the eagles, the partridges, the antlered deer, the geese, the spiders, the silent fishes of the deep, star-fishes, and creatures unseen to the eye—in short—all living things, all living things, having completed their mournful cycle, have been snuffed out. For thousands of years the earth has borne no living thing, and this poor moon now lights its lamp in vain. The cranes no longer wake in the meadows with a cry; no longer are May beetles heard humming in the groves of lime trees. It is cold, cold, cold. . . . It is deserted, deserted, deserted. . . . It is terrifying, terrifying, terrifying. [*pause*] All living bodies have turned to dust and the Eternal Matter has transformed them into stones, into water, into clouds, while their souls have all been merged into one. This common soul of the world is I—I. . . . The souls of Alexander the Great, of Caesar, of Shakespeare, of Napoleon, and of the basest leech are contained in me! In me the consciousness of men is merged with the instincts of the animals. I remember all, all, all, and live every single life anew in my own being!

Will-o'-the-wisps appear

ARKADINA   [*In a low voice*] This sounds like the Decadent school.

TREPLEV   [*Imploringly and reproachfully*] Mamma!

NINA   I am lonely. Once in a hundred years I open my lips to speak, and then my voice rings dismally through this void un-heard by anybody. . . . And you too, pale spirits, hear me not. The stagnant marsh gives birth to you before dawn, and you wander until day breaks—without thought, without will, without a quiver of life. The Devil, father of Eternal Matter, fearing lest life reappear in you, has created in you, as also in the rocks and water, a perpetual flux of atoms, so that you are constantly changing. The spirit alone remains constant and unchangeable in the whole universe. [*pause*] Like a prisoner cast into a deep and empty well, I know not where I am or what awaits me here. All I know is that I am destined to struggle with the Devil, and in cruel and stubborn battle to conquer the principle of material force, after which matter and spirit will merge in beautiful harmony and the Kingdom of Cosmic Will will come into being. But this will only happen after a long succession of millennia during which time the moon, bright Sirius, and this earth will all have been gradually turned to dust. Until then horror, horror . . .

A pause. Two red spots appear over the lake

And now my powerful enemy, the Devil, is approaching. I see his terrifying, blood-red eyes.

ARKADINA   There's a smell of sulfur. Is that right?

TREPLEV   Yes.

ARKADINA   [*Laughing*] Ah! It's quite a good effect!

TREPLEV   Mamma!

NINA   He is bored without Man. . . .

POLINA   [*To Dorn*] You've taken off your hat. Put it on before you catch cold.

ARKADINA   The doctor's taken his hat off to the Devil, the father of Eternal Matter.

TREPLEV   [*Flaring up, loudly*] The play's over! Enough of it! Curtain!

ARKADINA   But why get angry about it?

TREPLEV   That's enough! Curtain! Let down the curtain! [*stamping his foot*] Curtain!

The curtain drops

I apologize! I overlooked the fact that only a select few are permitted to write plays and act on the stage. I've encroached on the preserves of a monopoly! To me . . . I mean, I . . . [*tries to continue, then makes a resigned gesture and goes out to the left*]

ARKADINA   What is the matter with him?

SORIN   Irina, my dear, you shouldn't hurt a young man's self-esteem like this!

ARKADINA   But what have I said to him?

SORIN   You've offended him.

ARKADINA   He told us himself that it was going to be a joke, and I treated it as a joke.

SORIN   All the same . . .

ARKADINA   And now it turns out he's written a great work of art! Just think of that! So it wasn't for a joke that he got up this show and perfumed the air with sulfur, but in order to teach us something. He wanted to show us how we ought to write plays and what plays we should act in. Really this is becoming tedious! These perpetual jibes at my expense, these pinpricks—anyone would get tired of them, surely you'll grant me that! He's a conceited, difficult boy!

SORIN   He wanted to give you pleasure.

ARKADINA   Did he? Even so, he didn't choose an ordinary play but had to make us listen to these decadent ravings. I'm even prepared to listen to mad ravings for the sake of a joke, but here we have pretensions to new creative forms, to a new era in art. To my way of thinking, there are no new forms in this stuff at all, just a display of bad temper.

TRIGORIN   Everyone writes what he wants to and as he is able to.

ARKADINA   Let him write what he wants to and as he is able to, if only he leaves me out of it.

DORN   Jupiter! You are angry then.

ARKADINA   I'm not Jupiter; I'm a woman. [*lights a cigarette*] And I'm not angry. I'm merely irritated that a young man should spend his time in such a tiresome way. I had no wish to offend him.

MEDVEDENKO   There's no ground for making a distinction between spirit and matter, because spirit might consist of a combination of material atoms. [*with animation to Trigorin*] But you know, someone ought to write a play describing how our sort of people live—I mean we teachers—and get it produced somewhere. It's a hard life, a very hard life!

ARKADINA   That's not a bad idea. But let's not talk about plays now or atoms either. It's such a nice evening. Can you hear? There's someone singing.

All listen

How nice it is!

POLINA   It's on the other side of the lake. . . .

ARKADINA   [*After a pause, to Trigorin*] Sit down here beside me. Ten or fifteen years ago you could always hear music and singing on this lake—almost every night. There are six country houses around the lake. I remember such laughter and noise and shooting—and love affairs, love affairs all the time. . . . And the *jeune premier* and idol of all those houses was— allow me to introduce him— [*nods toward Dorn*] Doctor Yevgeni Sergeevich. He's fascinating still, but in those days he was irresistible. . . . Oh, dear! My conscience is beginning to torment me. Why did I hurt my poor boy's feelings? I'm so worried. [*loudly*] Kostya! Kostya, dear!

MASHA   I'll go and look for him.

ARKADINA   Please do, my dear!

MASHA   [*Walks to the left*] Yoo-hoo! Konstantin Gavriilovich! Yoo-hoo! [*goes off*]

NINA   [*Coming out from behind the stage*] Apparently we aren't going to continue, so I may as well come out. Good evening! [*kisses Arkadina and Polina*]

SORIN   Bravo! Bravo!

ARKADINA   Bravo! Bravo! We did admire you. You know, with your looks and your lovely voice, you really shouldn't stay in the country! It's a sin. I'm sure you have a gift for acting. Listen to me! You must go on the stage!

NINA   Oh, it's my one dream! [*sighs*] But it'll never come true.

ARKADINA   Who knows? Here now, let me introduce you—Mr. Trigorin, Boris Alekseevich Trigorin.

NINA   Oh, I'm so glad. [*overcome with embarrassment*] I always read everything you . . .

ARKADINA   [*Making her sit down beside them*] Don't be shy, my dear. He's a famous man, but he has a simple soul. You see, he's shy himself.

DORN I think the curtain might be raised now. This place gives me a sort of eerie feeling.

SHAMRAYEV [*Loudly*] Yakov, pull the curtain up, will you!

The curtain goes up

NINA [*To Trigorin*] It was a strange play, wasn't it?

TRIGORIN I didn't understand it at all. But I watched it with pleasure all the same. You acted with such sincerity. And the scenery was beautiful. [*pause*] There must be a lot of fish in this lake.

NINA Yes.

TRIGORIN I'm very fond of fishing. As far as I'm concerned, there's no greater pleasure than to sit on the bank of a river in the late afternoon and watch the float.

NINA I would have thought that for anyone who'd experienced the joy of doing creative work no other pleasure could exist.

ARKADINA [*Laughing*] You mustn't talk like that. When anyone talks high-flown language to him, he hasn't the least idea what to say.

SHAMRAYEV I remember hearing the great Silva sing lower C one night at the Moscow Opera. As it happened, a bass from our parish church choir was sitting in the gallery. Suddenly— imagine our utter amazement—we heard, "Bravo, Silva!" from the gallery . . . but a whole octave lower. Like this. [*in a deep bass*] Bravo, Silva! And after that—dead silence. You could hear a pin drop. . . .

DORN [*After a pause*] The angel of silence has flown over us!

NINA It's time for me to be going. Good-bye.

ARKADINA Where are you off to? Why so early? We won't let you go.

NINA My father is expecting me.

ARKADINA What a man, really! [*they embrace*] Well, if it can't be helped . . . We're sorry, very sorry to let you go.

NINA I wish you knew how hard it is for me to go.

ARKADINA Someone ought to see you home, my little one.

NINA [*Frightened*] Oh, no, no!

SORIN [*To Nina, imploringly*] Do stay!

NINA I can't, Pëtr Nikolaevich.

SORIN Stay just for an hour, that's all. Why must you, really?

NINA [*After a moment's thought, tearfully*] It's impossible. [*shakes hands with him and goes off quickly*]

ARKADINA She's an unfortunate girl, really. They say her mother left all her enormous fortune to her husband, every kopeck of it; and now this girl has nothing, since her father has already made a will in favor of his second wife. It's really scandalous.

DORN Yes, her charming father is a regular swine, to give him his due.

SORIN [*Rubbing his hands to warm them*] Let us go too, friends. The air is getting damp. My legs are hurting.

ARKADINA Your legs! They might as well be made of wood; you can hardly walk on them. Come along, you poor old man! [*takes his arm*]

SHAMRAYEV [*Offering his arm to his wife*] Madame?

SORIN I can hear that dog howling again. [*to Shamrayev*] Ilya Afanasievich, I wish you'd be good enough to tell them to let it off the chain.

SHAMRAYEV It isn't possible, Pëtr Nikolaevich. I'm afraid of thieves breaking into the barn. I've got millet there. [*to Medvedenko, who is walking beside him*] Yes, lower by a whole octave, "Bravo, Silva!" And he wasn't a professional singer either—just a fellow in the church choir.

MEDVEDENKO And what sort of pay does a fellow in the choir get?

All go out except Dorn

DORN [*Alone*] I don't know, maybe I don't understand anything, maybe I've gone off my head, but I did like that play. There is something in it. When that child was holding forth about loneliness, and later when the Devil's red eyes appeared, I was so moved that my hands were shaking. It was fresh, unaffected. . . . Ah! I think he's coming along now. I feel like telling him a lot of nice things about it.

TREPLEV [*Enters*] They've all gone already!

DORN I'm here.

TREPLEV   Mashenka has been looking for me all over the park. Insufferable creature!

DORN   Konstantin Gavriilovich, I liked your play exceedingly. It's a bit strange and, of course, I didn't hear the end, and yet it made a deep impression on me. You've got talent and you must carry on.

Treplev shakes his hand warmly and embraces him impulsively

Tut-tut! How strung up you are! Tears in your eyes! What I mean to say is this. You took your subject from the realm of abstract ideas. That was as it should be, because a work of art must without fail convey some great idea. Only things conceived in high seriousness can be beautiful. How pale you are!

TREPLEV   So you're telling me to carry on?

DORN   Yes. But you must depict only what is significant and permanent. You know, I've lived a varied life; I've chosen my pleasures with discrimination. I'm satisfied. But if it had ever been my lot to experience the exaltation an artist feels at the moment of creative achievement, I believe I would have come to despise this material body of mine and all that goes with it, and my soul would have taken wings and soared into the heights.

TREPLEV   Forgive me, where's Zarechnaya?

DORN   There's one more thing. A work of art must express a clear, definite idea. You must know what you are aiming at when you write; for if you follow the enchanted path of literature without a definite goal in mind, you'll lose your way and your talent will ruin you.

TREPLEV   [*Impatiently*] Where is Zarechnaya?

DORN   She's gone home.

TREPLEV   [*In despair*] What shall I do? I want to see her. . . . I've got to see her. . . . I'm going.

Enter Masha

DORN   [*To Treplev*] Do be a little calmer, my friend.

TREPLEV   But I'm going all the same. I must go.

MASHA Please, Konstantin Gavriilovich, come indoors. Your mamma is waiting for you. She's worried.

TREPLEV Tell her I've gone away. And I beg you—all of you—leave me alone! Leave me alone! Don't follow me around.

DORN But . . . but, my dear boy . . . You shouldn't. That's not right.

TREPLEV [*Tearfully*] Good-bye, Doctor. Thank you. [*goes out*]

DORN [*With a sigh*] Youth will have its own way! Youth!

MASHA When people can't think of anything else to say, they say, "Youth! Youth!" [*takes snuff*]

DORN [*Takes the snuff box from her and flings it into the bushes*] Disgusting! [*pause*] I think I can hear music in the house. We ought to go in.

MASHA Wait a moment.

DORN What is it?

MASHA There's something I want to tell you again. I feel like talking. [*agitated*] I'm not really fond of my father, but I've a soft spot in my heart for you. For some reason I feel a sort of deep affinity with you. . . . You must help me. Help me or I'll do something stupid, something that'll make a mockery of my life and mess it up. I can't go on like this.

DORN But what is it? How am I to help you?

MASHA I'm so unhappy. Nobody, nobody knows how unhappy I am! [*leaning her head against his breast, softly*] I love Konstantin.

DORN How distraught they all are! How distraught! And what a quantity of love around! It's the magic lake! [*tenderly*] But what can I do, my child? Tell me, what can I do? What?

CURTAIN

ACT TWO

A croquet lawn and flower beds. In the background on the right, a house with a large terrace. On the left, a view of the lake with bright sunlight reflected in the water. It is midday and hot. On one side of the croquet lawn Arkadina, Dorn, and Masha are sitting on a garden seat in the shade of an old lime tree. Dorn has an open book on his lap.

ARKADINA [*To Masha*] Come, let us get up. [*both get up*] Stand by my side. You are twenty-two, and I'm nearly twice that. Yevgeni Sergeevich, which of us looks the younger?

DORN You, of course.

ARKADINA There you are! And why is it? Because I work, I care about things, I'm always on the go, while you stay in the same place all the time. You don't really live. And I have a rule: never to wonder about the future! I never think of old age or of death. What is to be, will be.

MASHA And I feel as though I'd been born long, long ago, and I'm trailing my life behind me like a dress with an endless train. And often I don't feel like going on with life at all. Of course, that's all nonsense. One ought to shake oneself and throw it all off.

DORN [*Hums quietly*] "Tell her, my flowers . . ."

ARKADINA And one more thing—I am as particular about myself as an Englishman. Yes, my dear, I keep myself in hand, as they say. I'm always properly dressed and have my hair done just *comme il faut*. Do you think I'd permit myself to come out of the house, even into the garden, like this, in a dressing gown or with my hair untidy? Never. That's why it is I've kept so young looking—because I've never been sloppy or let myself go, as some women do. [*walks up and down the lawn, her hands on her hips*] There! You see? I'm as brisk as a bird. Fit to take the part of a fifteen-year-old girl!

DORN   Well, I may as well go on. [*picks up the book*] We'd just come to the corn merchant and the rats.

ARKADINA   Yes, the rats. Go on reading. [*sits down*] No, give it to me; I'll read. It's my turn. [*takes the book and looks for the place*] The rats . . . Here it is. [*reads*] "And it goes without saying that it is as dangerous for society people to pamper and encourage writers of novels, as it is for corn merchants to breed rats in their granaries. And yet novelists are very much sought after. Thus, when a woman has chosen a writer whom she wishes to capture, she lays siege to him with the aid of compliments, flattery, and favors." Well, that may be true of the French, but there's nothing like that with us. We don't plan ahead. Over here, a woman is usually head over heels in love with a writer long before she decides to capture him, don't you see? To go no further afield, take Trigorin and myself . . .

Sorin enters leaning on his stick with Nina walking beside him. They are followed by Medvedenko, who pushes an empty wheelchair

SORIN   [*Fondly, as to a child*] Indeed? So we're quite delighted, are we? We're feeling cheerful today after all? [*to his sister*] We're delighted! Our father and stepmother have gone off to Tver, and we are free now for three whole days.

NINA   [*Sits down beside Arkadina and embraces her*] I'm so happy! Now I belong to you.

SORIN   [*Sits down in his wheelchair*] She's looking very pretty today.

ARKADINA   Prettily dressed and interesting looking. That's a good girl. [*kisses her*] But we mustn't praise her too much or it may bring bad luck. Where's Boris Alekseevich?

NINA   He's down by the bathing shed—fishing.

ARKADINA   Surprising he doesn't get bored with it! [*prepares to go on reading*]

NINA   What is that?

ARKADINA   Maupassant's *Sur l'eau,* my dear. [*reads a few lines to herself*] Oh, well, the next bit isn't interesting or true either. [*closes the book*] I'm worried. Tell me, what is the matter with my son? Why is he so sullen and depressed? He spends day after day on the lake and I hardly ever see him.

MASHA   His heart is troubled. [*to Nina, timidly*] Please, will you read us something from his play?

NINA   [*Shrugging her shoulders*] Would you like me to? It's so uninteresting!

MASHA   [*Restraining her enthusiasm*] When he reads himself, his eyes blaze and his face turns pale. He has a beautiful, sad voice and the bearing of a poet.

Sorin is heard snoring

DORN   Good night!

ARKADINA   Petrusha!

SORIN   Eh?

ARKADINA   Are you asleep?

SORIN   Not in the least. . . .

ARKADINA   [*After a pause*] You're not taking any medical treatment, my friend. It's not wise, you know.

SORIN   I'd be glad to have some treatment, but the doctor here doesn't want me to.

DORN   Treatment! At sixty!

SORIN   Even at sixty, one wants to go on living.

DORN   [*Tartly*] Oh, all right then, take some valerian drops.

ARKADINA   I believe it would do him good to go and stay at a spa.

DORN   Well, he might go. Or he might not.

ARKADINA   What is one to make of that?

DORN   There's nothing to make of it. It's perfectly clear. . . .

MEDVEDENKO   [*After a pause*] Pëtr Nikolaevich ought to give up smoking.

SORIN   Nonsense.

DORN   No, it isn't nonsense. Wine and tobacco deprive you of your individuality. After a cigar or a glass of vodka you're no longer just Pëtr Nikolaevich, but Pëtr Nikolaevich plus somebody else. Your "I" becomes blurred, and you begin to think of yourself as if you were someone quite different—as "he."

SORIN [*Laughing*] It's all very well for you to talk. You've had a good life, but what about me? I've served in the Department of Justice for twenty-eight years, but I haven't really lived. I haven't really experienced anything yet, so obviously I feel very much like going on living. You're satisfied and you don't care anymore, so you're inclined to be philosophical. But I want to live. That's why I drink sherry at dinner and smoke cigars, and all that. And there it is.

DORN Life has to be taken seriously, but when it comes to taking cures at sixty and regretting that you didn't get enough enjoyment out of life when you were young—all that, forgive me, is just futile.

MASHA [*Getting up*] It must be about lunchtime. [*walking languidly and with an effort*] My leg's gone to sleep. [*goes out*]

DORN She'll go and have a couple of drinks before lunch.

SORIN She's not happy in her personal affairs, poor girl.

DORN Rubbish, Your Excellency!

SORIN You talk like a man who's had his fill of experience.

ARKADINA Oh, what could be more boring than this cloying country boredom! So hot, so still, nobody doing anything, everybody talking like a philosopher. It's nice to be here with you, my friends. It's pleasant to listen to you, but . . . how much better to be sitting alone in a hotel room learning a part!

NINA [*Enthusiastically*] How true! I do understand you!

SORIN It's better in town, of course. You sit in your study, your footman doesn't let anyone in unannounced, you have a telephone. There are cabs in the streets, and all that sort of thing.

DORN [*Hums*] "Tell her, my flowers . . ."

Shamrayev comes in, followed by Polina Andreyevna

SHAMRAYEV Here they are! Good morning to you! [*kisses Arkadina's hand, then Nina's*] So glad to see you looking so well. [*to Arkadina*] My wife tells me that you're thinking of going to town with her today. Is that right?

ARKADINA Yes, we are thinking of going.

SHAMRAYEV Hm! That's splendid. But, my dear lady, how do you propose to travel? We're carting the rye today, and all the men are busy. What horses are you going to have, may I ask?

ARKADINA What horses? How am I to know what horses?

SORIN But we have carriage horses.

SHAMRAYEV [*Agitated*] Carriage horses? Where am I to get collars for carriage horses? Where am I to get collars? It amazes me! It is really beyond my understanding! My dear lady! Forgive me, I have the greatest admiration for your talent; I'm prepared to give ten years of my life for you—but I can't let you have the horses.

ARKADINA But if I *have* to go? How very odd!

SHAMRAYEV My dear lady! You don't realize what farming means.

ARKADINA [*Flaring up*] The old, old story! All right, then, I'm leaving for Moscow this very day. Please have the horses hired for me in the village, or I'll walk to the station.

SHAMRAYEV [*Flaring up*] In that case, I'm giving up my post. You can look for another steward. [*goes out*]

ARKADINA Every summer it's like this. Every summer they insult me here. I won't set my foot in this place again! [*goes out to the left, in the direction of the bathing shed, which is offstage. A moment later she is seen entering the house, followed by Trigorin, who is carrying fishing rods and a pail*]

SORIN [*Flaring up*] This is pure insolence! It's the limit! I'm sick and tired of it, once and for all! Bring all the horses here this minute!

NINA [*To Polina Andreyevna*] To refuse Irina Nikolaevna, the famous actress! Surely, any wish of hers, even a mere whim, is more important than your farming? It's simply incredible.

POLINA [*In despair*] But what can I do? Put yourself in my position. What can I do?

SORIN [*To Nina*] Let us go along to my sister. We'll all try to persuade her not to go away, eh? [*looking in the direction in which Shamrayev has gone*] Insufferable fellow! Tyrant!

NINA [*Preventing him from rising*] Sit still, sit still. We'll take you along. [*she and Medvedenko push the wheelchair*] Oh, how dreadful all this is!

SORIN Yes, yes, it is dreadful. But he won't leave. I'll speak to him presently. [*they go out*]

Dorn and Polina Andreyevna are left alone

DORN People *are* tiresome. Speaking candidly, your husband ought to be simply chucked out of here. But the end of it all will be that this old woman, Pëtr Nikolaevich, and his sister will go and apologize to him. You'll see.

POLINA He's even sent the carriage horses to work in the fields. And misunderstandings like this happen every day. If you only knew how it upsets me! It makes me ill; you see I'm shaking. . . . I can't bear his rude manners. [*entreating him*] Yevgeni, my dear, dear man, won't you take me to live with you? Our time's passing; we're no longer young . . . and I wish we could stop concealing things and lying, now that we're so near the end of our lives.

DORN I'm fifty-five; it's too late for me to change my way of life.

POLINA I know you refuse me because there are other women you're intimate with. You can't take them all to live with you. I understand. Forgive me. You're tired of me.

Nina appears near the house. She is picking flowers

DORN No, not really.

POLINA I'm so tormented by jealousy. Of course, you're a doctor; you can't avoid women. I understand.

DORN [*To Nina, who comes up*] Well, how are things now?

NINA Irina Nikolaevna's crying and Pëtr Nikolaevich has gotten an attack of asthma.

DORN [*Getting up*] I'd better go and give them some valerian drops.

NINA [*Giving him the flowers*] For you!

DORN *Merci bien!* [*goes toward the house*]

POLINA [*Going with him*] What pretty flowers! [*near the house, in a low voice*] Give me those flowers!

> *Dorn gives them to her and she tears them to pieces and throws them aside. Both go into the house*

NINA [*Alone*] How strange it is to see a famous actress crying . . . and for such a trifling reason! And isn't it strange too? Here we have a famous author, a favorite with the public —they write about him in all the papers, they sell pictures of him everywhere, his works are translated into foreign languages—and he spends the whole day fishing and is quite delighted if he catches a couple of gudgeon. I used to think that famous people were proud and inaccessible and that they despised the crowd. I thought that the glory and luster of their names enabled them, as it were, to revenge themselves on people who put high birth and wealth above everything else. But here they are, crying, fishing, playing cards, laughing, and getting angry like anyone else.

TREPLEV [*Enters, hatless, carrying a gun and a dead sea gull*] Are you alone here?

NINA Yes, alone.

> *Treplev lays the sea gull at her feet*

What does this mean?

TREPLEV I was despicable enough to kill this sea gull today. I'm laying it at your feet.

NINA What is the matter with you? [*picks up the sea gull and looks at it*]

TREPLEV [*After a pause*] Soon I will kill myself in the same way.

NINA This is not like you at all!

TREPLEV True—but it's only since you've not been like yourself. You've changed toward me, you look at me coldly, my presence seems to embarrass you.

NINA You've grown so irritable lately, and most of the time you've been talking unintelligibly, in a sort of symbolic way. And now this sea gull here is apparently another symbol, but —you must forgive me—I don't understand it. [*puts the sea gull on the seat*] I'm too simpleminded to understand you.

TREPLEV It started that evening when my play was such a stupid fiasco. Women don't forgive failure. I burned it all, down to the last scrap. If you only knew how unhappy I am! Your growing coldness toward me is frightening; it's incredible! It is as if I woke up one day and saw this lake suddenly drying up or draining away into the ground. You said just now that you're too simpleminded to understand me. Oh, tell me— what is there to understand? My play wasn't liked, you despise my kind of inspiration, and now you think I'm commonplace and insignificant, just like all the rest. [*stamping his foot*] How well I understand it! I do indeed! It feels as though a nail has been knocked into my brain. Damn it—and my pride too, which is sucking my life blood, sucking it like a snake. [*seeing Trigorin, who comes in reading a book*] But here comes the real genius, stepping out like Hamlet himself, and with a book too. [*mimics*] "Words, words, words." The sun hasn't come near you yet, but you're smiling already and your eyes are melting in its rays. I won't inconvenience you further. [*goes out quickly*]

TRIGORIN [*Making notes in his book*] Takes snuff and drinks vodka. Always dresses in black. A schoolmaster in love with her . . .

NINA   Good morning, Boris Alekseevich!

TRIGORIN   Good morning. It turns out that we may have to leave here today, rather unexpectedly. It doesn't seem very likely that we will meet again. Girls don't often come my way, I mean girls who are young and interesting to meet. I've forgotten what it feels like to be eighteen or nineteen; indeed I can't imagine it at all clearly. That's why the girls in my novels and stories are usually so artificial. I wish I could exchange places with you, even if only for an hour, just to find out what your thoughts are, and what kind of a pretty little thing you are in a general sort of way.

NINA   And I would like to be in your place for a while.

TRIGORIN   Whatever for?

NINA   So that I could know what it feels like to be a famous, gifted writer. How does one experience fame? What sort of feeling does it give you to be famous?

TRIGORIN   What sort of feeling? Perhaps none. I've never

thought about it. [*after a moment's thought*] It's one thing or the other: either you exaggerate the extent of my fame, or I'm quite insensitive to it.

NINA But what if you read about yourself in the papers?

TRIGORIN When they praise me I am pleased, and when they attack me I feel in a bad mood for a couple of days.

NINA What a wonderful world you live in! How I envy you—if only you knew! How different people's destinies are! Some just drag out their obscure, tedious existences, all very much like one another, and all unhappy. And there are others—like you for instance, one in a million—who are given an interesting life, a life that is radiant and full of significance. You are fortunate!

TRIGORIN I? [*shrugs his shoulders*] Hm! You talk about fame and happiness, and this radiant and interesting life, but to me all these fine words of yours—you must forgive me—are just like so many delicious sweets, which I never eat. You are very young and very kind.

NINA Your life is beautiful.

TRIGORIN But what is there beautiful about it? [*looking at his watch*] I must go and do some writing presently. Forgive me, I haven't much time to spare. [*laughs*] You've stepped on my favorite corn, as the saying goes, and here I am getting excited and a little bit angry too. All the same, let's talk. Let's talk about my radiant and beautiful life. Well, where shall we begin? [*after a moment's thought*] You know what it is to have a *fixed idea,* for instance when a man keeps on thinking about the same thing day and night, about . . . let us say, the moon. Well, I too have a kind of moon of my own. I'm obsessed day and night by one thought: I must write, I must write, I just must. For some reason, as soon as I've finished one novel, I feel I must start writing another, then another, then another. I write in a rush, without stopping, and can't do anything else. What is there radiant or beautiful in that, I ask you? Oh, it's a fatuous life! Here I am with you, I'm quite worked up, and yet not for a single moment do I forget that there's an unfinished novel waiting for me. I look over there and I see a cloud shaped like a grand piano. At once I think I must put it into some story or other—the fact that a cloud looking like a grand piano has floated by. There's the scent of heliotrope in the air. I make a mental note: "sickly scent . . . flower—the color of a widow's dress . . . mention when describing a summer evening." I snatch at every word and sentence I utter, and every word you utter too and hurriedly lock them up in my literary pantry—in case they might come in useful! When I finish a piece of work, I dash off to the theater or go off on a fishing trip, and that's the time when I ought to relax and forget myself—but no! Something that feels like a heavy cast-iron ball begins to revolve in my brain—a new subject for a novel! So immediately I drag myself back to my desk again, and I have to push on with my writing once more, to keep on writing and writing. . . . And it's like that always, always . . . and I can't get any rest away from myself. I feel as though I'm devouring my own life, that for the sake of the honey I give to all and sundry I'm despoiling my best flowers of their pollen, that I'm plucking the flowers themselves and trampling on their roots. Am I out of my mind? Do you think my relatives and friends treat me like a sane person? "What are you jotting down now? What surprises have you in store for us?" It's the same thing over and over again, until I begin to imagine that this attentiveness on the part of my friends, all this praise and admiration, is just a sham, that they are trying to deceive me just as if I were insane. Sometimes I feel afraid of them stealing up on me from behind, seizing me and carrying me off, like Poprishchin,[1] to a lunatic asylum. As for the years when I was starting—my younger, better years—in those days my writing used to be one continuous torment. A minor writer, especially if he hasn't had much luck, sees himself as clumsy, awkward, and unwanted. He gets nervous and overwrought and feels irresistibly drawn toward people connected with literature or art; but then he just wanders among them unrecognized and unnoticed, unable to look them straight and courageously in the eye, like a passionate gambler who hasn't any money. I could not see my readers, but for some reason I always imagined

1. The principal character in the story *The Diary of a Madman*, by N. V. Gogol.

them as unfriendly and skeptical. I was afraid of the public—it terrified me—and whenever a new play of mine was produced, I always felt that the dark-haired people in the audience were hostile to it, and the fair-haired ones coldly indifferent. Oh, how dreadful it all was! What a torment!

NINA   But even so, don't you have moments of happiness and exaltation—moments when you feel inspired, when your creative work is actually in progress?

TRIGORIN   Yes, while I'm writing I enjoy it. I enjoy reading proofs too, but . . . as soon as the thing comes out in print I can no longer bear it. I immediately see that it's not what I intended, that it's a mistake, that it shouldn't have been written at all; and I feel angry and depressed. [*laughing*] And then the public reads it and says, "Yes, it's charming. So cleverly done. Charming, but a far cry from Tolstoy." Or "A very fine piece of work, but Turgenev's *Fathers and Children* is a better book." And so it will go on till my dying day—everything will be charming and clever—and nothing more. And when I die, my friends as they pass by my grave will say, "Here lies Trigorin. He was a good writer, but not as good as Turgenev."

NINA   You must forgive me, but I refuse to try to understand you. You've simply been spoiled by success.

TRIGORIN   What success? I've never liked myself. I dislike myself as a writer. But the worst of it is that I live in a sort of haze, and I often don't understand what I'm writing. I love this water here, the trees, the sky. I have a feeling for nature; it arouses a sort of passion in me, an irresistible desire to write. But you see, I'm not a mere landscape painter; I'm also a citizen of my country. I love it; I love its people. As an author, I feel I'm in duty bound to write about the people, their sufferings, their future—and about science, the rights of man, and so on, and so forth. And I write about everything in a great hurry while I'm being prodded and urged on from all sides and people keep getting angry with me; so that I dash around from one side to the other like a fox badgered by the hounds. I see science and society forging ahead, while I drop further and further behind, like a peasant who's just missed his train. And in the end I feel that all I can do is to paint landscapes, and that everything else I write is a sham—false to the very core.

NINA You've been working too hard. You haven't the time or the inclination to recognize your own importance. You may be dissatisfied with yourself, but to others you are a great and wonderful person! If I were a writer like you, I would give my whole life to the ordinary people, realizing at the same time that their happiness lay in striving to rise to my level—and then they'd have harnessed themselves to my chariot.

TRIGORIN Chariot, indeed! Am I an Agamemnon or what? [*both smile*]

NINA For the sake of being happy like that—of being a writer or an actress—I would put up with unfriendliness from my family, with poverty and disappointment, with living in a garret and having nothing to eat but rye bread. I would gladly suffer dissatisfaction with myself in the knowledge of my own imperfections, but in return I would demand fame . . . real, resounding fame. [*covering her face with her hands*] My head's going around! Ugh!

ARKADINA'S VOICE [*From the house*] Boris Alekseevich!

TRIGORIN They're calling me. To pack, I suppose. But I don't feel like leaving. [*looks around at the lake*] What a heavenly sight! How lovely it is!

NINA Do you see a house with a garden on the other side?

TRIGORIN Yes.

NINA It belonged to my mother when she was alive. I was born there. I've spent all my life beside this lake and I know every tiny island on it.

TRIGORIN It's a beautiful place! [*noticing the sea gull*] But what is this?

NINA A sea gull. Konstantin Gavriilovich killed it.

TRIGORIN What a beautiful bird! Really I don't feel like going away. Why don't you persuade Irina Nikolaevna to stay? [*writes in his notebook*]

NINA What are you writing?

TRIGORIN Just making a few notes. An idea suddenly came into my head. A subject for a short story: a young girl, like you, has lived beside a lake from childhood. She loves the lake as a sea gull does, and she's happy and free as a sea gull. But a man chances to come along, sees her, and, having nothing better to do, destroys her, just like this sea gull here.

A pause. Arkadina appears in the window

ARKADINA   Boris Alekseevich, where are you?
TRIGORIN   I'm coming! [*goes, then looks back at Nina. To Arkadina at the window*] What is it?
ARKADINA   We're staying.

Trigorin goes into the house

NINA   [*Advances to the footlights; after a few moments' meditation*] It's a dream!

CURTAIN

ACT THREE

The dining room in Sorin's house. Doors right and left. A side-board and a medicine cupboard. In the middle of the room a table. A trunk and some cardboard hat boxes indicate preparations for departure. Trigorin is having his breakfast while Masha stands beside the table.

MASHA   I'm telling you all this because you're a writer. You can make use of it if you like. I tell you honestly—if he had wounded himself badly, I wouldn't have lived another minute. But I've got courage all the same. I just decided I'd tear this love of mine out of my heart, tear it out by the roots.

TRIGORIN   But how?

MASHA   I'm getting married. To Medvedenko.

TRIGORIN   You mean the schoolmaster?

MASHA   Yes.

TRIGORIN   I don't see the point of it.

MASHA   What is the point of love without hope, of waiting whole years for something. . . . One doesn't know what. But when I'm married there'll be no time for love; new cares will drive out all the old ones. And anyway it'll be a change, you know. Shall we have another?

TRIGORIN   Do you think we ought to?

MASHA   Oh, come! [*fills two glasses*] Don't look at me like that. Women drink more often than you imagine. A few drink openly as I do, but most drink in secret. Yes. And it's always vodka or cognac. [*clinks glasses with him*] Here's good luck! You're a genuine, sincere man. I'm sorry to be parting from you. [*they drink*]

TRIGORIN   I don't feel like going away myself.

MASHA   Why don't you ask her to stay?

TRIGORIN   No, she won't stay now. Her son is behaving very tactlessly. First he shoots himself, and now they say he's going to challenge me to a duel. Whatever for? He sulks and snorts and preaches new forms of art. But there's room enough for all, for new and old alike. Why does he have to push and shove?

MASHA   There's jealousy too. However, it's not my affair.

A pause. Yakov passes from left to right carrying a suitcase. Nina comes in and stands by the window

My schoolmaster is not particularly clever, but he's kind-hearted and poor, and he's very fond of me. I'm sorry for him. I'm sorry for his old mother too. Well, let me wish you all the best. Don't think badly of me. [*shakes his hand warmly*] I'm very grateful to you for your friendly interest. Do send me your books and be sure to autograph them. Only don't write, "To the highly respected" and all that; but just put "To Marya, who doesn't know where she belongs and has no object in life." Good-bye! [*goes out*]

NINA   [*Holding out her hand toward Trigorin, with her fist clenched*] Odd or even?

TRIGORIN   Even.

NINA   [*With a sigh*] That means "no." I've only got one pea in my hand. I was trying to tell my fortune—whether to go on the stage or not. If only someone would give me advice!

TRIGORIN   One can't give advice about that. . . .

NINA   [*After a pause*] We are going to part now and . . . perhaps we will not meet again. Will you take this little medallion to remember me by? I had your initials engraved on it . . . and on the other side, the title of a book of yours— *Days and Nights.*

TRIGORIN   How exquisite! [*kisses the medallion*] A charming gift!

NINA   Think of me sometimes.

TRIGORIN   I will indeed. I will think of you as you were on that sunny day—do you remember?—a week ago, when you were wearing that light-colored dress. We talked. . . . There was a white sea gull lying on the seat.

NINA   [*Pensively*] Yes, a sea gull . . . [*pause*] We can't go on talking; someone's coming. Let me have two minutes with you before you go, I implore you. [*goes out on left*]

At the same time Arkadina and Sorin come in, the latter wearing a frock coat with the star of an order on it. They are followed by Yakov, who is looking after the packing

ARKADINA   Better stay at home, my friend. Are you really up to running around visiting people, with your rheumatism? [*to Trigorin*] Who was it just went out? Nina?

TRIGORIN   Yes.

ARKADINA   I'm sorry we've disturbed you. [*sits down*] I believe I've packed everything. I'm worn out.

TRIGORIN   [*Reading the inscription on the medallion*] *Days and Nights,* page 121, lines 11 and 12.

YAKOV   [*Clearing the table*] Am I to pack your fishing rods too, sir?

TRIGORIN   Yes, I will be wanting them again. But you can give the books away.

YAKOV   Yes, sir.

TRIGORIN   [*To himself*] Page 121, lines 11 and 12. What can they be? [*to Arkadina*] Are there any of my books in the house?

ARKADINA   Yes, in my brother's study, in the corner bookcase.

TRIGORIN   Page 121. [*goes out*]

ARKADINA   Really, Petrusha, you'd better stay at home.

SORIN   You are going away. I'll find it hard to stay at home without you.

ARKADINA   But what is there to do in town?

SORIN   Nothing special, but all the same . . . [*laughs*] There'll be the laying of the foundation stone of the County Hall, and all that sort of thing. I feel I'd like to shake myself out of this stagnant existence, if only for an hour or two. I've been lying around too long, like some old cigarette holder or something. I've ordered the horses for one o'clock, so that we'll be starting at the same time.

ARKADINA [*After a pause*] You must go on living here. Don't let yourself get bored and avoid catching cold. Watch over my son. Take care of him. Give him good advice. [*pause*] Here I am going away, and I won't even know why Konstantin tried to shoot himself. I believe jealousy was the chief reason, and the sooner I take Trigorin away from here, the better.

SORIN How shall I say it? There were other reasons too. It's not to be wondered at really—a young man, intelligent, living in the country, in the wilds . . . with no money, no position, no future. No occupation whatsoever. Ashamed and afraid of his idleness. I am extremely fond of him, and he's attached to me too. But all the same, he does feel in a way that he doesn't belong here, that he's a sponger, living on charity. It's not to be wondered at—he's got pride.

ARKADINA He's a great anxiety to me! [*pondering*] Should he get some sort of job?

SORIN [*Begins to whistle, then speaks irresolutely*] I think quite the best thing would be if you were to . . . give him a little money. In the first place, he ought to have proper clothes, and all that sort of thing. Just look at him; he's been wearing the same wretched jacket for the last three years, and he's got no overcoat. [*laughs*] And it wouldn't do the boy any harm to have a little fun . . . to go abroad or something. It wouldn't cost much.

ARKADINA All the same. I might manage the suit, perhaps, but as for going abroad . . . No, just at the moment I can't even manage the suit. [*resolutely*] I haven't got the money.

Sorin laughs

No!

SORIN [*Begins to whistle*] Quite so. Forgive me, my dear. Don't be annoyed. I believe you. You're a generous, noblehearted woman.

ARKADINA   [*Tearfully*] I have no money!

SORIN   Naturally, if I had any money I would give it to him myself, but I've got nothing, not a kopeck. [*laughs*] My steward takes all my pension and spends it on farming—on the cattle and the bees—and my money is all wasted. The bees die, the cows die, and I'm never allowed to use the horses.

ARKADINA   Well, I do have some money. But after all, I'm an actress: my dress bill alone is enough to ruin me.

SORIN   You're a dear, kindhearted woman. I respect you. Yes. . . . There's something the matter with me again. . . . [*sways*] I feel dizzy. [*holds on to the table*] I feel faint and all that sort of thing.

ARKADINA   [*Alarmed*] Petrusha! [*trying to support him*] Petrusha, my dear! [*calling*] Help! Help!

Treplev, with a bandage around his head, and Medvedenko come in

He's feeling faint!

SORIN   It's nothing, nothing. [*smiles and drinks some water*] It's gone away already . . . and all that sort of . . .

TREPLEV   [*To his mother*] Don't get alarmed, Mamma; it's not serious. Uncle often has these attacks nowadays. [*to his uncle*] You ought to lie down for a while, Uncle.

SORIN   Yes, for a while. . . . But I'll go to town all the same. I'll lie down for a bit; then go. That's definite. [*goes out leaning on his stick*]

MEDVEDENKO   [*Supporting him by the arm*] Here's a riddle for you: in the morning on four legs, at noon on two, in the evening on three.

SORIN   [*Laughing*] Quite so. And at night on its back. I can walk on my own, thank you.

MEDVEDENKO   Come, come, don't stand on ceremony. [*goes out with Sorin*]

ARKADINA   How he scared me!

TREPLEV   It doesn't do his health any good living in the country. He gets depressed. Suppose you suddenly felt generous, Mamma, and lent him a couple of thousand? Then he could spend a whole year in town.

ARKADINA   I have no money. I'm an actress, not a banker. . . .

TREPLEV   [*After a pause*] Mamma, will you change my bandage for me? You do it so well.

ARKADINA   [*Takes some iodoform and a box of bandages out of the medicine cupboard*] The doctor's late.

TREPLEV   He promised to be here by ten o'clock, and it's midday already.

ARKADINA   Sit down. [*takes the bandage off his head*] You look as if you're wearing a turban. Yesterday there was some stranger in the kitchen asking what nationality you were. But your wound is almost healed. There's only a tiny bit still open. [*kisses him on the head*] You won't play around with a gun again when I'm away, will you?

TREPLEV   No, Mamma. That was a moment of mad despair, when I had no control over myself. It won't happen again. [*kisses her hands*] You've got magic hands. I remember ever so long ago, when you were still playing in the state-aided theaters—I was quite young then—there was a fight in our courtyard. One of the tenants, a washerwoman, was badly hurt. Do you remember? She was taken off unconscious . . . and you went to see her several times and took medicine to her and bathed her children in a tub. Don't you remember?

ARKADINA   No. [*puts on a fresh bandage*]

TREPLEV   Two ballet dancers lived in the same house as we did then. They used to come and have coffee with you.

ARKADINA   That I do remember.

TREPLEV   They were so religious. [*pause*] Just lately, these last few days, I've felt that I loved you as tenderly and uncritically as I did when I was a child. I have no one left but you now. Only why, why did you let yourself fall under the influence of that man?

ARKADINA   You don't understand him, Konstantin. He's such an honorable man.

TREPLEV   And yet, when he was told I was going to challenge him, his honor didn't prevent him from behaving like a coward. He's leaving. Ignominious flight!

ARKADINA   What nonsense! I asked him to go myself.

TREPLEV   A most honorable man, indeed! Here we are on the

point of quarreling about him, while at this very moment he may be laughing at us in the garden or the drawing room . . . bringing out Nina's potentialities, trying to convince her finally that he's a genius.

ARKADINA You take a delight in saying these unpleasant things. I admire him, so please don't speak ill of him in my presence.

TREPLEV Well, I don't admire him. You want me to think he's a genius too, but you must forgive me—I can't lie. His books make me sick.

ARKADINA That's envy. Mediocre people trying to make unjustifiable claims about themselves have to run down people with real talent. Poor comfort, I must say!

TREPLEV [*Ironically*] Real talent! [*wrathfully*] I have more talent than the lot of you if it comes to that! [*tearing the bandage off his head*] It's conventional, hidebound people like you who have grabbed the best places in the arts today, who regard as genuine and legitimate only what you do yourselves! Everything else you have to smother and suppress! I refuse to accept you at your own valuation! I refuse to accept you or him!

ARKADINA You're decadent!

TREPLEV Take yourself off to your lovely theater and go on acting in your futile, miserable plays!

ARKADINA I've never acted in futile, miserable plays! Leave me alone! You're incapable of writing even a couple of miserable scenes! You're just a little upstart from Kiev! A parasite!

TREPLEV You miser!

ARKADINA You beggar!

Treplev sits down and weeps quietly

Nonentity! [*walks up and down in agitation, then stops*] Don't cry. . . . You mustn't cry! [*weeps*] You mustn't. [*kisses his forehead, then his cheeks and his head*] My darling child, forgive me. Forgive your wicked mother. Forgive an unhappy woman.

TREPLEV [*Embraces her*] If only you knew! I've lost everything. She doesn't love me, and I can't write anymore. . . . All my hopes are gone.

ARKADINA Don't despair. Everything will turn out all right.

He'll be leaving soon, and she'll love you again. [*wipes away his tears*] That's enough. We've made up now.

TREPLEV [*Kissing her hands*] Yes, Mamma.

ARKADINA [*Tenderly*] Make it up with him too. There's no need for a duel. Is there now?

TREPLEV Very well. Only, Mamma, don't make me see him. It's painful for me. It's too much for my strength.

Trigorin comes in

There. I'm going. [*quickly puts away the dressings in the cupboard*] The doctor will do the bandaging now.

TRIGORIN [*Looking through the book*] Page 121 . . . lines 11 and 12. Here it is. [*reads*] "If ever you need my life, come and take it."

Treplev picks up the bandage from the floor and goes out

ARKADINA [*Glancing at her watch*] The horses will soon be here.

TRIGORIN [*To himself*] "If ever you need my life, come and take it."

ARKADINA You've got all your things packed, I hope?

TRIGORIN [*Impatiently*] Yes, yes. [*musing*] Why does it seem so sad to me, this cry from a pure soul? Why does it wring my heart so agonizingly? "If ever you need my life, come and take it." [*to Arkadina*] Let us stay one more day!

Arkadina shakes her head

Let us stay!

ARKADINA Darling, I know what's holding you here. But do control yourself. You've become a little intoxicated. Try to sober down.

TRIGORIN You must try to be sober too—and sensible and reasonable. Do try to see all this like a true friend, I implore you. [*presses her hand*] You are capable of sacrifice. Be a friend to me; release me.

ARKADINA [*In great agitation*] Has she fascinated you as much as that?

TRIGORIN   I'm drawn to her! Perhaps it is just what I need.

ARKADINA   The love of a provincial girl? Oh, how little you know yourself!

TRIGORIN   Sometimes people go to sleep on their feet, and that's just the state I'm in as I talk to you. All the time I feel as if I were asleep and dreaming of her. I'm possessed by sweet and wonderful dreams. Let me go.

ARKADINA   [*Trembling*] No, no. . . . I'm just an ordinary woman. You mustn't talk to me like that. Don't torment me, Boris. I'm frightened.

TRIGORIN   You could be extraordinary, if you chose. Young love, enchanting, poetical—love that carries you off into a world of dreams—it's the only thing that can bring happiness on this earth! I've never yet known a love like that. In my youth I never had time; I was always hanging around on editors' doorsteps, struggling with poverty. And now it is here, it has come, it is beckoning to me. What's the sense in running away from it?

ARKADINA   [*Angrily*] You're out of your mind!

TRIGORIN   And why not?

ARKADINA   You've all been conspiring to torment me today! [*weeps*]

TRIGORIN   [*Clasping his head with his hands*] She doesn't understand! She doesn't want to understand!

ARKADINA   Am I really so old and ugly that you can talk to me about other women without embarrassment? [*embraces and kisses him*] Oh, you must have gone mad! My beautiful, my wonderful . . . You—the last page of my life! [*kneels before him*] My joy, my pride, my happiness! [*embraces his knees*] If you leave me even for a single hour I'll never survive it. I'll go out of my mind—my wonderful, magnificent man; my master.

TRIGORIN   Someone might come in. [*helps her to her feet*]

ARKADINA   Let them. I'm not ashamed of my love for you. [*kisses his hands*] My darling, reckless boy, you may want to behave as if you were mad, but I won't let you, I won't let you. [*laughs*] You're mine . . . mine. This forehead is mine, and these eyes, and this beautiful silky hair is mine too. All of you is mine. You're so gifted, so clever. You're the best of all the modern writers, the only hope of Russia. You have such sincerity, simplicity, freshness, stimulating humor. With a stroke of your pen you can convey the whole essence of a character or a landscape; people in your books are so alive. It is impossible to read your work and not be delighted by it. Do you think this is just hero worship? You think I'm flattering you? Come, look into my eyes. . . . Look. Do I look like a liar? There! You see —I alone know how to appreciate you. I'm the one person who tells you the truth, my darling, my wonderful man. Will you come? Yes? You'll not leave me?

TRIGORIN   I have no will of my own. I've never had a will of my own. Sluggish, flabby, always submissive—how can any woman like that sort of thing? Take me, carry me off, but don't let me ever move a step away from you.

ARKADINA   [*To herself*] Now he's mine! [*affecting an easy manner as if nothing had happened*] But, of course, you can stay if you want to. I'll go myself, and you can come on afterward, a week later. After all, why should you hurry?

TRIGORIN   No, we may as well go together.

ARKADINA   Just as you like. Let's go together then.

A pause. Trigorin wites in his notebook

What is it?

TRIGORIN   I heard a good phrase this morning: "The Maiden's Forest." . . . Might come in useful. [*stretches*] So we are going? More railway carriages, stations, refreshment bars, veal cutlets, conversations . . .

SHAMRAYEV   [*Coming in*] I have come to inform you that the horses are ready, I am sorry to say. It's time, my dear lady, we were off to the station; the train comes in at five minutes past two. You will do me that little favor, won't you, Irina Nikolaevna? You won't forget to inquire where the actor Suzdaltsev is now? Is he alive? Is he well? We used to stand each other drinks years ago. He used to be quite inimitable in *The Mail Robbery*. I remember at that time there was Izmailov, an actor who always played with him at Elizavetgrad. He was a remarkable personality too. . . . Don't be in a hurry, my dear lady. You needn't start for another five minutes. Once they were playing as conspirators in a melodrama, and when they were suddenly discovered they had to say, "We're caught in a trap." But Izmailov said, "We're taught in a cap." [*laughs loudly*] "Taught in a cap!"

While he is speaking, Yakov fusses with the suitcases; a maid brings Arkadina's hat, coat, umbrella, and gloves; and everyone helps her to put them on. The chef looks in through the door at left, and after some hesitation, enters. Then Polina Andreyevna, and finally Sorin and Medvedenko, come in

POLINA   [*With a small basket in her hand*] Here are some plums for your journey . . . very sweet. You might feel like having something refreshing.

ARKADINA   You are very kind, Polina Andreyevna.

POLINA   Good-bye, my dear! If there has been anything that wasn't quite as you like it, please forgive us. [*weeps*]

ARKADINA   [*Embracing her*] Everything was all right, everything! Only you shouldn't cry!

POLINA   Our days are passing!

ARKADINA   There's nothing we can do about it.

SORIN   [*Wearing an overcoat with a shoulder cape and a hat, and carrying a cane, comes in from the door at left. He speaks as he walks across the room*] It's time to go, Sister. Let's not be late for the train after all. I'm going to get into the carriage. [*goes out*]

MEDVEDENKO   I'll walk to the station . . . to see you off. I'll be there in no time. [*goes out*]

ARKADINA   Good-bye, my dears. If all goes well, we'll meet again next summer.

The maid, the chef, and Yakov kiss her hand

Don't forget me. [*gives the chef a ruble*] Here's a ruble between you three.

THE CHEF   Thank you kindly, madam. Good journey to you! We're most grateful for your kindness.

YAKOV   Godspeed to you!

SHAMRAYEV   Perhaps you'll write to us. It would make us so happy! Good-bye, Boris Alekseevich.

ARKADINA   Where is Konstantin? Tell him that I'm leaving. We must say good-bye. Think kindly of me. [*to Yakov*] I gave a ruble to the chef. It's between the three of you.

All go out at right. The stage is empty. There is the noise off-stage of people being seen off. The maid returns to fetch the basket of plums from the table and goes out again

TRIGORIN   [*Returning*] I've forgotten my cane. I believe it's out there, on the terrace. [*walks toward the door at the left and meets Nina, who comes in*] It's you! We're going.

NINA   I felt sure that we should see each other again. [*excitedly*] Boris Alekseevich, I've decided irrevocably, the die is cast— I'm going on the stage. I will be gone from here tomorrow. I'm leaving my father, leaving everything. I'm beginning a new life. I'm going to Moscow . . . like you. We'll see each other there.

TRIGORIN   [*Glancing behind him*] Stay at the Slavianski Bazaar. Let me know at once . . . at Molchanovka, Grokholski House. I must hurry.

NINA   [*After a pause*] One minute more. . . .

TRIGORIN   [*In an undertone*] You are so beautiful. Oh, how happy I am to think that we'll be seeing each other soon!

She leans her head on his breast

I will see these wonderful eyes again, this indescribably beautiful, tender smile . . . these sweet features, the expression of angelic purity! My darling. . . . [*a prolonged kiss*]

CURTAIN

Between the third and the fourth acts there is an interval of two years

ACT FOUR

A drawing room in Sorin's house, converted into a study by Konstantin Treplev. Doors right and left leading to other rooms. In the center, a French window opening onto the terrace. There is a writing desk in the corner on the right and an ottoman by the door on the left; also a bookcase and the usual drawing room furniture. Books are lying on the windowsills and on chairs. It is evening. The room is dimly lit by a shaded table lamp. There is the noise of wind in the trees and the chimneys.

A watchman is heard tapping.[1] *Enter Medvedenko and Masha.*

MASHA [*Calling*] Konstantin Gavriilovich! Konstantin Gavriilovich! [*looking around*] No, there's no one here. The old man keeps on asking: where's Kostya, where's Kostya. He just can't live without him.

MEDVEDENKO He's afraid of being alone. [*listening*] What dreadful weather! It's been like this for nearly two days.

MASHA [*Turning up the lamp*] There are waves on the lake, enormous ones.

MEDVEDENKO It's very dark outside. By the way, we might as well tell them to pull down that stage in the garden. It stands there naked and ugly like a skeleton, with the curtain flapping in the wind. You know, last night as I was walking past it, I thought I heard someone inside—crying.

1. In former days it was usual for a man to go around an estate, striking a wooden board with a stick to frighten away potential thieves.

MASHA   What next. . . .

MEDVEDENKO   [*After a pause*] Let's go home, Masha.

MASHA   [*Shaking her head*] No, I will stay here for the night.

MEDVEDENKO   [*Imploringly*] Masha, let us go! The baby may be hungry.

MASHA   What nonsense! Matrëna will feed him. . . .

MEDVEDENKO   [*After a pause*] I feel sorry for him. This is the third night he's been without his mother.

MASHA   How boring you've become! In the old days you did at least philosophize a bit now and again. Now all you talk about is baby and home, baby and home. I never hear anything else from you.

MEDVEDENKO   Let's go, Masha!

MASHA   You go by yourself.

MEDVEDENKO   Your father won't let me have a horse.

MASHA   Yes, he will. You go and ask him.

MEDVEDENKO   I suppose I might ask him. And you'll be coming home tomorrow then?

MASHA   [*Takes snuff*] Well, yes . . . tomorrow. How you pester me!

Enter Treplev and Polina Andreyevna. Treplev carries pillows and a blanket, and Polina Andreyevna, some sheets, which they put on the ottoman. Treplev then goes to his desk and sits down

What is this for, Mamma?

POLINA   It's for Pëtr Nikolaevich. He wants his bed made in Kostya's room.

MASHA   Let me. [*makes the bed*]

POLINA   [*Sighing*] Old people are like children. [*walks over to the writing desk and, leaning on her elbow, looks at an open manuscript*]

MEDVEDENKO   [*After a pause*] Well, I'd better go. Good-bye, Masha. [*kisses his wife's hand*] Good-bye, Mother. [*tries to kiss his mother-in-law's hand*]

POLINA   [*With irritation*] Go on with you! It's time you went if you are going.

MEDVEDENKO   Good-bye, Konstantin Gavriilovich.

*Treplev gives him his hand without speaking. Medvedenko
goes out*

POLINA [*Looking at the manuscript*] Who would have thought
that you would turn out to be a real writer, Kostya? But, thank
God, here you are getting money from magazines for your
work. [*strokes his hair*] You've grown so good-looking too.
Kostya, my dear, you're so kind; couldn't you be a little kinder
to my Mashenka?

MASHA [*Making the bed*] Leave him alone, Mamma.

POLINA [*To Treplev*] She's a nice girl, you know. [*pause*] Give a
woman a kind glance sometimes, Kostya, and she won't ask
for more. I know that.

Treplev gets up from his desk and goes out without speaking

MASHA There! Now you've made him angry. What's the point
of pestering him?

POLINA I feel so sorry for you, Mashenka!

MASHA A lot of use that is to me!

POLINA My heart's been aching for you. I see it all, you know. I
understand it all.

MASHA All this is just nonsense. Love without hope—it only
happens in novels. It's really nothing. You've only got to keep
a firm hold on yourself, to stop yourself hoping for . . . hoping for the tide to turn. If love sneaks into your heart the best
thing to do is to chuck it out. My husband's been promised a
transfer to another district. Once we get there, I'll forget it
all. . . . Tear it out of my heart, roots and all.

*A waltz with a melancholy tune is being played two rooms
away*

POLINA That's Kostya playing. He must be feeling sad.

MASHA [*Noiselessly takes two or three waltz turns*] The most
important thing, Mamma, is not to have him constantly in
front of me. Just let them give my Semën his transfer, and,
you'll see, I'll forget it all in a month. The whole thing is just
nonsense.

Door at left opens. Dorn and Medvedenko wheel in Sorin

MEDVEDENKO I've got six people at home now, and flour is two kopecks a pound.

DORN Yes, you've got to scrape and save!

MEDVEDENKO It's all very well for you to laugh. You've got more money than you know what to do with.

DORN Money? My dear fellow, in thirty years of practice—and very worrying practice at that, for I was day and night at everyone's beck and call—in all those years I've only managed to save two thousand rubles, and I've just spent that on a holiday abroad. I've got positively nothing.

MASHA [*To her husband*] So you haven't gone after all?

MEDVEDENKO [*Apologetically*] Well, how could I if they wouldn't let me have a horse?

MASHA [*Bitterly, in an undertone*] I just can't bear the sight of you!

Sorin is wheeled to the left side of the room. Polina, Masha, and Dorn sit down beside him. Medvedenko, looking depressed, stands a little apart from them

DORN What a lot of changes you've made though! You've turned this drawing room into a study.

MASHA Konstantin Gavriilovich is more comfortable working here. He can walk out into the garden whenever he likes, and he can think there.

The watchman can be heard tapping

SORIN Where's my sister?

DORN She's gone to the station to meet Trigorin. She'll be back soon.

SORIN I must be dangerously ill if you thought it necessary to send for my sister. [*after a short silence*] Isn't it odd? I'm dangerously ill; yet no one gives me any medicine.

DORN Well, what would you like to have? Valerian drops? Soda? Quinine?

SORIN There he goes again, the philosopher! Oh, how trying it all is! [*jerks his head in the direction of the ottoman*] Has that been gotten ready for me?

POLINA Yes, Pëtr Nikolaevich, it's for you.

SORIN Thank you.

DORN [*Hums*] "The moon floats through the night sky . . ."

SORIN You know, I'd like to give Kostya a subject for a novel. I'd call it *The Man Who Wished*. *"L'Homme qui a voulu."* Long ago in my young days I wanted to become a writer— and I didn't. I wanted to be a fine speaker, and I spoke abominably [*mimicking himself*] —"and all that sort of thing, and all the rest of it, and so on, and so forth . . ." When I tried to sum up my argument, I'd go plodding on and on until I broke into perspiration. I wanted to get married— and I didn't. I always wanted to live in town—and here I am finishing my life in the country, and all that sort of thing.

DORN You wanted to become a civil councillor—and you did.

SORIN [*Laughs*] That was something I didn't strive for. It just happened.

DORN Fancy expressing dissatisfaction with life at the age of sixty-two! It's a little indecent, you must admit.

SORIN What a persistent fellow he is! Can't you understand any-one wanting to live?

DORN That's just foolish. Every life must have an end—it's the law of nature.

SORIN You talk like a man who's had his fill of experience. You've satisfied your hunger, and so life means nothing to you; you don't care about it. But when it comes to dying, you'll be afraid too.

DORN The fear of death is an animal fear. You've got to suppress it. It's only religious people who consciously fear death, because they believe in a future life and are afraid they'll be punished for their sins. Your case is different: in the first place, you're not religious; and in the second, what sins have you committed? You've served in the Ministry of Justice for twenty-five years, that's all.

SORIN [*Laughs*] Twenty-eight.

Enter Treplev, who sits down on a low stool at Sorin's feet. Masha gazes at him continuously

DORN We're preventing Konstantin Gavriilovich from getting on with his work.

TREPLEV Oh, no, it doesn't matter. . . .

MEDVEDENKO [*After a pause*] If I might ask you, Doctor, which city do you like best of all those you've seen abroad?

DORN Genoa.

TREPLEV Why Genoa?

DORN Because there's something very fine about the street crowds there. You go out of your hotel at night, and the whole street is packed with people. You just wander among them aimlessly, anywhere you like, up and down. You live with them, become part of the crowd spiritually, and you end by almost believing that a world-soul can really exist—something like the world-soul in your play, the one Nina Zarechnaya acted in some time back. By the way, where is Zarechnaya now? Do you know how she is?

TREPLEV I suppose she's all right.

DORN Someone told me she's been leading a rather peculiar kind of life. What's been happening?

TREPLEV Well, Doctor, it's a long story.

DORN Never mind, you can make it short. . . .

TREPLEV [*After a pause*] She ran away from home and had an affair with Trigorin. You knew that, didn't you?

DORN Yes, I did know.

TREPLEV She had a child. It died. Trigorin fell out of love with her and went back to his former attachments, as might have been expected. In fact he never gave them up, but in his spineless way he somehow managed to keep them all going. As far as I can make it out from what I've heard, Nina's personal life turned out a complete failure.

DORN And what about the stage?

TREPLEV That was worse still, I believe. She started acting in a small theater at some holiday place near Moscow; then went to the provinces. I never lost sight of her at that time, and wherever she went, I followed. She would always take on big parts, but she acted them crudely, without distinction—with false intonations and violent gestures. There were moments when she showed talent—as when she uttered a cry, or died on the stage—but they were only moments.

DORN   Then she has some talent, after all?

TREPLEV   It's very hard to tell. I believe she has. I saw her, of course, but she refused to see me, and the servants wouldn't let me go up to her room at the hotel. I understood her state of mind and did not insist on seeing her. [*pause*] What more can I tell you? Afterward, when I got back home, I had letters from her—intelligent, warm, interesting letters. She did not complain, but I could feel that she was profoundly unhappy; every line was like an exposed, aching nerve. Her imagination seemed to be confused too. She signed herself "Sea Gull." You remember, in Pushkin's play *The River Nymph* the miller says he's a raven. So in the same way she kept calling herself "the sea gull" in her letters. By the way, she is here now.

DORN   What do you mean—here?

TREPLEV   I mean she's staying in the town, at a hotel. She's been there for four or five days. I did go to call on her, and Marya Ilyinichna here went too, but she won't see anyone. Semën Semënych insists that he saw her yesterday afternoon in the fields, a mile or so from here.

MEDVEDENKO   Yes, I did see her. She was walking away from here, toward the town. I bowed to her and asked why she didn't come to see us. She said she would.

TREPLEV   She won't come. [*pause*] Her father and stepmother won't have anything to do with her. They put men all around to make sure that she doesn't come near the house. [*goes with the doctor toward the writing desk*] How easy it is to be philosophical on paper, Doctor, and how difficult when it comes to real life.

SORIN   She was a most charming girl.

DORN   What?

SORIN   She was a most charming girl, I said. Councillor Sorin was actually in love with her for a time.

DORN   The old philanderer!

Offstage Shamrayev can be heard laughing

POLINA   I think they've arrived from the station.

TREPLEV   Yes, I can hear Mamma.

Enter Arkadina and Trigorin, followed by Shamrayev

SHAMRAYEV [*As he comes in*] We all of us get older; we wither
away like trees battered by the elements, but you, my dear
lady, you're still as young as ever. A light-colored blouse, viva-
cious manner . . . grace in all your movements . . .

ARKADINA You want to bring me ill luck again, you tiresome
man?

TRIGORIN [*To Sorin*] How do you do, Pëtr Nikolaevich? So
you're still doing poorly? That's not so good! [*seeing Masha,
happily*] Ah, Marya Ilyinichna!

MASHA So you remember me? [*shakes hands with him*]

TRIGORIN Married?

MASHA A long time now.

TRIGORIN Happy? [*bows to Dorn and Medvedenko, who bow
in return, then hesitatingly approaches Treplev*] Irina Nikolaevna has told me that you've forgotten the past and aren't
angry with me any longer.

Treplev holds out his hand

ARKADINA [*To her son*] Look, Boris Alekseevich has brought
the magazine with your new story in it.

TREPLEV [*Taking the magazine, to Trigorin*] Thank you, you're
very kind.

TRIGORIN Your admirers send their greetings to you. People in
Petersburg and Moscow are very intrigued by you—always
asking me what you are like, how old, and whether you're fair
or dark. For some reason they all think that you're getting on
in years. And no one knows your real name; you always pub-
lish your work under a pseudonym, don't you? You're as mysterious as the Man in the Iron Mask.

TREPLEV Will you be stopping with us for a while?

TRIGORIN No, I think I'll go back to Moscow tomorrow. I've
got to, really. I'm in a hurry to finish a novel, and besides, I've
promised to give them something for an anthology. In short
it's just the same as ever.

*While they talk Arkadina and Polina move a card table into
the middle of the room and open it. Shamrayev lights the can-*

dles and puts the chairs in place. A game of lotto is brought out of the cupboard

The weather isn't greeting me very kindly. There's a cruel wind. Tomorrow morning, if it drops, I'll go fishing on the lake. Besides, I want to have a look around the garden and see the place where your play was acted—you remember? I've a subject for a story. I only want to revive my memories of the scene where the action is supposed to take place.

MASHA   [*To her father*] Papa, do let Semën have a horse! He must get home somehow.

SHAMRAYEV   [*Mimics her*] A horse. . . . Must get home. [*sternly*] You saw the horses have just been to the station! How can I send them out again?

MASHA   But there are other horses. [*on seeing that her father says nothing, makes a gesture of discouragement*] Oh, you're hopeless.

MEDVEDENKO   I can walk, Masha. Really . . .

POLINA   [*With a sigh*] Walk in this weather! [*sits down at the card table*] Please come along, ladies and gentlemen.

MEDVEDENKO   It's only four miles after all. Good-bye. [*kisses his wife's hand*] Good-bye, Mother.

Polina reluctantly holds out her hand for him to kiss

I wouldn't have made any bother if it weren't for the baby. [*bows to the company*] Good-bye. [*goes out guiltily*]

SHAMRAYEV   He can walk all right! He's not a general, after all!

POLINA   [*Tapping on the table*] Come along, please! Let's not waste time; they'll be calling us to supper soon.

Shamrayev, Masha, and Dorn sit down at the table

ARKADINA   [*To Trigorin*] They always play lotto here when the long autumn evenings come on. Look, this is the same old set of lotto my mother used when she played with us children. Won't you have a game with us before supper? [*sits down at the table with Trigorin*] It's a dull game, but it's not so bad when you get used to it. [*deals three cards to everyone*]

TREPLEV   [*Turning over the pages of the magazine*] He's read his own story, but he hasn't even cut the pages of mine. [*puts the magazine down on his desk and walks toward the door at the left; as he passes his mother, he kisses her on the head*]

ARKADINA What about you, Kostya?

TREPLEV Please forgive me; I don't feel like it somehow. I'll go for a stroll. [*goes out*]

ARKADINA The stake is ten kopecks. Put it down for me, Doctor, will you?

DORN I will.

MASHA Have you all put down your money? I'm starting. Twenty-two!

ARKADINA Yes.

MASHA Three.

DORN Right!

MASHA Did you play three? Eight! Eighty-one! Ten!

SHAMRAYEV Don't be in such a hurry!

ARKADINA What a reception I had in Kharkov! My goodness! It makes my head go around even now!

MASHA Thirty-four!

A waltz with a melancholy tune is being played offstage

ARKADINA The students gave me a regular ovation. Three baskets of flowers, two garlands, and this as well. [*unfastens a brooch on her throat and tosses it onto the table*]

SHAMRAYEV Yes, that's really worth having.

MASHA Fifty!

DORN Just fifty?

ARKADINA I had a wonderful dress on. I know how to dress, if I know anything at all.

POLINA Kostya's playing the piano. He's depressed, poor boy.

SHAMRAYEV They've been attacking him a lot in the papers.

MASHA Seventy-seven!

ARKADINA He needn't take any notice of that!

TRIGORIN He's unlucky. He still can't manage to strike the right note somehow. There's something strange and vague about his writing; at times it even suggests the ravings of a sick man. And not a single living character!

MASHA Eleven!

ARKADINA [*Looking around at Sorin*] Petrusha, are you bored? [*pause*] He's asleep.

DORN The councillor is asleep.

MASHA Seven! Ninety!

TRIGORIN If I lived in a place like this, beside a lake, do you suppose I would ever write anything? I would overcome this passion of mine and do nothing but fish.

MASHA Twenty-eight!

TRIGORIN Just to catch a perch or a ruff—how delightful it is!

DORN Well, I believe in Konstantin Gavriilovich. He's got something! He certainly has! He thinks in images; his stories are vivid, full of color, and personally I'm deeply moved by them. But it's a pity he doesn't set himself any definite goal. He makes an impression, that's all, but an impression alone doesn't take you very far. Irina Nikolaevna, are you glad that you've got a writer for a son?

ARKADINA Can you imagine it? I haven't read anything of his yet. There's never any time.

MASHA Twenty-six!

Treplev comes in quietly and walks over to his desk

SHAMRAYEV [*To Trigorin*] By the way, Boris Alekseevich, we've still got something of yours down here.

TRIGORIN What is it?

SHAMRAYEV Konstantin Gavriilovich shot a gull once, and you asked me to get it stuffed for you.

TRIGORIN I don't remember. [*pondering*] No, I don't remember.

MASHA Sixty-one! One!

TREPLEV [*Throws open the window and listens*] How dark it is! I can't understand why I'm feeling so restless.

ARKADINA Kostya, will you shut the window? There's a draft.

Treplev shuts the window

MASHA Eighty-eight!

TRIGORIN The game is mine, my friends.

ARKADINA [*Gaily*] Bravo, bravo!

SHAMRAYEV Well done!

ARKADINA This man's a lucky fellow, always and everywhere! [*gets up*] But now let us go and have something to eat. Our famous man hasn't had a decent meal today. We'll go on with the game after supper. [*to her son*] Kostya, do leave your writing and come to supper.

TREPLEV I don't want any, Mamma. I'm not hungry.

ARKADINA Just as you like. [*wakes Sorin*] Petrusha, supper is ready! [*takes Shamrayev's arm*] Let me tell you about the reception I had at Kharkov.

Polina Andreyevna blows out the candles on the table, then she and Dorn wheel out Sorin's chair. Everyone goes out by the door on the left except for Treplev, who remains alone in the room sitting at his desk

TREPLEV [*Preparing to write, reads through what he has already written*] I used to talk such a lot about new forms in art, and now I feel I'm slipping into a rut myself, little by little. [*reads*] "The placard on the wall proclaimed. A pale face in its frame of dark hair." Proclaimed . . . a frame of dark hair. . . . This won't do at all! [*crosses out*] I'll start with the passage where the hero is awakened by the noise of the rain. The rest will have to come out. The description of the moonlit evening is too long and rather precious. Trigorin has worked out his own methods—it comes easily to him. He would just mention the neck of a broken bottle glistening on the dam and the black shadow of a mill wheel—and there you'd have a moonlit night. But I have to put in the tremulous light, the soft twinkling of the stars, and the distant sounds of a piano, dying away in the still, fragrant air. It's excruciating! [*pause*] Yes, I'm becoming more and more convinced that it isn't a matter of old or new forms. One must write without thinking about forms, and just because it pours freely from one's soul.

There is a tap on the window nearest to his desk

What's that? [*looks through the window*] I can't see anything. [*opens the French window and looks out into the garden*]

Someone ran down the steps. [*calls*] Who's there? [*goes out and is heard walking rapidly along the terrace; then returns half a minute later with Nina Zarechnaya*] Nina! Nina!

Nina leans her head against his breast and sobs quietly

[*deeply moved*] Nina! Nina! It's you . . . you. . . . I seem to have had a presentiment; my heart's been aching terribly all day. [*takes off her cape and hat*] Oh, my sweet, my precious girl, she's come at last! Don't cry, don't!

NINA   There's someone here.

TREPLEV   There isn't anyone.

NINA   Please lock the doors or someone will come in.

TREPLEV   No one will come in.

NINA   I know Irina Nikolaevna is here. Lock the doors.

TREPLEV   [*Locks the door on the right, then crosses to the left*] There's no lock on this one. I'll put a chair against it. [*puts an armchair against the door*] Don't be afraid; no one will come in.

NINA   [*Looks intently at his face*] Let me look at you for a little while. [*looking around*] How warm, how nice it is here! This used to be a drawing room. Have I changed a lot?

TREPLEV   Yes. You are thinner and your eyes have grown bigger. Nina, it's so strange to be seeing you! Why wouldn't you let me see you? Why haven't you come here before now? I know you've been in the town almost a week. I've been to your place every day, several times a day. I stood under your window like a beggar.

NINA   I was afraid that you might hate me. Every night I dream that you look at me and don't recognize me. If only you knew! Ever since I came I've been walking around here . . . beside the lake. I've been near this house many times, but I dared not come in. Let us sit down. [*they sit down*] Let us sit and talk, talk. . . . It's nice here, warm and comfortable. Do you hear the wind? There's a passage in Turgenev: "Fortunate is he who on such a night has a roof over him, who has a warm corner of his own." I am a sea gull. No, that's not it. [*rubs her forehead*] What was I saying? Yes. . . . Turgenev. . . . "And heaven help the homeless wayfarers." . . . Never mind. [*sobs*]

TREPLEV Nina, you're crying again! Nina!

NINA Never mind, it does me good. I haven't cried for two years. Yesterday, late in the evening I came into the garden to see whether our stage was still there. And it is still standing! I began to cry for the first time in two years, and it lifted the weight from my heart, and I felt more at ease. You see, I'm not crying now. [*takes his hand*] And so you've become a writer. You are a writer and I'm an actress. We've been drawn into the whirlpool too. I used to live here joyously, like a child. I used to wake up in the morning and burst into song. I loved you and dreamed of fame. . . . And now? Tomorrow morning early I have to go to Yelets in a third-class carriage . . . with the peasants; and at Yelets upstart businessmen will pester me with their attentions. Life is coarse!

TREPLEV Why do you have to go to Yelets?

NINA I've accepted an engagement for the whole winter. It's time to go.

TREPLEV Nina, I used to curse you: I hated you, I tore up your letters and photographs. But all the time I knew that I was bound to you heart and soul, and forever! It's not in my power to stop loving you, Nina. Ever since I lost you, ever since I began to get my work published, my life's been intolerable. I'm miserable. I feel as if my youth has been suddenly torn away from me, as if I've been inhabiting this world for ninety years. I call out your name; I kiss the ground where you've walked. Wherever I look I seem to see your face, that sweet smile that used to shine on me in the best years of my life.

NINA [*Bewildered*] Why does he talk like this? Why does he talk like this?

TREPLEV I am lonely. I've no one's love to warm me. I feel as cold as if I were in a cellar—and everything I write turns out lifeless and bitter and gloomy. Stay here, Nina, I entreat you, or let me come with you!

Nina quickly puts on her hat and cape

Nina, why—for heaven's sake—Nina . . . [*looks at her as she puts on her clothes*]

NINA [*After a pause*] The horses are waiting for me at the gate.

Don't see me off. I'll go by myself. [*tearfully*] Give me some water.

TREPLEV [*Gives her water*] Where are you going now?

NINA To the town. [*pause*] Irina Nikolaevna's here, isn't she?

TREPLEV Yes. My uncle had an attack on Thursday, so we telegraphed for her.

NINA Why did you say you kissed the ground where I walked? Someone ought to kill me. [*droops over the table*] I am so tired. Oh, I wish I could rest . . . just rest! [*raising her head*] I'm a sea gull. . . . No, that's not it. I'm an actress. Oh, well! [*she hears Arkadina and Trigorin laughing offstage, listens, then runs to the door at the left and looks through the keyhole*] So he is here too! [*returning to Treplev*] Oh, well! Never mind. . . . Yes. . . . He didn't believe in the theater. He was always laughing at my dreams, and so gradually I ceased to believe too and lost heart. . . . And then I was so preoccupied with love and jealousy and a constant fear for my baby. I became petty and common. When I acted I did it stupidly. I didn't know what to do with my hands or how to stand on the stage. I couldn't control my voice. But you can't imagine what it feels like—when you know that you are acting abominably. I'm a sea gull. No, that's not it again. . . . Do you remember you shot a sea gull? A man came along by chance, saw it, and destroyed it, just to pass the time. . . . A subject for a short story. . . . That's not it. [*rubs her forehead*] What was I talking about? . . . Yes, about the stage. I'm not like that now. Now I am a real actress. I act with intense enjoyment, with enthusiasm; on the stage I am intoxicated and I feel that I am beautiful. But now, while I'm living here, I go for walks a lot. I keep walking and thinking . . . thinking and feeling that I am growing stronger in spirit with every day that passes. I think I now know, Kostya, that what matters in our work— whether you act on the stage or write stories—what really matters is not fame or glamor, not the things I used to dream about—but knowing how to endure things. How to bear one's cross and have faith. I have faith now and I'm not suffering quite so much, and when I think of my vocation I'm not afraid of life.

TREPLEV [*Sadly*] You have found your right path; you know

131

which way you're going. But I'm still floating around in a cha-otic world of dreams and images, without knowing what use it all is. I have no faith, and I don't know what my vocation is.

NINA [*Listening*] Sh-sh! I'm going now. Good-bye. When I be-come a great actress, come and see me act. Promise? And now . . . [*presses his hand*] It's late. I can hardly stand up. I'm so tired and hungry.

TREPLEV Do stay; I'll give you some supper.

NINA No, no. Don't see me off; I'll go by myself. My horses are not far off. . . . So she brought him with her? Oh, well, it doesn't matter. When you see Trigorin don't tell him anything. I love him. I love him even more than before. A subject for a short story. . . . Yes, I love him, I love him passionately, I love him desperately! How nice it all used to be, Kostya! Do you remember? How tranquil, warm, and joyous, and pure our life was. What feelings we had—like tender, exquisite flowers. Do you remember? [*recites*] "The men, the lions, the eagles, the partridges, the antlered deer, the geese, the spiders, the silent fishes of the deep, starfishes, and creatures unseen to the eye—in short—all living things, all living things, all living things, having completed their mournful cycle, have been snuffed out. For thousands of years the earth has borne no liv-ing creature, and this poor moon now lights its lamp in vain. The cranes no longer wake up in the meadows with a cry; the May bugs are no longer heard humming in the groves of lime trees." [*impulsively embraces Treplev and runs out through the French window*]

TREPLEV [*After a pause*] It won't be very nice if someone meets her in the garden and tells Mamma. It might upset Mamma. [*he spends the next two minutes silently tearing up all his manuscripts and throwing them under the table, then unlocks the door at the right and goes out*]

DORN [*Trying to open the door at the left*] That's strange. The door seems to be locked. [*comes in and puts the armchair in its place*] Quite an obstacle race.

Enter Arkadina and Polina, followed by Yakov carrying drinks, then Masha, Shamrayev, and Trigorin

ARKADINA Put the red wine and the beer on the table here for Boris Alekseevich. We'll drink as we play. Let us sit down, friends.

POLINA [*To Yakov*] Bring the tea in as well. [*lights the candles and sits down at the card table*]

SHAMRAYEV [*Leads Trigorin to the cupboard*] Here is the thing I was telling you about just now. [*takes the stuffed sea gull out of the cupboard*] This is what you ordered.

TRIGORIN [*Looking at the sea gull*] I don't remember. [*musing*] No, I don't remember!

There is a sound of a shot offstage on the right. Everyone starts

DORN That's nothing. It must be something in my medicine chest that's gone off. Don't worry. [*goes out through the door at the right and returns in half a minute*] Just as I thought. A bottle of ether has burst. [*hums*] "Again I stand before you, enchanted."

ARKADINA [*Sitting down to the table*] Ough, how it frightened me! It reminded me of how . . . [*covers her face with her hands*] Everything went dark for a moment.

DORN [*Turning over the pages of a magazine, to Trigorin*] There was an article here about two months ago . . . a letter from America, and I wanted to ask you . . . [*puts his arm around Trigorin's waist and leads him to the footlights*] Because I'm very much interested in this question. . . . [*dropping his voice, in a lower tone*] Take Irina Nikolaevna away from here somehow. The fact is, Konstantin Gavriilovich has shot himself.

CURTAIN

THE THREE SISTERS

CHARACTERS

PROZOROV, Andrei Sergeevich

NATASHA (*Natalya Ivanovna*), his fiancée, afterward his wife

OLGA (*Olga Sergeevna, Olya, Olyushka, Olechka*) ⎫

MASHA (*Marya Sergeevna*) ⎬ his sisters

IRINA (*Irina Sergeevna, Irenushka*) ⎭

KULYGIN, Fëdor Ilyich, a teacher at the high school for boys and the husband of Masha

VERSHININ, Aleksandr Ignatievich, a lieutenant colonel and battery commander

TUTZENBACH, Nikolai Lvovich, baron and a lieutenant in the army

SOLENI, Vasili Vasilievich, a captain

CHEBUTYKIN, Ivan Romanovich, an army doctor

FEDOTIK, Aleksei Petrovich, a second lieutenant

RODÉ, Vladimir Karlovich, a second lieutenant

FERAPONT (*Ferapont Spiridonich*), an old porter from the County Council Office

ANFISA, the Prozorovs' former nurse, an old woman of eighty

The action takes place in a country town

ACT ONE

A drawing room in the Prozorovs' house; it is separated from a large ballroom[1] at the back by a row of columns. It is midday; there is cheerful sunshine outside. In the ballroom the table is being set for lunch. Olga, wearing the regulation dark blue dress of a secondary-school teacher, is correcting her pupils' work, standing or walking around as she does so. Masha, in a black dress, is sitting reading a book, her hat on her lap. Irina, in white, stands lost in thought.

OLGA It's exactly a year ago that Father died, isn't it? This very day, the fifth of May—your saint's day, Irina. I remember it was very cold and it was snowing. I felt then as if I would never survive his death; and you had fainted and were lying quite still, as if you were dead. And now—a year's gone by, and we talk about it so easily. You're wearing white, and your face is positively radiant.

A clock strikes twelve

The clock struck twelve then too. [*pause*] I remember when Father was being taken to the cemetery there was a military band, and a salute with rifle fire. That was because he was a general, in command of a brigade. And yet there weren't many

1. A large room, sparsely furnished, used for receptions and dances in Russian houses.

people at the funeral. Of course it was raining hard, raining and snowing.

IRINA Need we bring up all these memories?

Baron Tutzenbach, Chebutykin, and Soleni appear behind the columns by the table in the ballroom

OLGA It's so warm today that we can keep the windows wide open, and yet there aren't any leaves showing on the birch trees. Father was made a brigadier eleven years ago, and then he left Moscow and took us with him. I remember so well how everything in Moscow was in blossom by now; everything was soaked in sunlight and warmth. Eleven years have gone by, yet I remember everything about it as if we'd only left yesterday. Oh, heavens! When I woke up this morning and saw this flood of sunshine, all this spring sunshine, I felt so moved and so happy! I felt such a longing to get back home to Moscow!

CHEBUTYKIN [*To Tutzenbach*] The devil you have!

TUTZENBACH It's nonsense, I agree.

Masha, absorbed in her book, whistles a tune under her breath

OLGA Masha, stop whistling! How can you? [*pause*] I suppose I must get this continual headache because I have to go to school every day and go on teaching right into the evening. I seem to have the thoughts of someone quite old. Honestly, I've been feeling as if my strength and youth were running out of me drop by drop, day after day. Day after day, all these four years that I've been working at the school. I just have one longing and it seems to grow stronger and stronger.

IRINA If only we could go back to Moscow! Sell the house, finish with our life here, and go back to Moscow.

OLGA Yes, Moscow! As soon as we possibly can.

Chebutykin and Tutzenbach laugh

IRINA I suppose Andrei will soon get a professorship. He isn't likely to go on living here. The only problem is our poor Masha.

OLGA   Masha can come and stay the whole summer with us every year in Moscow.

Masha whistles a tune under her breath

IRINA   Everything will settle itself, with God's help. [*looks through the window*] What lovely weather it is today! Really I don't know why there's such joy in my heart. I remembered this morning that it was my saint's day, and suddenly I felt so happy; and I thought of the time when we were children and Mother was still alive. And then such wonderful thoughts came to me, such wonderful stirring thoughts!

OLGA   You're so lovely today; you really do look most attractive. Masha looks pretty today too. Andrei could be good-looking, but he's grown so fat. It doesn't suit him. As for me, I've just aged and grown a lot thinner. I suppose it's from getting so irritated with the girls at school. But today I'm at home, I'm free, and my headache's gone, and I feel much younger than I did yesterday. I'm only twenty-eight after all. . . . I suppose everything that God wills must be right and good, but I can't help thinking sometimes that if I'd gotten married and stayed at home, it would have been a better thing for me. [*pause*] I would have been very fond of my husband.

TUTZENBACH   [*To Soleni*] Really you talk such a lot of nonsense that I'm tired of listening to you. [*comes into the drawing room*] I forgot to tell you: Vershinin, our new battery commander, is going to call on you today. [*sits down by the piano*]

OLGA   I'm very glad to hear it.

IRINA   Is he old?

TUTZENBACH   No, not particularly. Forty, forty-five at the most. [*plays quietly*] He seems a nice fellow. Certainly not a fool. His only weakness is that he talks too much.

IRINA   Is he interesting?

TUTZENBACH   He's all right, only he's got a wife, a mother-in-law, and two little girls. What's more, she's his second wife. He calls on everybody and tells them that he's got a wife and two little girls. He'll tell you about it too; I'm sure of that. His wife seems to be a bit soft in the head. She wears a long braid like a girl, she is always philosophizing and talking in high-flown language, and then she often tries to commit suicide, apparently just to annoy her husband. I would have run away from a wife like that years ago, but he puts up with it and just grumbles about it.

SOLENI [*Enters the drawing room with Chebutykin*] Now I can only lift sixty pounds with one hand, but with two I can lift two hundred pounds or even two hundred and forty. So I conclude from that that two men are not just twice as strong as one, but three times as strong, if not more.

CHEBUTYKIN [*Reads the paper as he comes in*] Here's a recipe for falling hair: two ounces of naphthaline, half a bottle of wood alcohol. Dissolve and apply once a day. [*writes it down in a notebook*] Must make a note of it. [*to Soleni*] Well, as I was trying to explain to you, you cork the bottle and pass a glass tube through the cork. Then you take a pinch of ordinary powdered alum and . . .

IRINA Ivan Romanich, dear Ivan Romanich!

CHEBUTYKIN What is it, my child, what is it?

IRINA Tell me, why is it I'm so happy today? Just as if I were sailing along in a boat with big white sails, and above me the wide, blue sky, and in the sky great white birds floating around.

CHEBUTYKIN [*Kisses both her hands, tenderly*] My little white bird!

IRINA You know when I woke up this morning, and after I'd gotten up and washed, I suddenly felt as if everything in the world had become clear to me, and I knew the way I ought to live. I know it all now, my dear Ivan Romanich. Man must work by the sweat of his brow whatever his class, and that should make up the whole meaning and purpose of his life and happiness and contentment. Oh, how good it must be to be a workman, getting up with the sun and breaking stones by the roadside—or a shepherd—or a schoolteacher teaching the children—or an engine driver on the railway. Good heavens! It's better to be a mere ox or horse and work, than the sort of young woman who wakes up at twelve and drinks her coffee in bed and then takes two hours dressing. How dreadful! You know how you long for a cool drink in hot weather? Well, that's the way I long for work. And if I don't get up early from now on and really work, you can refuse to be friends with me anymore, Ivan Romanich.

CHEBUTYKIN   [*Tenderly*] So I will, so I will.

OLGA   Father taught us to get up at seven o'clock and so Irina always wakes up at seven—but then she stays in bed till at least nine, thinking about something or other. And with such a serious expression on her face too! [*laughs*]

IRINA   You think it's strange when I look serious because you always think of me as a little girl. I'm twenty, you know!

TUTZENBACH   All this longing for work. Heavens, how well I can understand it! I've never done a stroke of work in my life. I was born in Petersburg, an unfriendly, idle city—born into a family where work and worries were simply unknown. I remember a valet pulling off my boots for me when I came home from the cadet school. I grumbled at the way he did it, and my mother looked on in admiration. She was quite surprised when other people looked at me in any other way. I was so carefully protected from work! But I doubt whether they succeeded in protecting me for good and all—yes, I doubt it very much! The time's come: there's a terrific thundercloud advancing upon us; a mighty storm is coming to freshen us up! Yes, it's coming all right. It's quite near already, and it's going to blow away all this idleness and indifference and prejudice against work, this rot of boredom that our society is suffering from. I'm going to work, and in twenty-five or thirty years' time every man and woman will be working. Every one of us!

CHEBUTYKIN   I'm not going to work.

TUTZENBACH   You don't count.

SOLENI   In twenty-five years' time you won't be alive, thank goodness. In a couple of years you'll die from a stroke—or I'll lose my temper with you and put a bullet in your head, my good fellow. [*takes a cologne bottle from his pocket and sprinkles the scent over his chest and hands*]

CHEBUTYKIN   [*Laughs*] It's quite true that I never have done any work. Not a stroke since I left the university. I haven't even read a book, only newspapers. [*takes another newspaper out of his pocket*] For instance here. I know from the paper that there was a person called Dobrolyubov, but what he wrote about I haven't the faintest idea. God alone knows.

Someone knocks on the floor from downstairs

There! They're calling me to come down: there's someone come to see me. I'll be back in a moment. [*goes out hurriedly, stroking his beard*]

IRINA   He's up to one of his little games.

TUTZENBACH   Yes. He looked very solemn as he left. He's obviously going to give you a present.

IRINA   I do dislike that sort of thing.

OLGA   Yes, isn't it dreadful? He's always doing something silly.

MASHA   "A green oak grows by a curving shore, and round that oak hangs a golden chain . . ." [*gets up as she sings under her breath*]

OLGA   You're sad today, Masha.

Masha puts on her hat, singing

Where are you going?

MASHA   Home.

IRINA   What a strange thing to do.

TUTZENBACH   What! Going away from your sister's party?

MASHA   What does it matter? I'll be back this evening. Good-bye, my darling. [*kisses Irina*] And once again, I wish you all the happiness in the world. In the old days when Father was alive we used to have thirty or forty officers at our parties. What gay parties we had! And today—what have we got today? A man and a half, and the place is as quiet as a tomb. I'm going home. I'm depressed today, I'm sad; so don't listen to me. [*laughs through her tears*] We'll have a talk later, but good-bye for now, my dear. I'll go somewhere or other.

IRINA   [*Displeased*] Really you are a . . .

OLGA   [*Tearfully*] I understand you, Masha.

SOLENI   If a man starts philosophizing, you call that philosophy or possibly just sophistry; but if a woman or a couple of women start philosophizing you call that . . . What would you call it now? Ask me another!

MASHA   What are you talking about? You are a disconcerting person!

SOLENI   Nothing.

"He had no time to say 'Oh, oh!'
Before that bear had struck him low . . ."

MASHA [*After a pause, to Olga, crossly*] Do stop sniveling!

Enter Anfisa and Ferapont, the latter carrying a large cake

ANFISA Come along, my dear, this way. Come in, your boots are quite clean. [*to Irina*] A cake from Protopopov at the Council Office.

IRINA Thank you. Tell him I'm very grateful to him. [*takes the cake*]

FERAPONT What's that?

IRINA [*Louder*] Tell him I sent my thanks.

OLGA Nanny, will you give him a piece of cake? Go along, Ferapont; they'll give you some cake.

FERAPONT What's that?

ANFISA Come along with me, Ferapont Spiridonich, my dear. Come along. [*goes out with Ferapont*]

MASHA I don't like that Protopopov fellow, Mikhail Potapich or Ivanich or whatever it is. It's best not to invite him here.

IRINA I haven't invited him.

MASHA Thank goodness.

Enter Chebutykin, followed by a soldier carrying a silver samovar. Murmurs of astonishment and displeasure

OLGA [*Covering her face with her hands*] A samovar! But this is dreadful! [*goes through to the ballroom and stands by the table*]

IRINA My dear Ivan Romanich, what are you thinking about?

TUTZENBACH [*Laughs*] Didn't I tell you?

MASHA Ivan Romanich, you really ought to be ashamed of yourself!

CHEBUTYKIN My dear, sweet girls, I've no one in the world but you. You're dearer to me than anything in the world! I'm nearly sixty; I'm an old man—a lonely, utterly unimportant old man. The only thing that's worth anything in me is my love for you, and if it weren't for you, really I would have been dead long ago. [*to Irina*] My dear, my sweet little girl, haven't

I known you since the very day you were born? Didn't I carry you around in my arms? Didn't I love your dear mother?

IRINA But why do you get such expensive presents?

CHEBUTYKIN [*Tearfully and angrily*] Expensive presents! Get along with you! [*to the orderly*] Put the samovar over there. [*mimics Irina*] Expensive presents!

The orderly takes the samovar to the ballroom

ANFISA [*Crosses the drawing room*] My dears, there's a strange colonel just arrived. He's taken off his coat and he's coming up now. Irenushka, do be nice and polite to him, won't you? [*in the doorway*] And it's high time we had lunch too. Oh, dear! [*goes out*]

TUTZENBACH It's Vershinin, I suppose.

Enter Vershinin

Lieutenant Colonel Vershinin!

VERSHININ [*To Masha and Irina*] Allow me to introduce myself —Lieutenant Colonel Vershinin. I'm so glad, so very glad to be here at last. How you've changed! Dear, dear, how you've changed!

IRINA Please, do sit down. We're very pleased to see you, I'm sure.

VERSHININ [*Gaily*] I'm so glad to see you, so glad! But there were three of you, weren't there? Three sisters. I remember there were three little girls. I don't remember their faces, but I knew your father, Colonel Prozorov, and I remember he had three little girls. Oh, yes, I saw them myself. I remember them quite well. How time flies! Dear, dear, how it flies!

TUTZENBACH Aleksandr Ignatievich comes from Moscow.

IRINA From Moscow? You come from Moscow?

VERSHININ Yes, from Moscow. Your father was a battery commander there, and I was an officer in the same brigade. [*to Masha*] I seem to remember your face a little.

MASHA I don't remember you at all.

IRINA Olya, Olya! [*calls toward the ballroom*] Olya, do come!

Olga enters from the ballroom

It seems that Lieutenant Colonel Vershinin comes from Moscow.

VERSHININ   You must be Olga Sergeevna, the eldest. And you are Marya. And you are Irina, the youngest.

OLGA   You come from Moscow?

VERSHININ   Yes. I studied in Moscow and entered the service there. I stayed there quite a long time, but then I was put in charge of a battery here—so I moved out here, you see. I don't really remember you, you know; I only remember that there were three sisters. I remember your father, though; I remember him very well. All I need to do is to close my eyes and I can see him standing there as if he were alive. I used to visit you in Moscow.

OLGA   I thought I remembered everybody, and yet . . .

VERSHININ   My Christian names are Aleksandr Ignatievich.

IRINA   Aleksandr Ignatievich, and you come from Moscow! Well, what a surprise!

OLGA   We're going to live there you know.

IRINA   We hope to be there by the autumn. It's our hometown; we were born there. On Staraya Basmannaya Street. [*both laugh happily*]

MASHA   Fancy meeting a fellow townsman so unexpectedly! [*eagerly*] I remember now. Do you remember, Olga, there was someone they used to call "the lovesick major"? You were a lieutenant then, weren't you, and you were in love with someone or other, and everyone used to tease you about it. They called you "major" for some reason or other.

VERSHININ   [*Laughs*] That's it, that's it. "The lovesick major," that's what they called me.

MASHA   In those days you only had a mustache. Oh, dear, how much older you look! [*tearfully*] How much older!

VERSHININ   Yes, I was still a young man in the days when they called me "the lovesick major." I was in love then. It's different now.

OLGA   But you haven't got a single gray hair! You've aged, yes, but you're certainly not an old man.

VERSHININ   Nevertheless, I've turned forty-two. Is it long since you left Moscow?

IRINA   Eleven years. Now what are you crying for, Masha, you funny girl? [*tearfully*] You'll make me cry too.

MASHA   I'm not crying. What was the street you lived on?

VERSHININ   On the Staraya Basmannaya.

OLGA   We did too.

VERSHININ   At one time I lived on Nemetskaya Street. I used to walk from there to the Krasny Barracks, and I remember there was such a gloomy bridge I had to cross. I used to hear the noise of the water rushing under it. I remember how lonely and sad I felt there. [*pause*] But what a magnificently wide river you have here! It's a marvelous river!

OLGA   Yes, but this is a cold place. It's cold here, and there are too many mosquitoes.

VERSHININ   Really? I would have said you had a really good, healthy climate here, a real Russian climate. Forest, river . . . birch trees too. The dear, unpretentious birch trees— I love them more than any of the other trees. It's nice living here. But there's one rather strange thing: the station is fifteen miles from the town. And no one knows why.

SOLENI   I know why it is.

Everyone looks at him

Because if the station were nearer, it wouldn't be so far away; and since it is so far away, it can't be nearer.

An awkward silence

TUTZENBACH   You like your little joke, Vasili Vasilievich.

OLGA   I'm sure I remember you now. I know I do.

VERSHININ   I knew your mother.

CHEBUTYKIN   She was a good woman, God bless her memory!

IRINA   Mamma was buried in Moscow.

OLGA   At the convent of Novodyevichi.

MASHA   You know, I'm even beginning to forget what she looked like. I suppose people will lose all memory of us in just the same way. We'll be forgotten.

VERSHININ Yes, we will all be forgotten. Such is our fate, and we can't do anything about it. And all the things that seem serious, important, and full of meaning to us now will be forgotten one day—or anyway they won't seem important anymore. [*pause*] It's strange to think that we're utterly unable to tell what will be regarded as great and important in the future and what will be thought of as just paltry and ridiculous. Didn't the great discoveries of Copernicus—or of Columbus, if you like—appear useless and unimportant to begin with? Whereas some rubbish, written up by an eccentric fool, was regarded as a revelation of great truth? It may well be that in time to come the life we live today will seem strange and uncomfortable and stupid and not too clean either and perhaps even wicked.

TUTZENBACH Who can tell? It's just as possible that future generations will think that we lived our lives on a very high plane and remember us with respect. After all we no longer have tortures and public executions and invasions, though there's still a great deal of suffering!

SOLENI [*In a high-pitched voice as if calling to chickens*] Cluck, cluck, cluck! There's nothing our good baron loves as much as a nice bit of philosophizing.

TUTZENBACH Vasili Vasilievich, will you kindly leave me alone? [*moves to another chair*] It's becoming tiresome.

SOLENI [*As before*] Cluck, cluck, cluck!

TUTZENBACH [*To Vershinin*] The suffering that we see around us—and there's so much of it—itself proves that our society has at least achieved a level of morality that is higher.

VERSHININ Yes, yes, of course.

CHEBUTYKIN You said just now, Baron, that our age will be called great; but people are small all the same. [*gets up*] Look how small I am.

A violin is played offstage

MASHA That's Andrei playing the violin; he's our brother, you know.

IRINA We've got quite a clever brother. We're expecting him to be a professor. Papa was a military man, but Andrei chose an academic career.

OLGA   We've been teasing him today. We think he's in love, just a little.

IRINA   With a girl who lives down here. She'll be calling in today most likely.

MASHA   The way she dresses herself is awful! It's not that her clothes are just ugly and old-fashioned, they're simply pathetic. She'll put on some weird-looking, bright yellow skirt with a crude sort of fringe affair, and then a red blouse to go with it. And her cheeks look as though they've been scrubbed, they're so shiny! Andrei's not in love with her—I can't believe it; after all he has got some taste. I think he's just playing the fool just to annoy us. I heard yesterday that she's going to get married to Protopopov, the chairman of the local council. I thought it was an excellent idea. [*calls through the side door*] Andrei, come here, will you? Just for a moment, dear.

Enter Andrei

OLGA   This is my brother, Andrei Sergeevich.

VERSHININ   Vershinin.

ANDREI   Prozorov. [*wipes the perspiration from his face*] I believe you've been appointed battery commander here?

OLGA   What do you think, dear? Aleksandr Ignatievich comes from Moscow.

ANDREI   Do you really? Congratulations! You'll get no peace from my sisters now.

VERSHININ   I'm afraid your sisters must be getting tired of me already.

IRINA   Just look, Andrei gave me this little picture frame today. [*shows him the frame*] He made it himself.

VERSHININ   [*Looks at the frame, not knowing what to say*] Yes, it's . . . it's very nice indeed.

IRINA   Do you see that little frame over the piano? He made that one too.

Andrei waves his hand impatiently and walks off

OLGA   He's awfully clever and he plays the violin and he makes all sorts of things too. In fact he's very gifted all around. Andrei, please don't go. He's got such a bad habit—always going off like this. Come here!

Masha and Irina take him by the arms and lead him back, laughing

MASHA Now just you come here!

ANDREI Leave me alone, please!

MASHA You are a silly! They used to call Aleksandr Ignatievich "the lovesick major," and he didn't get annoyed.

VERSHININ Not in the least.

MASHA I feel like calling you a "lovesick fiddler."

IRINA Or a "lovesick professor."

OLGA He's fallen in love! Our Andryusha's in love!

IRINA [*Clapping her hands*] Three cheers for Andryusha! Andryusha's in love!

CHEBUTYKIN [*Comes up behind Andrei and puts his arms around his waist*] "Nature created us for love alone." [*laughs loudly, still holding his paper in his hand*]

ANDREI That's enough of it, that's enough. [*wipes his face*] I couldn't get to sleep all night, and I'm not feeling too grand just now. I read till four o'clock and then I went to bed, but nothing happened. I kept thinking about one thing and another. And it gets light so early; the sun just pours into my room. I'd like to translate a book from the English while I'm here during the summer.

VERSHININ You read English then?

ANDREI Yes. My father—God bless his memory—used to simply wear us out with learning. It sounds silly, I know, but I must confess that since he died I've begun to grow fat, as if I'd been physically relieved of the strain. I've grown quite stout in a year. Yes, thanks to Father, my sisters and I know French and German and English, and Irina here knows Italian too. But what an effort it all cost us!

MASHA Knowing three languages in a town like this is an unnecessary luxury. In fact, not even a luxury, but just a sort of useless encumbrance. It's rather like having a sixth finger on your hand. We know a lot of stuff that's just useless.

VERSHININ Really! [*laughs*] You know a lot of stuff that's useless! It seems to me that there's no place on earth, however dull and depressing it may be, where intelligence and education can be useless. Let us suppose that among the hundred thousand people in this town—all of them, no doubt, very backward and uncultured—there are just three people like yourselves. Obviously you can't hope to triumph over all the mass of ignorance around you. As your life goes by, you'll have to keep giving in little by little until you get lost in the crowd, in the hundred thousand. Life will swallow you up, but you'll not quite disappear; you'll make some impression on it. After you've gone perhaps six more people like you will turn up, then twelve, and so on, until in the end most people will have become like you. So in two or three hundred years life on this old earth of ours will have become marvelously beautiful. Man longs for a life like that, and if it isn't here yet, he must imagine it, wait for it, dream about it, prepare for it. He must know and see more than his father and his grandfather did. [*laughs*] And you're complaining because you know a lot of stuff that's useless.

MASHA [*Takes off her hat*] I'll be staying to lunch.

IRINA [*With a sigh*] Really someone should have written all that down.

Andrei has left the room, unnoticed

TUTZENBACH You say that in time to come life will be marvelously beautiful. That's probably true. But in order to share in it now, at a distance so to speak, we must prepare for it and work for it.

VERSHININ [*Gets up*] Yes. . . . What a lot of flowers you've got here! [*looks around*] And what a marvelous house! I do envy you! All my life I seem to have been huddling in small flats, with two chairs and a sofa and a stove that always smokes. It's the flowers that I've missed in my life, flowers like these! [*rubs his hands*] Oh, well, never mind!

TUTZENBACH Yes, we must work. I suppose you're thinking I'm a sentimental German. But I assure you I'm not—I'm Russian. I don't speak a word of German. My father was brought up in the Greek Orthodox faith.

VERSHININ [*Walks up and down the room*] You know, I often
wonder what it would be like if you could start your life over
again—deliberately, I mean, consciously. Suppose you could
put aside the life you'd lived already, as though it were just a
sort of rough draft, and then start another one like a clean
copy. If that happened I think the thing you'd want most of all
would be not to repeat yourself. You'd try at least to create a
new environment for yourself, a flat like this one, for instance,
with some flowers and plenty of light. I have a wife, you
know, and two little girls; and my wife's not very well, and all
that. Well, if I had to start my life all over again, I wouldn't
marry. No, no!

Enter Kulygin, in the uniform of a teacher

KULYGIN [*Approaches Irina*] Congratulations, dear sister—
from the bottom of my heart—congratulations on your
saint's day. I wish you good health and everything a girl of
your age ought to have! And allow me to present you with this
little book. [*hands her a book*] It's the history of our school
covering the whole fifty years of its existence. I wrote it myself.
Quite a trifle, of course—I wrote it in my spare time when I
had nothing better to do—but I hope you'll read it nevertheless. Good morning to you all! [*to Vershinin*] Allow me to introduce myself. Kulygin's the name; I'm a teacher at the
secondary school here. And a town councillor. [*to Irina*] You'll
find a list in the book of all the pupils who have completed
their studies at our school during the last fifty years. *Feci quod
potui, faciant meliora potentes.* [*kisses Masha*]
IRINA But you gave me this book last Easter!
KULYGIN [*Laughs*] Did I really? In that case give it back to me
—or no, better give it to the colonel. Please do take it, Colonel.
Maybe you'll read it sometime when you've nothing better to
do.
VERSHININ Thank you very much. [*then prepares to leave*] I'm
so very glad to have made your acquaintance.
OLGA You aren't going, are you? Really, you mustn't.
IRINA But you'll stay and have lunch with us! Please.
OLGA Please do.

VERSHININ [*Bows*] I see I've intruded on your saint's day party. I didn't know. Forgive me for not offering you my congratulations. [*then goes into the ballroom with Olga*]

KULYGIN Today is Sunday, my friends, a day of rest; let us rest and enjoy it, each according to his age and position in life! We will have to roll up the carpets and put them away till the winter. We must remember to put some naphthaline on them or Persian powder. . . . The Romans enjoyed good health because they knew how to work *and* how to rest. They had *mens sana in corpore sano*. Their life had a definite shape, a form. The director of the school says that the most important thing about life is form. A thing that loses its form is finished— that's just as true of our ordinary, everyday lives. [*takes Masha by the waist and laughs*] Masha loves me. My wife loves me. Yes, and the curtains will have to be put away with the carpets too. . . . I'm cheerful today; I'm in quite excellent spirits. Masha, we're invited to the director's at four o'clock today. A country walk has been arranged for the teachers and their families.

MASHA I'm not going.

KULYGIN [*Distressed*] Masha, darling, why not?

MASHA I'll tell you later. [*peevishly*] All right, I'll come, only leave me alone now. [*walks off*]

KULYGIN And after the walk we will all spend the evening at the director's house. In spite of weak health that man is certainly sparing no pains to be sociable. A first-rate, thoroughly enlightened man! A most excellent person! After the conference yesterday he said to me, "I'm tired, Fëdor Ilyich. I'm tired!" [*looks at the clock, then at his watch*] Your clock is seven minutes fast. Yes, "I'm tired," he said.

The sound of the violin is heard offstage

OLGA Will you all come and sit down, please! Lunch is ready. There's a pie.

KULYGIN Ah, Olga, my dear girl! Last night I worked up to eleven o'clock and I felt tired, but today I'm quite happy. [*goes to the table in the ballroom*] My dear Olga!

CHEBUTYKIN [*Puts the newspaper in his pocket and combs his beard*] A pie? Excellent!

MASHA [*Sternly to Chebutykin*] Remember, you mustn't take anything to drink today. Do you hear? It's bad for you.

CHEBUTYKIN Never mind. I've gotten over that weakness long ago! I haven't done any heavy drinking for two years. [*impatiently*] Anyway, my dear, what does it matter?

MASHA All the same, don't you dare drink anything. See that you don't now! [*petulantly, but taking care that her husband does not hear*] So now I've got to spend another of these damnably boring evenings at the director's!

TUTZENBACH I wouldn't go if I were you, and that's that.

CHEBUTYKIN Don't you go, my dear.

MASHA Don't go, indeed! Oh, what a damnable life! It's intolerable. [*goes into the ballroom*]

CHEBUTYKIN [*Follows her*] Well, well!

SOLENI [*As he passes Tutzenbach on the way to the ballroom*] Cluck, cluck, cluck!

TUTZENBACH Do stop it, Vasili Vasilievich. I've really had enough of it.

SOLENI Cluck, cluck, cluck!

KULYGIN [*Gaily*] Your health, Colonel! I'm a schoolteacher and I'm quite one of the family here, as it were. I'm Masha's husband. She's got a sweet nature, such a very sweet nature!

VERSHININ I think I'll have a little of this dark vodka. [*drinks*] Your health! [*to Olga*] I do feel so happy with you people!

Only Irina and Tutzenbach remain in the drawing room

IRINA Masha's in a bit of a bad mood today. You know, she got married when she was eighteen, and then her husband seemed the cleverest man in the world to her. It's different now. He's the kindest of men, but not the cleverest.

OLGA [*Impatiently*] Andrei, will you please come?

ANDREI [*Offstage*] Just coming. [*enters and goes to the table*]

TUTZENBACH What are you thinking about?

IRINA Oh, nothing special. You know, I don't like this man Soleni; I'm quite afraid of him. Whenever he opens his mouth he says something silly.

TUTZENBACH He's a strange fellow. I'm sorry for him, even though he irritates me. In fact I feel more sorry for him than irritated. I think he's shy. When he's alone with me, he can be quite sensible and friendly, but in company he's offensive and bullying. Don't go over there just yet; let them get settled down at the table. Let me stay with you for a bit. Tell me what you're thinking about. [*pause*] You're twenty and I'm not thirty yet myself. What years and years we still have ahead of us—a whole long succession of years, all full of my love for you!

IRINA Don't talk to me about love, Nikolai Lvovich.

TUTZENBACH [*Not listening*] Oh, I long so passionately for life; I long to work and strive so much. And all this longing is somehow mingled with my love for you, Irina. And just because you happen to be beautiful, life appears beautiful to me! What are you thinking about?

IRINA You say that life is beautiful. Maybe it is—but what if it only seems to be beautiful? Our lives, I mean the lives of us three sisters, haven't been beautiful up to now. The truth is that life has been stifling us, like weeds in a garden. I'm afraid I'm crying. . . . So unnecessary. [*quickly dries her eyes and smiles*] We must work, work! The reason we feel depressed and take such a gloomy view of life is that we've never known what it is to make a real effort. We're the children of parents who despised work.

Enter Natalya Ivanovna. She is wearing a pink dress with a green belt

NATASHA They've gone in to lunch already. I'm late. [*glances at herself in a mirror and adjusts her dress*] My hair seems to be all right. [*catches sight of Irina*] My dear Irina Sergeevna, congratulations! [*gives her a vigorous and prolonged kiss*] You've got such a lot of visitors. I feel quite shy. How do you do, Baron?

OLGA [*Enters the drawing room*] Oh, there you are, Natalya Ivanovna! How are you, my dear? [*they kiss each other*]

NATASHA Congratulations! You've such a lot of people here that I feel dreadfully shy.

OLGA It's all right; they're all old friends. [*alarmed, dropping her voice*] You've got a green belt on! My dear, that's surely a mistake!

NATASHA   Why, is it a bad omen or what?

OLGA   No, but it just doesn't go with your dress. It looks so strange.

NATASHA   [*Tearfully*] Really? But it isn't really green you know; it's a sort of dull color. [*follows Olga to the ballroom*]

All are now seated at the table; the drawing room is empty

KULYGIN   Irina, you know, I do wish you'd find yourself a good husband. In my view it's high time you got married.

CHEBUTYKIN   You ought to get yourself a nice little husband too, Natalya Ivanovna.

KULYGIN   Natalya Ivanovna already has a husband in view.

MASHA   [*Strikes her plate with her fork*] A glass of wine for me, please! Three cheers for our jolly old life! We keep our end up, we do!

KULYGIN   Masha, you won't get more than five out of ten for good conduct!

VERSHININ   Say there, this liqueur's very nice. What is it made of?

SOLENI   Cockroaches!

IRINA   Ugh! Ugh! How disgusting!

OLGA   We're having roast turkey for dinner tonight, and then apple tart. Thank goodness I'll be here all day today. . . . This evening too. You must all come this evening.

VERSHININ   May I come in the evening too?

IRINA   Yes, please do.

NATASHA   They don't stand on ceremony here.

CHEBUTYKIN   "Nature created us for love alone." [*laughs*]

ANDREI   [*Irritably*] Will you stop it please? Aren't you tired of it yet?

Fedotik and Rodé come in with a large basket of flowers

FEDOTIK   Just look here, they're having lunch already!

RODÉ   [*In a loud voice*] Having their lunch? So they are; they're having lunch already.

FEDOTIK   Wait half a minute. [*takes a snapshot*] One! Just a minute more! [*takes another snapshot*] Two! All over now.

They pick up the basket and go into the ballroom, where they are greeted uproariously

RODÉ [*Loudly*] Congratulations, Irina Sergeevna! I wish you all the best—everything you'd wish for yourself! Gorgeous weather today, absolutely marvelous. I've been out walking the whole morning with the boys. You do know that I teach gym at the high school, don't you?

FEDOTIK You may move now, Irina Sergeevna, that is, if you want to. [*takes a snapshot*] You do look attractive today. [*takes a top out of his pocket*] By the way, look at this top. It's got a wonderful hum.

IRINA What a sweet little thing!

MASHA "A green oak grows by a curving shore, and round that oak hangs a golden chain . . ." A golden chain around that oak. [*peevishly*] Why do I keep on saying that? Those lines have been worrying me all day long!

KULYGIN Do you know, we're thirteen at table?

RODÉ [*Loudly*] You don't really believe in these old superstitions, do you? [*laughs*]

KULYGIN When thirteen people sit down at the table, it means that some of them are in love. Is it you, by any chance, Ivan Romanich?

CHEBUTYKIN Oh, I'm just an old sinner. But what I can't make out is why Natalya Ivanovna looks so embarrassed.

Loud laughter. Natasha runs out into the drawing room. Andrei follows her

ANDREI Please, Natasha, don't pay any attention to them! Stop. . . . Wait a moment. Please!

NATASHA I feel so ashamed. I don't know what's the matter with me, and they're all laughing at me. It's awful of me to leave the table like that, but I couldn't help it. I just couldn't. [*covers her face with her hands*]

ANDREI My dear girl, please, please don't get upset. Honestly they don't mean any harm; they're just teasing. My dear, sweet girl, they're really good-natured folks, they all are, and they're fond of us both. Come over to the window; they can't see us there. [*looks around*]

NATASHA You see, I'm not used to being with a lot of people.

ANDREI Oh, how young you are, Natasha—how wonderfully, beautifully young! My dear, sweet girl, don't get so upset! Do believe me, believe me. I'm so happy, so full of love, of joy. . . . No, they can't see us here! They can't see us! How did I come to love you? When was it? I don't understand anything. My precious, my sweet, my innocent girl, please—I want you to marry me! I love you; I love you as I've never loved anybody. [*kisses her*]

Enter two officers and, seeing Natasha and Andrei kissing, stand and stare in amazement

CURTAIN

ACT TWO

The scene is the same as in Act One. It is eight o'clock in the evening. The faint sound of an accordion is heard coming from the street.

The stage is unlighted. Enter Natalya Ivanovna in a dressing gown, carrying a candle. She crosses the stage and stops by the door leading to Andrei's room.

NATASHA What are you doing, Andryusha? Reading? It's all right; I only wanted to know. [*goes to another door, opens it, looks inside, and shuts it again*] No one's left a light anywhere.

ANDREI [*Enters with a book in his hand*] What is it, Natasha?

NATASHA I was just going around to see if anyone had left a light anywhere. It's carnival week, and the servants are so excited about it . . . anything might happen! You've got to watch them. Last night about twelve o'clock I happened to go into the dining room, and—would you believe it?—there was a lighted candle on the table. I haven't found out who lit it. [*puts the candle down*] What time is it?

ANDREI [*Glances at his watch*] Quarter past eight.

NATASHA And Olga and Irina still out. They aren't back from work yet, poor things! Olga's still at some teachers' conference, and Irina's at the post office. [*sighs*] This morning I said to Irina, "Do take care of yourself, my dear." But she won't listen. Did you say it was a quarter past eight? I'm afraid Bobik is not at all well. Why does he get so cold? Yesterday he had a temperature, but today he feels quite cold when you touch him. I'm so afraid!

ANDREI   It's all right, Natasha. The boy's well enough.

NATASHA   Still, I think he ought to have a special diet. I'm so anxious about him. By the way they tell me that some carnival party's supposed to be coming here soon after nine. I'd rather they didn't come, Andryusha.

ANDREI   Well, I really don't know what I can do. They've been asked to come.

NATASHA   This morning the dear little fellow woke up and looked at me, and then suddenly he smiled. He recognized me, you see. "Good morning, Bobik," I said, "good morning, darling precious!" And then he laughed. Babies understand everything, you know; they understand us perfectly well. Anyway, Andryusha, I'll tell the servants not to let that carnival party in.

ANDREI   [*Irresolutely*] Well . . . it's really for my sisters to decide, isn't it? It's their house after all.

NATASHA   Yes, it's their house as well. I'll tell them too. They're so kind. [*walks off then*] I've ordered sour milk for supper. The doctor says you ought to eat nothing but sour milk or you'll never get any thinner. [*stops*] Bobik feels so cold. I'm afraid his room is too cold for him. He ought to move into a warmer room, at least until the warm weather comes. Irina's room for instance. That's just a perfect room for a baby: it's dry and it gets the sun all day long. We must tell her. Perhaps she'd share Olga's room for a bit. In any case she's never at home during the day; she only sleeps there. [*then pause*] Andryusha, why don't you say anything?

ANDREI   I was just daydreaming. There's nothing to say anyway.

NATASHA   Well. What was it I was going to tell you? Oh, yes! Ferapont from the Council Office wants to see you about something.

ANDREI   [*Yawns*] Tell him to come up.

Natasha goes out. Andrei, bending over the candle, which she has left behind, begins to read his book. Enter Ferapont in an old shabby overcoat, his collar turned up, his ears muffled in a scarf

Hello, my friend! What did you want to see me about?

FERAPONT   The chairman's sent you the register and a letter or something. Here they are. [*hands him the book and the letter*]

ANDREI   Thanks. That's all right. Incidentally, why have you come so late? It's past eight already.

FERAPONT   What's that?

ANDREI   [*Raising his voice*] I said, why have you come so late? It's past eight already.

FERAPONT   That's right. It was still daylight when I came first, but they wouldn't let me see you. "The master's busy," they said. Well, if you're busy, you're busy. I'm not in a hurry. [*thinking that Andrei has said something*] What's that?

ANDREI   Nothing. [*turns over the pages of the register*] Tomorrow's Friday. There's no meeting, but I'll go to the office just the same. Do some work. I'm so bored at home! [*pause*] Yes, my dear old fellow, how things do change. What a fraud life is! So strange! Today I picked up this book, just out of boredom, because I hadn't anything to do. It's a copy of some lectures I attended at the university. Good heavens! Just think — I'm secretary of the local council now, and Protopopov's chairman. And the most I can ever hope for is to become a member of the council myself! Me—a member of the local council! I, who dream every night that I'm a professor in Moscow University, a famous academician, the pride of all Russia!

FERAPONT   I'm sorry, I can't tell you. I don't hear very well.

ANDREI   If you could hear properly I don't think I'd be talking to you like this. I must talk to someone, but my wife doesn't seem to understand me. And as for my sisters . . . I'm afraid of them for some reason or other; I'm afraid of them laughing at me and pulling my leg. I don't drink and I don't like going to bars, but oh, man! how I'd enjoy an hour or so at Testov's or the Great Moscow Restaurant! Yes, my dear fellow, I would indeed!

FERAPONT   The other day at the office a contractor was telling me about some businessmen who were eating pancakes in Moscow. One of them ate forty pancakes and died. It was either forty or fifty; I can't remember exactly.

ANDREI   You can sit in some huge restaurant in Moscow without knowing anyone, and no one knowing you; yet somehow you don't feel that you don't belong there. Whereas here you know everybody, and everybody knows you, and yet you don't feel you belong here; you feel you don't belong at all. You're lonely and you feel like a stranger.

FERAPONT   What's that? [*pause*] It was the same man that told me—of course he may have been lying—he said that there's an enormous rope stretched right across Moscow.

ANDREI   Whatever for?

FERAPONT   I'm sorry, I can't tell you. That's what he said.

ANDREI   What nonsense! [*reads the book*] Have you ever been to Moscow?

FERAPONT   [*After a pause*] No. It wasn't God's wish. [*pause*] Shall I go now?

ANDREI   Yes, you may go. Good-bye.

Ferapont goes out

Good-bye. [*reading*] Come in the morning to take some letters. You can go now. [*pause*] He's gone.

A bell rings

Yes, that's how it is. [*stretches and slowly goes to his room*]

Singing is heard offstage; a nurse is putting a baby to sleep. Enter Masha and Vershinin. While they talk together, a maid lights a lamp and candles in the ballroom

MASHA   I don't know. [*pause*] I don't know. Habit's very important of course. For instance, after Father died, for a long time we couldn't get accustomed to the idea that we hadn't any orderlies to wait on us. But, habit aside, I think it's quite right what I was saying. Perhaps it's different in other places, but in this town the military certainly do seem to be the nicest and most generous and best-mannered people.

VERSHININ   I'm thirsty. I could do with a nice glass of tea.

MASHA   [*Glances at her watch*] They'll bring it in presently. You see, they married me off when I was eighteen. I was afraid of my husband because he was a schoolteacher, and I had only just left school myself. He seemed terribly learned then, very clever and important. Now it's quite different, unfortunately.

VERSHININ Yes. I see.

MASHA I don't say anything against my husband—I'm used to him now—but there are such a lot of vulgar and unpleasant and offensive people among the other civilians. Vulgarity upsets me; it makes me feel insulted. I actually suffer when I meet someone who lacks refinement and gentle manners and courtesy. When I'm with the other teachers, my husband's friends, I just suffer.

VERSHININ Yes, of course. But I would have thought that in a town like this the civilians and the army people were equally uninteresting. There's no difference between them. If you talk to any educated person here, civilian or military, he'll generally tell you that he's just worn out. It's either his wife or his house or his estate or his horse or something. We Russians are capable of such elevated thoughts, but why do we have such low ideals in practical life? Why is it, why?

MASHA Why?

VERSHININ Yes, why does his wife wear him out? Why do his children wear him out? And what about *him* wearing out his wife and children?

MASHA You're a bit low-spirited today, aren't you?

VERSHININ Perhaps. I haven't had any dinner today. I've had nothing to eat since morning. One of my daughters is a bit under the weather, and when the children are ill, I get so worried. I feel utterly conscience-stricken at having given them a mother like theirs. Oh, if only you could have seen her this morning! What a despicable woman! We started quarreling at seven o'clock, and at nine I just walked out and slammed the door. [*pause*] I never talk about these things in the ordinary way. It's a strange thing, but you're the only person I feel I dare complain to. [*kisses her hand*] Don't be angry with me. I've nobody, nobody but you.

MASHA [*After a pause*] What a noise the wind's making in the stove! Just before Father died the wind howled in the chimney just like that.

VERSHININ Are you superstitious?

MASHA Yes.

VERSHININ   How strange. [*kisses her hand*] You really are a
wonderful creature, a marvelous creature! Wonderful, marvelous! It's quite dark here, but I can see your eyes shining.

MASHA   [*Moves to another chair*] There's more light over here.

VERSHININ   I love you, I love you, I love you. I love your eyes. I
love your movements. I dream about them. A wonderful, marvelous being!

MASHA   [*Laughing softly*] When you talk to me like that, somehow I can't help laughing, although I'm afraid at the same
time. Don't say it again, please. [*half audibly*] Well, no. . . .
Go on. I don't mind. [*covers her face with her hands*] I don't
mind. . . . Someone's coming. Let's talk about something
else.

Enter Irina and Tutzenbach through the ballroom

TUTZENBACH   I have a triple-barreled name—Baron Tutzen-
bach-Krone-Altschauer—but actually I'm a Russian. I was
baptized in the Greek Orthodox faith just like yourself. I
haven't really got any German characteristics, except maybe
the obstinate, patient way I keep on pestering you. Look how
I bring you home every evening.

IRINA   How tired I am!

TUTZENBACH   And I'll go on meeting you at the post office and
bringing you home every evening for the next twenty years—
unless you send me away. [*noticing Masha and Vershinin, with
pleasure*] Oh, it's you! How are you?

IRINA   Well, here I am, home at last! [*to Masha*] A woman came
into the post office just before I left. She wanted to send a wire
to her brother in Saratov to tell him her son had just died, but
she couldn't remember the address. So we had to send the wire
without an address, just to Saratov. She was crying and I was
rude to her for no reason at all. "I've no time to waste," I told
her. So stupid of me. We're having the carnival crowd today,
aren't we?

MASHA   Yes.

IRINA   [*Sits down*] How nice it is to rest! I am tired!

TUTZENBACH   [*Smiling*] When you come back from work, you
look so young, so pathetic, somehow.

167

IRINA I'm tired. No, I don't like working at the post office. I don't like it at all.

MASHA You've gotten thinner. [*whistles*] You look younger too, and your face looks quite boyish.

TUTZENBACH It's the way she does her hair.

IRINA I must look for another job. This one doesn't suit me. It hasn't got what I always longed for and dreamed about. It's the sort of work you do without inspiration, without even thinking.

Someone knocks at the floor from below

That's the doctor knocking. [*to Tutzenbach*] Will you answer him, dear? I can't. I'm so tired.

Tutzenbach knocks on the floor

He'll be up in a moment. We must do something about all this. Andrei and the doctor went to the club last night and lost at cards again. They say Andrei lost two hundred rubles.

MASHA [*With indifference*] Well, what are we to do about it?

IRINA He lost two weeks ago, and he lost in December too. I wish to goodness he'd lose everything we've got, and soon too, and then perhaps we'd move out of this place. Good heavens, I dream of Moscow every night. Sometimes I feel as if I were going mad. [*laughs*] We're going to Moscow in June. How many months are there till June? February, March, April, May . . . Nearly half a year!

MASHA We must take care that Natasha doesn't get to know about his losing at cards.

IRINA I don't think she cares.

Enter Chebutykin. He has been resting on his bed since dinner and has just gotten up. He combs his beard, then sits down at the table and takes out a newspaper

MASHA There he is. Has he paid his rent yet?

IRINA [*Laughs*] No. Not a kopeck for the last eight months. I suppose he's forgotten.

MASHA [*Laughs*] How solemn he looks sitting there!

They all laugh. A pause

IRINA Why don't you say something, Aleksandr Ignatievich?

VERSHININ I don't know. I'm just longing for some tea. I'd give my life for a glass of tea! I've had nothing to eat since morning.

CHEBUTYKIN Irina Sergeevna!

IRINA What is it?

CHEBUTYKIN Please come here. *Venez ici!*

Irina goes over to him and sits down at the table

I can't do without you.

Irina lays out the cards for a game of solitaire

VERSHININ Well, if we can't have any tea, let's do a bit of philosophizing anyway.

TUTZENBACH Yes, let's. What about?

VERSHININ What about? Well . . . let's try to imagine what life will be like after we're dead, say in two or three hundred years.

TUTZENBACH All right then. After we're dead, people will fly around in balloons, the cut of their coats will be different, the sixth sense will be discovered and possibly even developed and used for all I know. But I believe life itself will remain the same; it will still be difficult and full of mystery and full of happiness. And in a thousand years' time people will still be sighing and complaining, "How hard this business of living is!" And yet they'll still be scared of death and unwilling to die just as they are now.

VERSHININ [*After a moment's thought*] Well, you know . . . How shall I put it? I think everything in the world is bound to change gradually—in fact it's changing before our very eyes. In two or three hundred years or maybe in a thousand years—it doesn't matter how long exactly—life will be different. It will be happy. Of course we won't be able to enjoy that future life, but all the same what we're living for now is to create it; we work and . . . yes, we suffer in order to create it.

That's the goal of our life, and you might say that's the only happiness we will ever achieve.

Masha laughs quietly

TUTZENBACH Why are you laughing?

MASHA I don't know. I've been laughing all day today.

VERSHININ [*To Tutzenbach*] I went to the same cadet school as you did but I never went on to the military academy. I read a great deal, of course, but I never know what books I ought to choose, and probably I read a lot of stuff that's not worth anything. But the longer I live the more I seem to long for knowledge. My hair's turning gray and I'm getting on in years, and yet how little I know, how little! All the same I think I do know one thing, which is not only true but also most important. I'm sure of it. Oh, if only I could convince you that there's not going to be any happiness for our own generation, that there mustn't be and won't be. We've just got to work and work. All the happiness is reserved for our descendants, our remote descendants. [*pause*] Anyway if I'm not to be happy, then at least my children's children will be.

Fedotik and Rodé enter the ballroom. They sit down and sing quietly, one of them playing a guitar

TUTZENBACH So you won't even allow us to dream of happiness! But what if I *am* happy?

VERSHININ You're not.

TUTZENBACH [*Flinging up his hands and laughing*] We don't understand one another, that's obvious. How can I convince you?

Masha laughs quietly

[*holds up a finger to her*] Show a finger to her and she'll laugh! [*to Vershinin*] And life will be just the same as ever not merely in a couple of hundred years' time, but in a million years. Life doesn't change. It always goes on the same; it follows its own laws, which don't concern us, which we can't discover anyway. Think of the birds that migrate in the autumn—the cranes, for instance: they just fly on and on. It doesn't matter what sort of thoughts they've got in their heads—great thoughts or little thoughts—they just fly on and on, not knowing where or why. And they'll go on flying no matter how many philosophers they happen to have flying with them. Let them philosophize as much as they like, as long as they go on flying.

MASHA   Isn't there some meaning?

TUTZENBACH   Meaning? Look out there. It's snowing. What's the meaning of that?

MASHA   I think a human being has got to have some faith, or at least he's got to seek faith. Otherwise his life will be empty, empty. How can you live and not know why the cranes fly, why children are born, why the stars shine in the sky! You must either know why you live or else . . . nothing matters. . . . Everything's just wild grass.

VERSHININ   All the same I'm sorry my youth's over.

MASHA   "It's a bore to be alive in this world, friends." That's what Gogol says.

TUTZENBACH   And I feel like saying: it's hopeless arguing with you, friends! I give you up.

CHEBUTYKIN   [*Reads out of the paper*] Balzac's marriage took place at Berdichev.[1]

Irina sings softly to herself

Must write this down in my notebook. [*writes*] Balzac's marriage took place at Berdichev. [*reads on*]

IRINA   [*Playing solitaire, pensively*] Balzac's marriage took place at Berdichev.

TUTZENBACH   Well, I've thrown in my hand. Did you know that I sent in my resignation, Marya Sergeevna?

MASHA   Yes, I heard about it. I don't see anything good in it either. I don't like civilians.

TUTZENBACH   Never mind. [*gets up*] What sort of a soldier do I

1. A town in western Russia well known for its almost exclusively Jewish population.

make anyway? I'm not even good-looking. Well, what does it matter? I'll work. I'd like to do such a hard day's work that when I came home in the evening I'd fall on my bed exhausted and go to sleep at once. [*goes to the ballroom*] I would think working men sleep well at nights!

FEDOTIK [*To Irina*] I've gotten you some colored crayons at Pyzhikov's, on Moscow Street. And this little penknife too.

IRINA You still treat me as if I were a little girl. I wish you'd remember I'm grown up now. [*takes the crayons and the penknife joyfully*] They're awfully nice!

FEDOTIK Look, I bought a knife for myself too. You see, it's got another blade here, and then another. This thing's for cleaning your ears, and these are nail scissors, and this is for cleaning your nails.

RODÉ [*In a loud voice*] Doctor, how old are you?

CHEBUTYKIN Me? Thirty-two.

Laughter

FEDOTIK I'll show you another kind of solitaire. [*sets out the cards*]

The samovar is brought in, and Anfisa attends to it. Shortly afterward Natasha comes in and begins to fuss around the table. Soleni enters, bows to the company, and sits down at the table

VERSHININ What a wind though!

MASHA Yes. I'm tired of winter. I've almost forgotten what summer is like.

IRINA [*Playing solitaire*] It's coming out. We'll get to Moscow!

FEDOTIK No, it's not coming out. You see, the eight has to go on the two of spades. [*laughs*] That means you won't go to Moscow.

CHEBUTYKIN [*Reads the paper*] Tsitsihar. Smallpox is raging.

ANFISA [*Goes up to Masha*] Masha, the tea's ready, dear. [*to Vershinin*] Will you please come to the table, Your Excellency? Forgive me, your name's slipped my memory.

MASHA Bring it here, Nanny. I'm not coming over there.

IRINA Nanny!

ANFISA Comi-ing!

NATASHA [*To Soleni*] You know, even tiny babies understand what we say perfectly well! "Good morning, Bobik," I said to him only today, "good morning, my precious!" And then he looked at me in such a special sort of way. You may say it's only a mother's imagination, but it isn't, I do assure you. No, no! He really is an extraordinary child!

SOLENI If that child were mine, I'd cook him up in a frying pan and eat him. [*picks up his glass, goes into the drawing room, and sits down in a corner*]

NATASHA [*Covers her face with her hands*] What a rude, ill-mannered person!

MASHA People who don't even notice whether it's summer or winter are lucky! I think I'd be indifferent to the weather if I were living in Moscow.

VERSHININ I've just been reading the diary of some French cabinet minister—he wrote it in prison. He got sent to prison in connection with the Panama affair. He writes with such a passionate delight about the birds he can see through the prison window—the birds he never even noticed when he was a cabinet minister. Of course now that he's released he won't notice them anymore. And in the same way you won't notice Moscow once you live there again. We're not happy and we can't be happy: we only want happiness.

TUTZENBACH [*Picks up a box from the table*] Say there, where are all the chocolates?

IRINA Soleni's eaten them.

TUTZENBACH All of them?

ANFISA [*Serving Vershinin tea*] Here's a letter for you, sir.

VERSHININ For me? [*takes the letter*] From my daughter. [*reads it*] Yes, of course. Forgive me, Marya Sergeevna, I'll just leave quietly. I won't have any tea. [*gets up, agitated*] Always the same thing.

MASHA What is it? Secret?

VERSHININ [*In a low voice*] My wife's taken poison again. I must go. I'll get away without them seeing me. All this is so dreadfully unpleasant. [*kisses Masha's hand*] My dear, good, sweet girl. I'll go out this way quietly. [*goes out*]

ANFISA   Where's he off to? And I've just brought him some tea! What a queer fellow!

MASHA   [*Flaring up*] Leave me alone! Why do you keep worrying me? Why don't you leave me in peace? [*goes to the table, cup in hand*] I'm sick and tired of you, silly old woman!

ANFISA   Why . . . I didn't mean to offend you, dear.

ANDREI'S VOICE   [*Offstage*] Anfisa!

ANFISA   [*Mimics him*] Anfisa! Sitting there in his den! [*goes out*]

MASHA   [*By the table in the ballroom, crossly*] Do let me sit down somewhere! [*jumbles up the cards laid out on the table*] You take up the whole table with your cards! Why don't you get on with your tea?

IRINA   How bad-tempered you are, Mashka!

MASHA   Well, if I'm bad-tempered, don't talk to me then. Don't touch me!

CHEBUTYKIN   [*Laughs*] Don't touch her! Take care you don't touch her!

MASHA   You may be sixty, but you're always babbling some damn nonsense or other just like a child.

NATASHA   [*Sighs*] My dear Masha, need you use such expressions? You know, with your good looks you'd be thought so charming, even by the best people—yes, I honestly mean it— if only you wouldn't use these expressions of yours! *Je vous prie, pardonnez-moi, Marie, mais vous avez des manières un peu grossières.*

TUTZENBACH   [*With suppressed laughter*] Pass me . . . Say there, will you please pass me . . . Is that cognac over there or what?

NATASHA   *Il paraît que mon Bobik déjà ne dort pas.* I think he's awake. He's not been too well today. I must go and see him. Excuse me. [*goes out*]

IRINA   And where has Aleksandr Ignatievich gone to?

MASHA   He's gone home. His wife's done something queer again.

TUTZENBACH   [*Goes over to Soleni with a decanter of cognac*] You always sit alone brooding over something or other— though what it's all about nobody knows. Well, let's make up. Let's have a cognac together. [*they drink*] I suppose I'll have to play the piano all night tonight—a lot of rubbishy tunes of course. Never mind!

SOLENI   Why did you say, "Let's make up"? We haven't quarreled.

TUTZENBACH   You always give me the feeling that there's something wrong between us. You're a strange character, no doubt about it.

SOLENI   [*Recites*] "I am strange, but who's not so? Don't be angry, Aleko!"

TUTZENBACH   What's Aleko got to do with it?

SOLENI   [*After a pause*] When I'm alone with somebody I'm all right; I'm just like other people. But in company I get depressed and shy, and . . . I talk all sorts of nonsense. All the same I'm a good deal more honest and well intentioned than plenty of others. I can prove I am.

TUTZENBACH   You often make me angry because you keep on pestering me when we're in company. But all the same I do like you for some reason. I'm going to get drunk tonight, whatever happens! Let's have another drink!

SOLENI   Yes, let's. [*pause*] I've never had anything against you personally, Baron. But my temperament's rather like Lermontov's. [*in a low voice*] I even look a little like Lermontov, I've been told. [*takes a cologne bottle from his pocket and sprinkles some cologne on his hands*]

TUTZENBACH   I have sent in my resignation! Finished! I've been considering it for five years, and now I've made up my mind at last. I'm going to work.

SOLENI   [*Recites*] "Don't be angry, Aleko! . . . Away, away with all your dreams!"

During the conversation Andrei enters quietly with a book in his hand and sits down by the candle

TUTZENBACH   I'm going to work!

CHEBUTYKIN   [*Comes into the drawing room with Irina*] And the food they treated me to was the genuine Caucasian stuff: onion soup, followed by chehartma—that's a meat dish, you know.

SOLENI   Cheremsha isn't meat at all; it's a plant, something like an onion.

CHEBUTYKIN No-o, my dear friend. Chehartma isn't an onion; it's roast mutton.

SOLENI I tell you cheremsha is a kind of onion.

CHEBUTYKIN Well, why should I argue about it with you? You've never been to the Caucasus and you've never tasted chehartma.

SOLENI I haven't tasted it because I can't stand the smell of it. Cheremsha stinks just like garlic.

ANDREI [*Imploringly*] Do stop it, friends! Please stop it!

TUTZENBACH When's the carnival crowd coming?

IRINA They promised to be here by nine—that means any moment now.

TUTZENBACH [*Embraces Andrei and sings*] "Ah, my beautiful porch, my lovely new porch, my . . ."[1]

ANDREI [*Dances and sings*] "My new porch all made of maple wood."

CHEBUTYKIN [*Dances*] "With fancy carving over the door."

Laughter

TUTZENBACH [*Kisses Andrei*] Let's have a drink, the hell with it! Andryusha, let's drink to eternal friendship. I'll come with you when you go back to Moscow University.

SOLENI Which university? There are two universities in Moscow.

ANDREI There's only one.

SOLENI I tell you there are two.

ANDREI Never mind, make it three. The more the merrier.

SOLENI There are two universities in Moscow.

Murmurs of protest and cries of "hush!"

There are two universities in Moscow, an old one and a new one. But if you don't want to listen to what I'm saying, if my conversation irritates you, I can keep silent. In fact I can go to another room. [*goes out through one of the doors*]

1. A traditional Russian dance song.

TUTZENBACH Bravo, bravo! [*laughs*] Let's get started, my friends. I'll play for you. What a funny creature that Soleni is! [*sits down at the piano and plays a waltz*]

MASHA [*Dances alone*] The baron is drunk, the baron is drunk, the baron is drunk.

Enter Natasha

NATASHA [*To Chebutykin*] Ivan Romanovich! [*speaks to him, then goes out quietly*]

Chebutykin touches Tutzenbach on the shoulder and whispers to him

IRINA What is it?

CHEBUTYKIN It's time we were going. Good night.

IRINA But really . . . What about the carnival party?

ANDREI [*Embarrassed*] The carnival party's not coming. You see, my dear, Natasha says that Bobik isn't very well, and so . . . Anyway, I don't know . . . and I certainly don't care.

IRINA [*Shrugs her shoulders*] Bobik's not very well!

MASHA Never mind, we'll keep our end up! If they turn us out, out we must go! [*to Irina*] It isn't Bobik who's not well; it's her. There! [*taps her forehead with her finger*] Petty little bourgeois housewife!

Andrei goes to his room on the right. Chebutykin follows him. The guests say good-bye in the ballroom

FEDOTIK What a pity! I'd been hoping to spend the evening here, but of course, if the baby's ill . . . I'll bring him some toys tomorrow.

RODÉ [*In a loud voice*] I had a good long sleep after lunch today on purpose. I thought I'd be dancing all night. I mean to say, it's only just nine o'clock.

MASHA Let's go outside and talk it over. We can decide what to do then.

Voices are heard saying, "Good-bye! God bless you!" and Tu-
tzenbach is heard laughing gaily. Everyone goes out. Anfisa
and a maid clear the table and put out the lights. The nurse
sings to the baby offstage. Enter Andrei, wearing an overcoat
and hat, followed by Chebutykin. They move quietly

CHEBUTYKIN I've never found time to get married, somehow . . . partly because my life's just flashed past me like
lightning, and partly because I was always madly in love with
your mother and she was married.

ANDREI One shouldn't marry. One shouldn't marry because it's
so boring.

CHEBUTYKIN That may be so, but what about loneliness? You
can philosophize as much as you like, dear boy, but loneliness
is a dreadful thing. Although really . . . Well, it doesn't make
a damn bit of difference of course!

ANDREI Let's go quickly.

CHEBUTYKIN What's the hurry? There's plenty of time.

ANDREI I'm afraid my wife may try to stop me.

CHEBUTYKIN Ah!

ANDREI I won't play cards tonight; I'll just sit and watch. I'm
not feeling too well. What should I do for this breathlessness,
Ivan Romanovich?

CHEBUTYKIN Why ask me, dear boy? I can't remember. I simply don't know.

ANDREI Let's go through the kitchen.

They go out. A bell rings. The ring is repeated; then voices and
laughter are heard

IRINA [*Coming in*] What's that?

ANFISA [*In a whisper*] The carnival party.

The bell rings again

IRINA Tell them there's no one at home, Nanny. Apologize to
them.

Anfisa goes out. Irina walks up and down the room, lost in thought. She seems agitated. Enter Soleni

SOLENI [*Puzzled*] There's no one here. Where is everybody?

IRINA They've gone home.

SOLENI How strange! Then you're alone here?

IRINA Yes, alone. [*pause*] Well, good night.

SOLENI I know I behaved tactlessly just now. I lost control of myself. But you're different from the others; you stand out high above them. You're pure; you can see where the truth lies. You're the only person in the world who can possibly understand me. I love you. I love you with a deep, infinite . . .

IRINA Do please go away. Good night!

SOLENI I can't live without you. [*follows her*] Oh, it's such a delight just to look at you! [*with tears*] Oh, my happiness! Your glorious, marvelous, entrancing eyes—eyes like no other woman's I've ever seen.

IRINA [*Coldly*] Please stop it, Vasili Vasilievich!

SOLENI I've never spoken to you of my love before. It makes me feel as if I were living on a different planet. [*rubs his forehead*] Never mind! I can't force you to love me, obviously. But I don't intend to have any rivals—successful rivals, I mean. No, no! I swear to you by everything I hold sacred that if there's anyone else, I'll kill him. Oh, how wonderful you are!

Enter Natasha carrying a candle

NATASHA [*Pokes her head into one room, then into another, but passes the door leading to her husband's room*] Andrei's reading in there. Better let him read. Forgive me, Vasili Vasilievich, I didn't know you were here. I'm afraid I'm not properly dressed.

SOLENI I don't care. Good-bye. [*goes out*]

NATASHA You must be tired, my poor dear girl. [*kisses Irina*] You ought to go to bed earlier.

IRINA Is Bobik alseep?

NATASHA Yes, he's asleep. But he's not sleeping peacefully. By the way, my dear, I've been meaning to speak to you for some time but there's always been something. Either you're not here, or I'm too busy. You see, I think that Bobik's nursery is so cold and damp. And your room is just ideal for a baby. Darling, do you think you could move into Olga's room?

IRINA   [*Not understanding her*] Where to?

The sound of bells is heard outside, as a troika is driven up to the house

NATASHA   You can share a room with Olya for the time being, and Bobik can have your room. He is such a darling! This morning I said to him, "Bobik, you're my very own! My very own!" And he just gazed at me with his dear little eyes.

The doorbell rings

That must be Olga. How late she is!

A maid comes up to Natasha and whispers in her ear

Protopopov! What a funny fellow! Protopopov's come to ask me to go for a drive with him. In a troika! [*laughs*] Aren't these men strange creatures!

The doorbell rings again

Someone's ringing. Shall I go for a short drive? Just for a quarter of an hour? [*to the maid*] Tell him I'll be down in a minute.

The doorbell rings

That's the bell again. I suppose it's Olga. [*goes out*]

The maid runs out. Irina sits lost in thought. Enter Kulygin and Olga, followed by Vershinin

KULYGIN Well! What's the meaning of this? You said you were going to have a party.

VERSHININ It's a strange thing. I left here about half an hour ago, and they were expecting a carnival party then.

IRINA They've all gone.

KULYGIN Masha's gone too? Where has she gone to? And why is Protopopov waiting outside in a troika? Who's he waiting for?

IRINA Please don't ask me questions. I'm tired.

KULYGIN You spoiled child!

OLGA The conference has only just ended. I'm quite worn out. The headmistress is ill and I'm substituting for her. My head's aching, oh, my head, my head. [*sits down*] Andrei lost two hundred rubles at cards last night. The whole town's talking about it.

KULYGIN Yes, the conference exhausted me too. [*sits down*]

VERSHININ So now my wife's taken it into her head to try to frighten me. She tried to poison herself. However, everything's all right now, so I can relax, thank goodness. So we've got to go away? Well, good night to you, all the best. Fëdor Ilyich, would you care to come along with me somewhere or other? I can't stay at home tonight, I really can't. Do come!

KULYGIN I'm tired. I don't think I'll come. [*gets up*] I'm tired. Has my wife gone home?

IRINA I think so.

KULYGIN [*Kisses Irina's hand*] Good night. We can rest tomorrow and the day after tomorrow, two whole days! Well, I wish you all the best. [*going out*] How I long for some tea! I planned on spending the evening in congenial company, but— *o fallacem hominum spem!* Always use the accusative case in exclamations.

VERSHININ Well, it looks as if I'll have to go somewhere by myself. [*goes out with Kulygin, whistling*]

OLGA My head aches, oh, my head. Andrei lost at cards. The whole town's talking. I'll go and lie down. [*going out*] Tomorrow I'm free. Heavens what a joy! Tomorrow I'm free, and the day after tomorrow I'm free. My head's aching, oh, my poor head.

IRINA   [*Alone*] They've all gone. No one's left.

Someone is playing an accordion in the street. The nurse sings in the next room

NATASHA   [*Crosses the ballroom, wearing a fur coat and cap. She is followed by the maid*] I'll be back in half an hour. I'm just going for a little drive. [*goes out*]
IRINA   [*Alone, with intense longing*] Moscow! Moscow! Moscow!

CURTAIN

ACT THREE

A bedroom now shared by Olga and Irina. There are two beds, one on the right, the other on the left, each screened off from the center of the room. It is past two o'clock in the morning. Offstage the alarm is being sounded on account of a fire, which has been raging for some time. No one in the house has been to bed yet. Masha is lying on a couch, dressed as usual in black. Olga and Anfisa come in.

ANFISA   Now they're sitting down there, under the stairs. I keep telling them to come upstairs, that they shouldn't sit down there, but they just cry. "We don't know where our papa is," they say, "perhaps he got burned in the fire." What an idea! And there are people in the yard too . . . half-dressed.

OLGA   [*Takes a dress out of a wardrobe*] Take this gray dress, Nanny. . . . And this one . . . This blouse too . . . And this skirt. Oh, heavens! What is happening! Apparently the whole of the Kirsanovski Street's been burned down. Take this . . . And this too . . . [*throws the clothes into Anfisa's arms*] The poor Vershinins had a fright. Their house only just escaped being burned down. They'll have to spend the night here. We mustn't let them go home. Poor Fedotik's lost everything; he's got nothing left.

ANFISA   I'd better call Ferapont, Olyushka; I can't carry all this.

OLGA   [*Rings*] No one pays any attention when I ring. [*calls *through the door*] Is anyone there? Will someone come up, please!

A window, red with the glow of the fire, can be seen through the open door. The sound of a passing fire engine is heard

How dreadful it all is! And how tired of it I am!

Enter Ferapont

Take this downstairs please. The Kolotilin girls are sitting under the stairs. Give it to them. And this too.

FERAPONT   Very good, madam. Moscow was burned down in 1812 just the same. Mercy on us! Yes, the French were surprised all right.

OLGA   Go ahead now, take this down.

FERAPONT   Very good. [*goes out*]

OLGA   Give it all away, Nanny dear. We won't keep anything. Give it all away. I'm so tired. I can hardly keep on my feet. We mustn't let the Vershinins go home. The little girls can sleep in the drawing room, and Aleksandr Ignatievich can share the downstairs room with the baron. Fedotik can go in with the baron too, or maybe he'd better sleep in the ballroom. The doctor's gone and gotten drunk—you'd think he'd done it on purpose; he's so hopelessly drunk that we can't let anyone go into his room. Vershinin's wife will have to go into the drawing room too.

ANFISA   [*Wearily*] Don't send me away, Olyushka, darling! Don't send me away!

OLGA   What nonsense you're talking, Nanny! No one's sending you away.

ANFISA   [*Leans her head against Olga's breast*] My dearest girl! I do work, you know; I work as hard as I can. I suppose now that I'm getting weaker, I'll be told to go. But where can I go? Where? I'm eighty years old. I'm over eighty-one!

OLGA   You sit down for a while, Nanny. You're tired, you poor dear. [*makes her sit down*] Just rest a bit. You've turned quite pale.

Enter Natasha

NATASHA They're saying we ought to start a drive in aid of the victims of the fire. You know—form a society or something for the purpose. Well, why not? It's an excellent idea! In any case it's up to us to help the poor as best we can. Bobik and Sofochka are fast asleep as if nothing had happened. We've got such a crowd of people in the house; the place seems full of people whichever way you turn. There's flu around in the town. I'm so afraid the children might catch it.

OLGA [*Without listening to her*] You can't see the fire from this room; it's quiet in here.

NATASHA Yes. I suppose my hair is all over the place. [*stands in front of the mirror*] They say I've gotten fatter, but it's not true! I'm not a bit fatter. Masha's asleep. She's tired, poor girl. [*to Anfisa, coldly*] How dare you sit down in my presence! Get up! Get out of here!

Anfisa goes out. A pause

I can't understand why you keep that old woman in the house.

OLGA [*Taken aback*] Forgive me for saying it, but I can't understand how you . . .

NATASHA She's quite useless here. She's just a peasant woman; her right place is in the country. You're spoiling her. I do like order in the home. I don't like having useless people around. [*strokes Olga's cheek*] You're tired, my poor dear! Our head-mistress is tired! You know, when my Sofochka grows up and goes to school, I'll be frightened of you.

OLGA I'm not going to be a headmistress.

NATASHA You'll be asked to, Olechka. It's settled.

OLGA I'll refuse. I couldn't do it. I wouldn't be strong enough. [*drinks water*] You spoke so harshly to Nanny just now. You must forgive me for saying so, but I just can't stand that sort of thing. It made me feel quite faint.

NATASHA [*Agitated*] Forgive me, Olya, forgive me. I didn't mean to upset you.

Masha gets up, picks up a pillow, and starts to go out in a huff

OLGA   Please try to understand me, dear. It may be that we've been brought up in a peculiar way, but anyway I just can't bear it. When people are treated like that, it gets me down, I feel quite ill. . . . I simply get unnerved.

NATASHA   Forgive me, dear, forgive me! [*kisses her*]

OLGA   Any cruel or tactless remark, even the slightest discourtesy, upsets me.

NATASHA   It's quite true, I know I often say things that would be better left unsaid—but you must agree with me, dear, that she'd be better in the country somewhere.

OLGA   She's been with us for thirty years.

NATASHA   But she can't do any work now, can she? Either I don't understand you, or you don't want to understand me. She can't work; she just sleeps or sits around.

OLGA   Well, let her sit around.

NATASHA   [*In surprise*] What do you mean, let her sit around? Surely she is a servant! [*tearfully*] No, I don't understand you, Olya! I have a nurse for the children and a wet nurse and we share a maid and a cook. Whatever do we want this old woman for? What for?

The alarm is sounded again

OLGA   I've aged ten years tonight.

NATASHA   We must sort things out, Olya. You're working at your school, and I'm working at home. You're teaching and I'm running the house. And when I say anything about the servants, I know what I'm talking about. That old thief, that old witch, must get out of this house tomorrow! [*stamps her feet*] How dare you annoy me like this? How dare you? [*recovering her self-control*] Really if you don't move downstairs, we'll always be quarreling. This is quite dreadful!

Enter Kulygin

KULYGIN   Where's Masha? It's time we went home. They say the fire's getting less fierce. [*stretches*] Only one block got burned down, but to begin with it looked as if the whole town was going to be set on fire by that wind. [*sits down*] I'm so tired,

Olechka, my dear. You know, I've often thought that if I hadn't married Masha, I'd have married you, Olechka. You're so kind. I'm worn out. [*listens*]

OLGA   What is it?

KULYGIN   The doctor's gotten drunk just as if he'd done it on purpose. Hopelessly drunk. As if he'd done it on purpose. [*gets up*] I think he's coming up here. Can you hear him? Yes, he's coming up. [*laughs*] What a fellow really! I'm going to hide myself. [*goes to the wardrobe and stands between it and the wall*] What a scoundrel!

OLGA   He's been off drinking for two years, and now suddenly he goes and gets drunk. [*walks with Natasha toward the back of the room*]

Chebutykin enters; walking firmly and soberly he crosses the room, stops, looks around, then goes to the washstand, and begins to wash his hands

CHEBUTYKIN   [*Glumly*] The devil take them all . . . all the lot of them! They think I can treat anything just because I'm a doctor, but I know positively nothing at all. I've forgotten everything I used to know. I remember nothing, positively nothing.

Olga and Natasha leave the room without his noticing

The devil take them! Last Wednesday I attended a woman at Zasyp. She died, and it's all my fault that she did die. Yes. I used to know a thing or two twenty-five years ago, but now I don't remember anything. Not a thing! Perhaps I'm not a man at all, but I just imagine that I've got hands and feet and a head. Perhaps I don't exist at all, and I only imagine that I'm walking around and eating and sleeping. [*weeps*] Oh, if only I could simply stop existing! [*stops crying, glumly*] God knows. . . . The other day they were talking about Shakespeare and Voltaire at the club. I haven't read either—never read a single line of either—but I tried to make out by my expression that I had. The others did the same. How petty it all is! How despicable! And then suddenly I thought of the woman I killed on Wednesday. It all came back to me, and I felt like such a swine, so sick of myself that I went and got drunk.

Enter Irina, Vershinin, and Tutzenbach. Tutzenbach is wearing a fashionable, new civilian suit

IRINA   Let's sit down here for a while. No one will come in here.

VERSHININ   The whole town would have been burned down if it weren't for the soldiers. They're a fine lot of fellows! [*rubs his hands with pleasure*] Excellent fellows! Yes, they're a fine lot!

KULYGIN   [*Approaches them*] What's the time?

TUTZENBACH   It's past three. It's beginning to get light.

IRINA   Everyone's sitting in the ballroom and nobody thinks of leaving. That man Soleni's there too. [*to Chebutykin*] You ought to go to bed, Doctor.

CHEBUTYKIN   I'm all right. Thanks. [*combs his beard*]

KULYGIN   [*Laughs*] A bit tipsy, Ivan Romanovich! [*slaps him on the shoulder*] You're a fine one! *In vino veritas,* as they used to say in Rome.

TUTZENBACH   Everyone keeps asking me to arrange a concert in aid of the victims of the fire.

IRINA   Well, who'd you get to perform in it?

TUTZENBACH   It could be done if we wanted to. Marya Sergeevna plays the piano wonderfully well, in my opinion.

KULYGIN   Yes, wonderfully well!

IRINA   She's forgotten how to. She hasn't played for three years . . . or maybe it's four.

TUTZENBACH   Nobody understands music in this town, not a single person. But I do—I really do—and I assure you quite definitely that Marya Sergeevna plays magnificently. She's almost a genius for it.

KULYGIN   You're right, Baron. I'm very fond of Masha. She's such a nice girl.

TUTZENBACH   Fancy being able to play so exquisitely, and yet having nobody, nobody at all, to appreciate it!

KULYGIN   [*Sighs*] Yes. But would it be quite proper for her to play in a concert? [*pause*] I don't know anything about these matters, my friends. Perhaps it'll be perfectly all right. But you know, although our director is a good man, a very good man indeed and most intelligent, I know that he does hold certain views. . . . Of course this doesn't really concern him, but I'll have a word with him about it all the same, if you like.

Chebutykin picks up a china clock and examines it

VERSHININ   I've gotten my clothes in such a mess helping to put out the fire, I must look like nothing on earth. [*pause*] I believe they were saying yesterday that our brigade might be transferred to somewhere a long way away. Some said it was to be Poland, and some said it was Chita, in Siberia.

TUTZENBACH   I heard that too. Well, the town will seem quite deserted.

IRINA   We'll go away too!

CHEBUTYKIN   [*Drops the clock and breaks it*] Smashed to smithereens!

A pause. Everyone looks upset and embarrassed

KULYGIN   [*Picks up the pieces*] Fancy breaking such a valuable thing! Ah, Ivan Romanich, Ivan Romanich! You'll get a bad mark for that!

IRINA   It was my mother's clock.

CHEBUTYKIN   Well, supposing it was. If it was your mother's, then it was your mother's. Perhaps I didn't smash it. Perhaps it only appears that I did. Perhaps it only appears to us that we exist, whereas in reality we don't exist at all. I don't know anything; no one knows anything. [*stops at the door*] Why are you staring at me? Natasha's having a nice little affair with Protopopov, and you don't see it. You sit here seeing nothing, and meanwhile Natasha's having a nice little affair with Protopopov. [*sings*] Would you like a date? [*goes out*]

VERSHININ   So. [*laughs*] How odd it all is really! [*pause*] When the fire started, I ran home as fast as I could. When I got near, I could see that our house was all right and out of danger, but the two little girls were standing there, in the doorway, in their night clothes. Their mother wasn't there. People were rushing around, horses, dogs . . . And in the kids' faces I saw a frightened, anxious, appealing look, I don't know what! My heart sank when I saw their faces. My God, I thought, what will these children have to go through in the course of their poor lives? And they may live a long time too! I picked them up and ran back here with them, and all the time I was running, I was thinking the same thing: what will they have to go through?

The alarm is sounded. A pause

When I got here, my wife was here already . . . angry, shouting!

Enter Masha carrying a pillow. She sits down on the couch

And when my little girls were standing in the doorway with nothing on but their night clothes, and the street was red with the glow of the fire and full of terrifying noises, it struck me that the same sort of thing used to happen years ago, when armies used to make sudden raids on towns and plunder them and set them on fire. Anyway is there any essential difference between things as they were and as they are now? And before very long, say, in another two or three hundred years, people may be looking at our present life just as we look at the past now, with horror and scorn. Our own times may seem uncouth to them, boring and frightfully uncomfortable and strange. Oh, what a great life it'll be then, what a life! [*laughs*] Forgive me, I'm philosophizing my head off again . . . but may I go on, please? I'm bursting to philosophize just at the moment. I'm in the mood for it. [*pause*] You seem as if you've all gone to sleep. As I was saying: what a great life it will be in the future! Just try to imagine it. . . . At the present time there are only three people of your intellectual caliber in the whole of this town, but future generations will be more productive of people like you. They'll go on producing more and more of the same sort until at last the time will come when everything will be just as you'd wish it yourselves. People will live their lives in your way, and then even you may be outmoded, and a new lot will come along who will be even better than you are. [*laughs*] I'm in quite a special mood today. I feel full of a tremendous urge to live. [*sings*]

"To Love all ages are in fee,
    The passion's good for you and me." [*laughs*]
MASHA   [*Sings*] Tara-tara-tara . . .
VERSHININ   Tum-tum . . .
MASHA   Tara-tara . . .
VERSHININ   Tum-tum, tum-tum . . . [*laughs*]

Enter Fedotik

FEDOTIK   [*Dancing about*] Burned, burned! Everything I've got
    burned!

All laugh

IRINA   It's hardly a joking matter. Has everything really been
    burned?
FEDOTIK   [*Laughs*] Everything, completely. I've got nothing left.
    My guitar's burned, my photographs are burned, all my letters
    are burned. Even the little notebook I was going to give you
    has been burned.

Enter Soleni

IRINA   No, please go away, Vasili Vasilievich. You can't come in
    here.
SOLENI   Can't I? Why can the baron come in here if I can't?
VERSHININ   We really must go, all of us. What's the fire doing?
SOLENI   It's dying down, they say. Well, I must say it's a peculiar
    thing that the baron can come in here and I can't. [*takes a
    cologne bottle from his pocket and sprinkles himself with
    cologne*]
VERSHININ   Tara-tara.
MASHA   Tum-tum, tum-tum.
VERSHININ   [*Laughs, to Soleni*] Let's go to the ballroom.
SOLENI   Very well, we'll make a note of this. "I hardly need to
    make my moral yet more clear: that might be teasing geese, I
    fear!"[1] [*looks at Tutzenbach*] Cluck, cluck, cluck! [*goes out
    with Vershinin and Fedotik*]

1. From Krylov's fable "Geese."

IRINA That Soleni has smoked the room out. [*puzzled*] The baron's asleep. Baron! Baron!

TUTZENBACH [*Waking out of his doze*] I must be tired. The brickworks . . . No, I'm not talking in my sleep. I really do intend to go to the brickworks and start working there quite soon. I've had a talk with the manager. [*to Irina, tenderly*] You are so pale, so beautiful, so fascinating. Your pallor seems to light up the darkness around you, as if it were luminous, somehow. You're sad; you're dissatisfied with the life you have to live. Oh, come away with me; let's go away and work together!

MASHA Nikolai Lvovich, I wish you'd go away.

TUTZENBACH [*Laughs*] Oh, you're here, are you? I didn't see you. [*kisses Irina's hand*] Good-bye, I'm going. You know, as I look at you now, I keep thinking of the day—it was a long time ago, your saint's day—when you talked to us about the joy of work. You were so gay and high-spirited then. And what a happy life I saw ahead of me! Where is it all now? [*kisses her hand*] There are tears in your eyes. You should go to bed; it's beginning to get light. It's almost morning. Oh, if only I could give my life for you!

MASHA Nikolai Lvovich, please go away! Really now.

TUTZENBACH I'm going. [*goes out*]

MASHA [*Lies down*] Are you asleep, Fëdor?

KULYGIN Eh?

MASHA Why don't you go home?

KULYGIN My darling Masha, my sweet, my precious Masha . . .

IRINA She's tired. Let her rest awhile, Fedya.

KULYGIN I'll go in a moment. My wife, my dear, good wife! How I love you! Only you!

MASHA [*Crossly*] Amo, amas, amat, amamus, amatis, amant!

KULYGIN [*Laughs*] Really, she's an amazing woman! I've been married to you for seven years, but I feel as if we were only married yesterday. Yes, on my word of honor, I do! You really are amazing! Oh, I'm so happy, happy, happy!

MASHA And I'm so bored, bored, bored! [*sits up*] I can't get it out of my head. It's simply disgusting. It's like having a nail driven into my head. No, I can't keep silent about it anymore.

It's about Andrei. He's actually mortgaged this house to a bank, and his wife's got hold of all the money. And yet the house doesn't belong to him; it belongs to all four of us! Surely, he must realize that, if he's got any honesty.

KULYGIN Why bring all this up, Masha? Why bother about it now? Andryusha owes money everywhere. Leave him alone.

MASHA Anyway it's disgusting. [*lies down*]

KULYGIN Well, we aren't poor, Masha. I've got work, I teach at the county school, I give private lessons in my spare time. I'm just a plain, honest man. *Omnia mea mecum porto,* as they say.

MASHA I don't ask for anything, but I'm just disgusted by injustice. [*pause*] Why don't you go home, Fëdor?

KULYGIN [*Kisses her*] You're tired. Just rest here for a while. I'll go home and wait for you. Go to sleep. [*goes to the door*] I'm happy, happy, happy! [*goes out*]

IRINA The truth is that Andrei is getting to be shallow-minded. He's aging and since he's been living with that woman he's lost all the inspiration he used to have! Not long ago he was working for a professorship, and yet yesterday he boasted of having at last been elected a member of the County Council. Fancy him a member, with Protopopov as chairman! They say the whole town's laughing at him; he's the only one who doesn't know anything or see anything. And now, you see, everyone's at the fire, while he's just sitting in his room, not taking the slightest notice of it. Just playing his violin. [*agitated*] Oh, how dreadful it is, how dreadful, how dreadful! I can't bear it any longer, I can't, I really can't!

Enter Olga. She starts arranging things on her bedside table

[*sobs loudly*] You must turn me out of here! Turn me out; I can't stand it anymore!

OLGA [*Alarmed*] What is it? What is it, darling?

IRINA [*Sobbing*] Where? Where has it all gone to? Where is it? Oh, God! I've forgotten. I've forgotten everything. . . . There's nothing but a muddle in my head. I don't remember what the Italian for "window" is or for "ceiling." . . . Every day I'm forgetting more and more, and life's slipping by, and it will never, never come back. We will never go to Moscow. I can see that we will never go.

OLGA   Don't, my dear, don't.

IRINA   [*Trying to control herself*] Oh, I'm so miserable! I can't work! I won't work! I've had enough of it, enough! First I worked on the telegraph, now I'm in the County Council office, and I hate and despise everything they give me to do there. I'm twenty-three years old, I've been working all this time, and I feel as if my brain's dried up. I know I've gotten thinner and uglier and older, and I find no kind of satisfaction in anything, none at all. And the time's passing . . . and I feel as if I'm moving away from any hope of a genuine, fine life. I'm moving further and further away and sinking into a kind of abyss. I feel in despair, and I don't know why I'm still alive, why I haven't killed myself.

OLGA   Don't cry, my dear child, don't cry. It hurts me.

IRINA   I'm not crying anymore. That's enough of it. Look, I'm not crying now. Enough of it, enough!

OLGA   Darling, let me tell you something. I just want to speak as your sister, as your friend, That is, if you want my advice. Why don't you marry the baron?

Irina weeps quietly

After all you do respect him; you think a lot of him. It's true, he's not good-looking, but he's such a decent, clean-minded sort of man. After all one doesn't marry for love, but to fulfill a duty. At least I think so, and I'd marry even if I weren't in love. I'd marry anyone that proposed to me, as long as he was a decent man. I'd even marry an old man.

IRINA   I've been waiting all this time, imagining that we'd be moving to Moscow, and I'd meet the man I'm meant for there. I've dreamed about him and I've loved him in my dreams. But it's all turned out to be nonsense. . . . Nonsense.

OLGA   [*Embracing her*] My darling sweetheart, I understand everything perfectly. When the baron resigned his commission and came to see us in his civilian clothes, I thought he looked so plain that I actually started to cry. He asked me why I was crying. How could I tell him? But, of course, if it were God's will that he should marry you, I'd feel perfectly happy about it. That's quite a different matter, quite different!

Natasha, carrying a candle, comes out of the door on the right, crosses the stage, and goes out through the door on the left without saying anything

MASHA [*Sits up*] She goes around looking as if she'd started the fire.

OLGA You're silly, Masha. You're the stupidest person in our family. Forgive me for saying so. . . .

MASHA [*After a pause*] My dear sisters, I've got something to confess to you. I must get some relief; I feel the need of it in my heart. I'll confess it to you two alone, and then never again, never to anybody! I'll tell you in a minute. [*in a low voice*] It's a secret, but you'll have to know everything. I can't keep silent anymore. [*pause*] I'm in love, in love. I love that man. You saw him there just now. Well, what's the use? I love Vershinin.

OLGA [*Goes behind her screen*] Don't say it. I don't want to hear it.

MASHA Well, what's to be done? [*holding her head*] I thought he was queer at first; then I started to pity him. Then I began to love him . . . love everything about him—his voice, his talk, his misfortunes, his two little girls.

OLGA Nevertheless, I don't want to hear it. You can say any nonsense you like, I'm not listening.

MASHA Oh, you're stupid, Olya! If I love him, well—that's my fate! That's my destiny. He loves me too. It's all rather frightening, isn't it? Not a good thing, is it? [*takes Irina by the hand and draws her to her*] Oh, my dear! How are we going to live through the rest of our lives? What's going to become of us? When you read a novel, everything in it seems so old and obvious. But when you fall in love yourself, you suddenly discover that you don't really know anything, and you've got to make your own decisions. . . . My dear sisters, my dear sisters! I've confessed it all to you, and now I'll keep quiet. I'll be like that madman in the story by Gogol—silence . . . silence!

Enter Andrei followed by Ferapont

ANDREI [*Irritably*] What do you want? I don't understand you.

FERAPONT [*Stopping in the doorway, impatiently*] I've asked you about ten times already, Andrei Sergeevich.

ANDREI In the first place you're not to call me Andrei Sergeevich; call me "Your Honor."

FERAPONT The firemen are asking Your Honor if they may drive through your garden to get to the river. They've been going a long way around all this time—it's a terrible business!

ANDREI All right. Tell them it's all right.

Ferapont goes out

They keep on plaguing me. Where's Olga?

Olga comes from behind the screen

I wanted to see you. Will you give me the key to the cupboard? I've lost mine. You know the key I mean, the small one you've got.

Olga silently hands him the key. Irina goes behind the screen on her side of the room

What a terrific fire! It's going down though. That Ferapont annoyed me, the devil take him! Silly thing he made me say. Telling him to call me "Your Honor"! [*pause*] Why don't you say anything, Olya? [*pause*] It's about time you stopped this nonsense. Sulking like this for no reason whatever. . . . You here, Masha? And Irina's here too. That's excellent! We can talk it over then, frankly once and for all. What have you got against me? What is it?

OLGA Drop it now, Andryusha. Let's talk it over tomorrow. [*agitated*] What a dreadful night!

ANDREI [*In great embarrassment*] Don't get upset. I'm asking you quite calmly: what have you got against me? Tell me frankly.

VERSHININ'S VOICE [*Offstage*] Tum-tum-tum!

MASHA [*In a loud voice, getting up*] Tara-tara-tara! [*to Olga*] Good-bye, Olya, God bless you! [*goes behind the screen and kisses Irina*] Sleep well. Good-bye, Andrei. I would leave them now; they're tired. Talk it over tomorrow. [*goes out*]

OLGA Really, Andryusha, let's leave it till tomorrow. [*goes behind the screen on her side of the room*] It's time to go to bed.

ANDREI I only want to say one thing; then I'll go. In a moment. First of all, you've got something against my wife, against Natasha. I've always been conscious of it from the day we got married. Natasha is a fine woman; she's honest and straightforward and high-principled. That's my opinion. I love and respect my wife. You understand that I respect her, and I expect others to respect her too. I repeat: she's an honest, high-principled woman, and all your grievances against her—if you don't mind my saying so—are just imagination and nothing more. [*pause*] Secondly, you seem to be annoyed with me for not making myself a professor and not doing any academic work. But I'm working in the Council Office, I'm a member of the County Council, and I feel my service there is just as fine and valuable as any academic work I might do. I'm a member of the County Council, and if you want to know, I'm proud of it! [*pause*] Thirdly, there's something else I must tell you. . . . I know I mortgaged the house without asking your permission. That was wrong, I admit it, and I ask you to forgive me. I was driven to it by my debts. I'm in debt for about thirty-five thousand rubles. I don't play cards anymore; I've given it up long ago. The only thing I can say to justify myself is that you girls get an annuity, while I don't get anything. No income, I mean.

KULYGIN [*Calling through the door*] Is Masha there? She's not there? [*alarmed*] Where can she be then? It's very strange. [*goes away*]

ANDREI So you won't listen? Natasha is a good, honest woman, I tell you. [*walks up and down the stage, then stops*] When I married her, I thought we were going to be happy; I thought we would all be happy. But . . . oh, my God! [*weeps*] My dear sisters, my dear, good sisters, don't believe what I've been saying, don't believe it. [*goes out*]

KULYGIN [*Through the door, agitated*] Where's Masha? Isn't Masha here? Extraordinary! [*goes away*]

The alarm is heard again. The stage is empty

IRINA [*Speaking from behind the screen*] Olya! Who's that knocking on the floor?

OLGA It's the doctor, Ivan Romanovich. He's drunk.

IRINA It's been one thing after another all night. [*pause*] Olya! [*peeps out from behind the screen*] Have you heard? The troops are being moved from the district. They're being sent somewhere a long way off.

OLGA That's only a rumor.

IRINA We'll be left quite alone then. Olya!

OLGA Well?

IRINA Olya, darling, I do respect the baron. I think a lot of him; he's a very good man. I'll marry him, Olya. I'll agree to marry him, if only we can go to Moscow! Let's go! Please let's go! There's nowhere in all the world like Moscow. Let's go, Olya! Let's go!

CURTAIN

ACT FOUR

The old garden belonging to the Prozorovs' house. A river is seen at the end of a long avenue of fir trees, and on the far bank of the river, a forest. On the right of the stage there is a veranda with a table on which champagne bottles and glasses have been left. It is midday. From time to time people from the street pass through the garden to get to the river. Five or six soldiers march through quickly.

Chebutykin, radiating a mood of benevolence, which does not leave him throughout the act, is sitting in a chair in the garden. He is wearing his army cap and is holding a walking stick, as if ready to be called away at any moment. Kulygin, with a decoration around his neck and with his mustache shaved off, Tutzenbach, and Irina are standing on the veranda saying good-bye to Fedotik and Rodé, who are coming down the steps. Both officers are in marching uniform.

TUTZENBACH [*Embracing Fedotik*] You're a good fellow, Fedotik; we've been good friends! [*embraces Rodé*] Once more then. . . . Good-bye, my dear friends!

IRINA *Au revoir!*

FEDOTIK It's not *au revoir*. It's good-bye. We will never meet again!

KULYGIN Who knows? [*wipes his eyes, smiling*] There! You've made me cry.

IRINA We'll meet some time.

FEDOTIK   Perhaps in ten or fifteen years' time. But then we'll hardly know one another. We will just meet and say "how are you?" coldly. [*takes a snapshot*] Wait a moment. Just one more, for the last time.

RODÉ   [*Embraces Tutzenbach*] We're not likely to meet again. [*kisses Irina's hand*] Thank you for everything . . . everything!

FEDOTIK   [*Annoyed*] Just wait a second!

TUTZENBACH   We'll meet again if we're fated to meet. Do write to us. Be sure to write.

RODÉ   [*Glancing around the garden*] Good-bye, trees! [*shouts*] Hey! [*pauses*] Good-bye, echo!

KULYGIN   I wouldn't be surprised if you got married out there, in Poland. You'll get a Polish wife, and she'll put her arms around you and say, *"kochany"!*[1] [*laughs*]

FEDOTIK   [*Glances at his watch*] There's less than an hour to go. Soleni is the only one from our battery who's going down the river on the barge. All the others are marching with the division. Three batteries are leaving today by road and three more tomorrow—then the town will be quite peaceful.

TUTZENBACH   Yes, and dreadfully dull too.

RODÉ   By the way, where's Marya Sergeevna?

KULYGIN   She's somewhere in the garden.

FEDOTIK   We must say good-bye to her.

RODÉ   Good-bye. I really must go or I'll burst into tears. [*quickly embraces Tutzenbach and Kulygin, then kisses Irina's hand*] Life's been very pleasant here.

FEDOTIK   [*To Kulygin*] Here's something for a souvenir for you —a notebook with a pencil. We'll go down to the river through here. [*they go off, glancing back*]

RODÉ   [*Shouts*] Heigh-ho!

KULYGIN   [*Shouts*] Good-bye!

At the back of the stage Fedotik and Rodé meet Masha and say good-bye to her. She goes off with them

IRINA   They've gone. . . . [*sits down on the bottom step of the veranda*]

1. A Polish word meaning "beloved."

CHEBUTYKIN   They forgot to say good-bye to me.

IRINA   Well, what about you?

CHEBUTYKIN   That's true; I forgot too. Never mind, I'll be seeing them again quite soon. I'll be leaving tomorrow. Yes . . . only one more day. And then in a year's time I'll be retiring. I'll come back here and finish the rest of my life near you. There's just one more year to go and then I get my pension. [*puts a newspaper in his pocket and takes out another*] I'll come back here and lead a reformed life. I'll be a nice, quiet, well-behaved little man.

IRINA   Yes, it's really time you reformed, my dear friend. You ought to live a different sort of life somehow.

CHEBUTYKIN   Yes, I think so too. [*sings quietly*] Tarara-boom-di-ay. . . . I'm sitting on a tomb-di-ay.

KULYGIN   Ivan Romanovich is incorrigible! Incorrigible!

CHEBUTYKIN   Yes, you ought to have taken me in hand. You'd have reformed me!

IRINA   Fëdor's shaved his mustache off. I can't bear to look at him.

KULYGIN   Why not?

CHEBUTYKIN   If I could just tell you what your face looks like now—but I don't dare.

KULYGIN   Well! Such are the conventions of life! *Modus vivendi*, you know. The director shaved his mustache off, so I shaved mine off when they gave me an inspectorship. No one likes it, but personally I'm quite indifferent. I'm content. Whether I've got a mustache or not, it's all the same to me. [*sits down*]

Andrei passes across the back of the stage pushing a carriage with a child asleep in it

IRINA   Ivan Romanovich, my dear friend, I'm awfully worried about something. You were out in the town garden last night. Tell me what happened there.

CHEBUTYKIN   What happened? Nothing. Just a trifling thing. [*reads his paper*] It doesn't matter anyway.

KULYGIN   They say that Soleni and the baron met in the town garden outside the theater last night and . . .

TUTZENBACH   Don't, please! What's the good? [*waves his hand at him deprecatingly and goes into the house*]

KULYGIN   It was outside the theater. Soleni started badgering the baron, and he lost patience and said something that offended him.

CHEBUTYKIN   I don't know anything about it. It's all nonsense.

KULYGIN   A schoolteacher once wrote "nonsense" in Russian over a pupil's essay, and the pupil puzzled over it, thinking it was a Latin word. [*laughs*] Frightfully funny, you know! They say that Soleni's in love with Irina and that he got to hate the baron more and more. Well, that's understandable. Irina's a very nice girl. She's a bit like Masha; she tends to get wrapped up in her own thoughts. [*to Irina*] But your disposition is more easygoing than Masha's. And yet Masha has a very nice disposition too. I love her, I love my Masha.

From the back of the stage comes a shout: "Yoo-hoo!"

IRINA   [*Starts*] Anything seems to startle me today. [*pause*] I've got everything ready too. I'm sending my luggage off after lunch. The baron and I are going to get married tomorrow, and directly afterward we're moving to the brickworks, and the day after tomorrow I'm starting work at the school. So our new life will begin, God willing! When I was sitting for my teacher's diploma, I suddenly started crying for sheer joy, with a sort of feeling of blessedness. [*pause*] The carrier will be coming for my luggage in a minute.

KULYGIN   That's all very well, but somehow I can't feel that it's meant to be serious. All ideas and theories, but nothing really serious. Anyway I wish you luck from the bottom of my heart.

CHEBUTYKIN   [*Moved*] My dearest girl, my precious child! You've gone on so far ahead of me, I'll never catch up now. I've gotten left behind like a bird that has grown too old and can't keep up with the rest of the flock. Fly away, my dears, fly away, and God be with you! [*pause*] It's a pity you've shaved your mustache off, Fëdor Ilyich.

KULYGIN   Don't keep on about it, please! [*sighs*] Well, the soldiers will be leaving today, and everything will go back to what it was before. Anyway whatever they say, Masha is a good, loyal wife. Yes, I love her dearly and I'm thankful for what God has given me. Fate treats people so differently. For instance there's an excise clerk here called Kozyrev. He was at school with me and he was expelled in his fifth year because he just couldn't grasp the *ut consecutivum*. He's dreadfully hard up now and in bad health too, and whenever I meet him, I just say to him, "Hello, *ut consecutivum!*" "Yes," he replies, "that's just the trouble—*consecutivum*" and he starts coughing. Whereas I—I've been lucky all my life. I'm happy; I've actually been awarded the order of Saint Stanislav, second class—and now I'm teaching the children the same old *ut consecutivum*. Of course, I'm clever, cleverer than plenty of other people, but happiness does not consist of merely being clever.

In the house someone plays "The Maiden's Prayer"

IRINA   Tomorrow night I won't have to listen to "The Maiden's Prayer." I won't have to meet Protopopov. [*pause*] By the way, he's in the sitting room. He's come again.

KULYGIN   Hasn't our headmistress arrived yet?

IRINA   No, we've sent for her. If you only knew how difficult it is for me to live here by myself, without Olya! She lives at the school now; she's the headmistress and she's busy the whole day. And I'm here alone, bored, with nothing to do, and I hate the very room I live in. So I've just made up my mind—if I'm really not going to be able to live in Moscow, that's that. It's my fate, that's all. Nothing can be done about it. It's God's will, everything that happens, and that's the truth. Nikolai Lvovich proposed to me. Well, I thought it over, and I made up my mind. He's such a nice man; it's really extraordinary how nice he is. And then suddenly I felt as though my soul had grown wings; I felt more cheerful and so relieved somehow that I wanted to work again. Just to start work! Only something happened yesterday, and now I feel as though something mysterious is hanging over me.

CHEBUTYKIN   Nonsense!

NATASHA   [*Speaking through the window*] Our headmistress!

KULYGIN   Our headmistress has arrived! Let's go indoors. [*goes indoors with Irina*]

CHEBUTYKIN   [*Reads his paper and sings quietly to himself*] Tarara-boom-di-ay. I'm sitting on a tomb-di-ay.

Masha walks up to him. Andrei passes across the back of the stage pushing the carriage

MASHA You look very comfortable sitting here.

CHEBUTYKIN Well, why not? Anything happening?

MASHA [*Sits down*] No, nothing. [*pause*] Tell me something. Were you in love with my mother?

CHEBUTYKIN Yes, very much in love.

MASHA Did she love you?

CHEBUTYKIN [*After a pause*] I can't remember now.

MASHA Is my man here? Our cook Marfa always used to call her policeman "my man." Is he here?

CHEBUTYKIN Not yet.

MASHA When you have to take your happiness in snatches, in little bits, as I do, and then lose it, as I've lost it, you gradually get hardened and bad-tempered. [*points at her breast*] Something's boiling over inside me, here. [*looking at Andrei, who again crosses the stage with the carriage*] There's Andrei, our dear brother. All our hopes are gone. It's the same as when thousands of people haul a huge bell up into a tower. Untold labor and money is spent on it, and then suddenly it falls and gets smashed. Suddenly, without rhyme or reason. It was the same with Andrei.

ANDREI When are they going to settle down in the house? They're making such a row.

CHEBUTYKIN They will soon. [*looks at his watch*] This is an old-fashioned watch: it strikes. [*winds his watch, which then strikes*] The first, second, and fifth batteries will be leaving punctually at one o'clock. [*pause*] And I will leave tomorrow.

ANDREI For good?

CHEBUTYKIN I don't know. I may return in about a year. Although God knows, it's all the same.

The sounds of a harp and a violin are heard

ANDREI The town will seem quite empty. Life will be snuffed out like a candle. [*pause*] Something happened yesterday outside the theater; everybody's talking about it. I'm the only one that doesn't seem to know about it.

CHEBUTYKIN It was nothing. A lot of nonsense. Soleni started badgering the baron or something. The baron lost his temper and insulted him, and in the end Soleni had to challenge him to a duel. [*looks at his watch*] I think it's time to go. At half past twelve, in the forest over there, on the other side of the river . . . Bang-bang! [*laughs*] Soleni imagines he's like Lermontov. He actually writes poems. But, joking apart, this is his third duel.

MASHA Whose third duel?

CHEBUTYKIN Soleni's.

MASHA What about the baron?

CHEBUTYKIN Well, what about him?

MASHA My thoughts are all in a muddle. But what I mean to say is that they shouldn't be allowed to fight. He might wound the baron or even kill him.

CHEBUTYKIN The baron's a good enough fellow, but what does it really matter if there's one baron more or less in the world? Well, let it be! It's all the same.

The shouts of "ah-hoo!" and "yoo-hoo!" are heard from beyond the garden

That's Skvortsov, the second, shouting from the boat. He can wait.

ANDREI I think it's simply immoral to fight a duel, or even to be present at one as a doctor.

CHEBUTYKIN That's only how it seems. We don't exist; nothing exists. It only seems to us that we do. And what difference does it make?

MASHA Talk, talk, nothing but talk all day long! [*starts to go*] Having to live in this awful climate with the snow threatening to fall at any moment, and then on top of it having to listen to all this sort of talk. [*stops*] I won't go into the house; I can't bear going in there. Will you let me know when Vershinin comes? [*walks off along the avenue*] Look, the birds are beginning to fly away already! [*looks up*] Swans or geese . . . Dear birds, happy birds . . . [*goes off*]

ANDREI Our house will seem quite deserted. The officers will go, you'll go, my sister will get married, and I'll be left alone in the house.

CHEBUTYKIN What about your wife?

Enter Ferapont with some papers

ANDREI My wife is my wife. She's a good, decent sort of woman. She's really very kind too, but there's something about her that pulls her down to the level of an animal—a sort of mean, blind, thick-skinned animal—anyway not a human being. I'm telling you this as a friend, the only person I can talk openly to. I love Natasha, it's true. But at times she appears to me so utterly vulgar that I feel quite bewildered by it, and then I can't understand why, for what reasons I love her —or anyway did love her.

CHEBUTYKIN [*Gets up*] Well, dear boy, I'm going away tomorrow and it may be we will never see each other again. So I'll give you a bit of advice. Put on your hat, take a walking stick, and go away. Go away and don't ever look back. And the farther you go, the better.

Soleni passes across the back of the stage accompanied by two officers. Seeing Chebutykin, he turns toward him, while the officers walk on

SOLENI It's time, Doctor. Half past twelve already. [*shakes hands with Andrei*]

CHEBUTYKIN In a moment. Oh, I'm tired of you all. [*to Andrei*] Andryusha, if anyone asks for me, tell them I'll be back presently. [*sighs*] Oh-ho-ho!

SOLENI
"He had not time to say 'Oh, oh!'
Before that bear had struck him low."
[*walks off with him*] What are you groaning about, old man?

CHEBUTYKIN Oh, well!

SOLENI How do you feel?

CHEBUTYKIN [*Sourly*] Like a last year's bird's nest.

SOLENI You don't have to be so agitated about it, old boy. I won't indulge in anything much; I'll just scorch his wings a little, like a woodcock's. [*takes out a cologne bottle and sprinkles cologne over his hands*] I've used up a whole bottle today, but my hands still smell. They smell like a corpse. [*pause*] Yes. Do you remember that poem of Lermontov's?

"And he, rebellious, seeks a storm,
  As if in storms there were tranquillity."
CHEBUTYKIN   Yes.
  "He had not time to say 'Oh, oh!'
  Before that bear had struck him low."
[*goes out with Soleni*]

Shouts of "yoo-hoo, ah-hoo!" are heard. Enter Andrei and Ferapont

FERAPONT   Will you sign these papers please?
ANDREI   [*With irritation*] Leave me alone! Leave me alone, for heaven's sake. [*goes off with the carriage*]
FERAPONT   Well, what am I supposed to do with the papers then? They are meant to be signed, aren't they? [*goes to back of stage*]

Enter Irina and Tutzenbach, the latter wearing a straw hat. Kulygin crosses the stage, calling, "Yoo-hoo, Masha! Yoo-hoo!"

TUTZENBACH   I think he's the only person in the whole town who's glad that the army is leaving.
IRINA   That's quite understandable really. [*pause*] The town will look quite empty.
TUTZENBACH   My dear, I'll be back in a moment.
IRINA   Where are you going?
TUTZENBACH   I must slip back to the town, and then . . . I want to see some of my colleagues off.
IRINA   It's not true. Nikolai, why are you so absentminded today? [*pause*] What happened outside the theater last night?
TUTZENBACH   [*With a movement of impatience*] I'll be back in an hour. I'll be back with you again. [*kisses her hands*] My treasure! [*gazes into her eyes*] It's five years since I first began to love you, and still I can't get used to it, and you seem more beautiful every day. What wonderful, lovely hair! What marvelous eyes! I'll take you away tomorrow. We'll work, we'll be rich, my dreams will come to life again. And you'll be happy! But—there's only one "but," only one—you don't love me!

IRINA   I can't help that! I'll be your wife. I'll be loyal and obedient to you, but I can't love you. What's to be done? [*weeps*] I've never loved anyone in my life. Oh, I've had such dreams about being in love! I've been dreaming about it for ever so long, day and night. But somehow my soul seems like an expensive piano that someone has locked up and the key's gotten lost. [*pause*] Your eyes are so restless.

TUTZENBACH   I was awake all night. Not that there's anything to be afraid of in my life, nothing threatening. Only the thought of that lost key torments me and keeps me awake. Say something to me. [*pause*] Say something!

IRINA   What? What am I to say? What?

TUTZENBACH   Anything.

IRINA   Don't, my dear, don't.

TUTZENBACH   Such trifles, such silly little things, sometimes become so important suddenly for no apparent reason! You laugh at them, just as you always have done, you still regard them as trifles, and yet you suddenly find they're in control, and you haven't the power to stop them. But let's not talk about all that! Really I feel quite elated. I feel as if I were seeing those fir trees and maples and birches for the first time in my life. They all seem to be looking at me with a sort of inquisitive look and waiting for something. What beautiful trees— and how beautiful, when you think of it, life ought to be with trees like these!

Shouts of "ah-hoo, yoo-hoo!" are heard

I must go; it's time. Look at that dead tree; it's all dried up, but it's still swaying in the wind along with the others. And in the same way, it seems to me that, if I die, I will still have a share in life somehow or other. Good-bye, my dear. [*kisses her hands*] Your papers, the ones you gave me, are on my desk, under the calendar.

IRINA   I'm coming with you.

TUTZENBACH   [*Alarmed*] No, no! [*goes off quickly, then stops in the avenue*] Irina!

IRINA   What?

TUTZENBACH   [*Not knowing what to say*] I didn't have any cof-

fee this morning. Will you tell them to get some ready for me?
[*goes off quickly*]

*Irina stands lost in thought, then goes to the back of the stage
and sits down on a swing. Enter Andrei with the carriage.
Ferapont appears*

FERAPONT   Andrei Sergeevich, the papers aren't mine, you
know; they're the office papers. I didn't make them up.

ANDREI   Oh, where has all my past life gone to? The time when I
was young and gay and clever, when I used to have fine
dreams and great thoughts, and the present and the future
were bright with hope? Why do we become so dull and commonplace and uninteresting almost before we've begun to live?
Why do we get lazy, indifferent, useless, unhappy? This town's
been in existence for two hundred years; a hundred thousand
people live in it, but there's not one who's any different from
all the others! There's never been a scholar or an artist or a
saint in this place, never a single man sufficiently outstanding
to make you feel passionately that you wanted to emulate him.
People here do nothing but eat, drink, and sleep. Then they die
and some more take their places, and they eat, drink, and sleep
too. And just to introduce a bit of variety into their lives, so
they'll avoid getting completely stupid with boredom, they indulge in their disgusting gossip and vodka and gambling and
lawsuits. The wives deceive their husbands, and the husbands
lie to their wives and pretend they don't see anything and don't
hear anything. And all this overwhelming vulgarity and petti-
ness crushes the children and puts out any spark they might
have in them, so that they too become miserable, half-dead
creatures, just like one another and just like their parents! [*to
Ferapont, curtly*] What do you want?

FERAPONT   What? Here are the papers to sign.

ANDREI   What a nuisance you are!

FERAPONT   [*Hands him the papers*] The porter at the finance department told me just now; he said last winter they had two
hundred degrees of frost in Petersburg.

ANDREI   I hate the life I live at present, but oh, the sense of ela-
tion when I think of the future! Then I feel so lighthearted,

such a sense of release! I seem to see light ahead, light and freedom. I see myself free, and my children too—free from idleness, free from kvass, free from eternal meals of goose and cabbage, free from afterdinner naps, free from all this degrading parasitism!

FERAPONT   They say two thousand people were frozen to death. They say everyone was scared stiff. It was either in Petersburg or in Moscow; I can't remember exactly.

ANDREI   [*With sudden emotion, tenderly*] My dear sisters, my dear good sisters! [*tearfully*] Masha, my dear sister!

NATASHA   [*Through the window*] Who's that talking so loudly there? Is that you, Andryusha? You'll wake Sofochka. *Il ne faut pas faire du bruit; la Sophie est déjà dormie. Vous êtes un ours.* [*getting angry*] If you want to talk, give the baby buggy to someone else. Ferapont, take the carriage from the master.

FERAPONT   Yes, madam. [*takes the carriage*]

ANDREI   [*Embarrassed*] I was talking quietly.

NATASHA   [*In the window, caressing her small son*] Bobik! Naughty Bobik! Aren't you a naughty boy!

ANDREI   [*Glancing through the papers*] All right, I'll go through them and sign them if they need it. You can take them back to the office later. [*goes into the house, reading the papers*]

Ferapont wheels the carriage into the garden

NATASHA   [*In the window*] What's Mommy's name, Bobik? You darling! And who's that lady? Auntie Olya. Say, "Hello, Auntie Olya."

Two street musicians, a man and a girl, enter and begin to play on a violin and a harp. Vershinin, Olga, and Anfisa come out of the house and listen in silence for a few moments. Then Irina approaches them

OLGA   Our garden's like a public road; everybody goes through it. Nanny, give something to the musicians.

ANFISA   [*Giving them money*] Go along now. God bless you, good people!

The musicians bow and go away

Poor, homeless folk! Whoever would go dragging around the streets playing tunes if he had enough to eat? [*to Irina*] How are you, Irenushka? [*kisses her*] Ah, my child, what a life I'm having! Such comfort! In a large flat at the school with Olyushka—and no rent to pay either! The Lord's been kind to me in my old age. I've never had such a comfortable time in my life, old sinner that I am! A big flat, and no rent to pay, and a whole room to myself, with my own bed. All free. Sometimes when I wake up in the night I begin to think, and then—Oh, Lord! Oh, Holy Mother of God!—there's no one happier in the world than me!

VERSHININ [*Glances at his watch*] We will be starting in a moment, Olga Sergeevna. It's time I went. [*pause*] I wish you all the happiness in the world. . . . Everything. Where's Marya Sergeevna?

IRINA She's somewhere in the garden. I'll go and look for her.

VERSHININ That's kind of you. I really must hurry.

ANFISA I'll come and help to look for her. [*calls out*] Mashenka, yoo-hoo! [*goes with Irina toward the far end of the garden*] Yoo-hoo! Yoo-hoo!

VERSHININ Everything comes to an end. Well, here we are— and now it's going to be good-bye. [*looks at his watch*] The city gave us a sort of farewell lunch. There was champagne, and the mayor made a speech, and I ate and listened, but in spirit I was with you here. [*glances around the garden*] I've grown so . . . so accustomed to you.

OLGA Will we meet again some day I wonder?

VERSHININ Most likely not! [*pause*] My wife and the two little girls will be staying on here for a month or two. Please, if anything happens, if they need anything . . .

OLGA Yes, yes, of course. You needn't worry about that. [*pause*] Tomorrow there won't be a single officer or soldier in the town. All that will be just a memory, and, of course, a new life will begin for us here. [*pause*] Nothing ever happens as we'd like it to. I didn't want to be a headmistress, and yet now I am one. It means we won't be going to live in Moscow.

VERSHININ Well, thank you for everything. Forgive me if ever I've done anything. . . . I've talked a lot too much, far too much. Forgive me for that; don't think too unkindly of me.

OLGA [*Wipes her eyes*] Now . . . why is Masha so long in coming?

VERSHININ What else can I tell you now that it's time to say good-bye? What shall I philosophize about now? [*laughs*] Yes, life is difficult. It seems quite hopeless for a lot of us, just a kind of impasse. And yet you must admit that it is gradually getting easier and brighter, and it's clear that the time isn't far off when the light will spread everywhere. [*looks at his watch*] Time, it's time for me to go. In the old days the human race was always making war; its entire existence was taken up with campaigns, advances, retreats, victories. But now all that's out of date, and in its place there's a huge vacuum, clamoring to be filled. Humanity is passionately seeking something to fill it with and, of course, it will find something some day. Oh, if only it would happen soon! [*pause*] If only we could educate the industrious people and make the educated people industrious. [*looks at his watch*] I really must go.

OLGA Here she comes!

Enter Masha

VERSHININ I've come to say good-bye.

Olga walks off and stands a little to one side so as not to interfere with their parting

MASHA [*Looking into his face*] Good-bye! [*a long kiss*]

OLGA That'll do, that'll do.

Masha sobs loudly

VERSHININ Write to me. Don't forget me! Let me go. . . . It's time. Olga Sergeevna, please take her away. . . . I must go. . . . I'm late already. [*deeply moved, kisses Olga's hands, then embraces Masha once again, and goes out quickly*]

OLGA That'll do, Masha! Don't, my dear, don't.

Enter Kulygin

KULYGIN [*Embarrassed*] Never mind, let her cry, let her. My dear Masha, my dear, sweet Masha. You're my wife, and I'm happy in spite of everything. I'm not complaining; I've no reproach to make—not a single one. Olga here is my witness. We'll start our life over again in the same old way, and you won't hear a word from me . . . not a hint.

MASHA [*Suppressing her sobs*] "A green oak grows by a curving shore, and round that oak hangs a golden chain . . ." A golden chain round that oak. . . . Oh, I'm going mad. By a curving shore . . . a green oak . . .

OLGA Calm yourself, Masha, calm yourself. Give her some water.

MASHA I'm not crying anymore.

KULYGIN She's not crying anymore. She's a good girl.

The hollow sound of a gunshot is heard in the distance

MASHA "A green oak grows by a curving shore, and round that oak hangs a golden chain . . ." A green cat . . . A green oak . . . I've got it all mixed up. [*drinks water*] My life's messed up. . . . I don't want anything now. . . . I'll calm down in a moment. . . . It doesn't matter. . . . What *is* "the curving shore"? Why does it keep coming into my head all the time? My thoughts are all mixed up.

Enter Irina

OLGA Calm down, Masha. That's right. . . . Good girl! Let's go indoors.

MASHA [*Irritably*] I'm not going in there! [*sobs, but immediately checks herself*] I won't go into that house now, and I'm not going to . . .

IRINA Let's sit down together for a moment and not talk about anything. I'm going away tomorrow, you know. . . .

KULYGIN [*After a pause*] Yesterday I took away a false beard and a mustache from a boy in the third grade. I've got them here. [*puts them on*] Do I look like our German teacher? [*laughs*] I do, don't I? The boys are funny.

MASHA It's true, you do look like that German of yours.

OLGA [*Laughs*] Yes, he does.

Masha cries

IRINA That's enough, Masha!

KULYGIN Very much like him, I think!

Enter Natasha

NATASHA [*To the maid*] What? Oh, yes. Mr. Protopopov is going to keep an eye on Sofochka, and Andrei Sergeevich is going to take Bobik out in the baby buggy. What a lot of work these children make! [*to Irina*] Irina, you're really leaving tomorrow? What a pity! Stay just another week, won't you? [*catching sight of Kulygin, shrieks; he laughs and takes off the false beard and mustache*] Get away with you! How you scared me! [*to Irina*] I've grown so accustomed to you being here. You mustn't think it's going to be easy for me to be without you. I'll get Andrei and his old violin to move into your room: he can saw away at it as much as he likes there. And then we'll move Sofochka into his room. She's such a wonderful child, really! Such a lovely little girl! This morning she looked at me with such a sweet expression, and then she said, "Mamma!"

KULYGIN It's quite true; she is a beautiful child.

NATASHA So tomorrow I'll be alone here. [*sighs*] I'll have this fir tree avenue cut down first, then that maple tree over there. It looks so awful in the evenings. [*to Irina*] My dear, that belt you're wearing doesn't suit you at all. Not at all good taste. You want something brighter to go with that dress. I'll tell them to put flowers all around here, lots of flowers, so that we get plenty of scent from them. [*sternly*] Why is there a fork lying on this seat? [*going into the house, to the maid*] Why is that fork left on the seat there? [*shouts*] Don't answer me back!

KULYGIN There she goes again!

A band plays a military march offstage. All listen

OLGA They're going.

Enter Chebutykin

MASHA The soldiers are going. Well, happy journey to them! [*to her husband*] We must go home. Where's my hat and cape?

KULYGIN I took them indoors. I'll bring them at once.

OLGA Yes, we can go home now. It's time.

CHEBUTYKIN Olga Sergeevna!

OLGA What is it? [*pause*] What?

CHEBUTYKIN Nothing. I don't know quite how to tell you. [*whispers into her ear*]

OLGA [*Frightened*] It can't be true!

CHEBUTYKIN Yes. . . . A bad business. I'm so tired. . . . Quite worn out. I don't want to say another word. [*with annoyance*] Anyway nothing matters!

MASHA What's happened?

OLGA [*Puts her arms around Irina*] What a dreadful day! I don't know how to tell you, dear.

IRINA What is it? Tell me quickly, what is it? For heaven's sake! [*cries*]

CHEBUTYKIN The baron's just been killed in a duel.

IRINA [*Cries quietly*] I knew it, I knew it.

CHEBUTYKIN [*Goes to the back of the stage and sits down*] I'm tired. [*takes a newspaper out of his pocket*] Let them cry for a bit. [*sings quietly to himself*] Tarara-boom-di-ay, I'm sitting on a tomb-di-ay. What difference does it make?

The three sisters stand huddled together

MASHA Oh, listen to that band! They're leaving us. . . . One of them's gone for good . . . forever! We're left alone . . . to start our lives all over again. We must go on living. . . . We must go on living.

IRINA [*Puts her head on Olga's breast*] Someday people will know why such things happen, and what the purpose of all this suffering is. Then there won't be any more riddles. Meanwhile we must go on living . . . and working. Yes, we must just go on working! Tomorrow I'll go away alone and teach in a school somewhere; I'll give my life to people who need it. It's autumn now, winter will soon be here, and the snow will cover everything. . . . But I'll go on working and working!

OLGA [*Puts her arms around both her sisters*] How cheerfully and jauntily that band's playing—really I feel as if I wanted to live! Merciful God! The years will pass, and we will all be gone for good and quite forgotten. Our faces and our voices will be forgotten and people won't even know that there were once three of us here. But our sufferings may mean happiness for the people who come after us. There'll be a time when peace and happiness reign in the world, and then we will be remembered kindly and blessed. No, my dear sisters, life isn't finished for us yet! We're going to live! The band is playing so cheerfully and joyfully—maybe if we wait a little longer, we will find out why we live, why we suffer. . . . Oh, if we only knew, if only we knew!

The music grows fainter and fainter. Kulygin, smiling happily, brings out the hat and the cape. Andrei enters; he is pushing the carriage with Bobik sitting in it

CHEBUTYKIN [*Sings quietly to himself*] Tarara-boom-di-ay . . . I'm sitting on a tomb-di-ay. [*reads the paper*] What does it matter? Nothing matters!

OLGA   If only we knew, if only we knew!

CURTAIN

UNCLE VANYA

CHARACTERS

SEREBRYAKOV, Aleksandr Vladimirovich, a retired professor

YELENA ANDREYEVNA (*Hélène Lenochka*), his wife, aged twenty-seven

SONYA (*Sofya Aleksandrovna, Sonechka, Sonyushka*), his daughter by his first wife

VOYNITSKAYA, Marya Vasilievna, widow of a privy councillor and mother of the professor's first wife

VOYNITSKI, Ivan Petrovich (*Vanya*), her son

ASTROV, Mikhail Lvovich, a doctor

TELEGIN, Ilya Ilyich (*nicknamed "Waffles"*), a landowner reduced to poverty

MARINA TIMOFEEVNA, an old children's nurse

A WORKMAN

The action takes place on Serebryakov's estate

ACT ONE

A garden. Part of a house with a terrace can be seen. There is a table set for tea under an old poplar in the avenue. Garden seats and chairs; on one of them lies a guitar. Not far from the table there is a swing. It is between two and three o'clock in the afternoon. The sky is overcast.

Marina, a small, plump, slow-moving, elderly woman, is sitting beside the samovar, knitting a stocking. Astrov is pacing up and down the avenue near her.

MARINA [*Pours out a glass of tea*] Here, drink it, dearie.

ASTROV [*Reluctantly accepting the glass*] I don't feel like it somehow.

MARINA Perhaps you'd like a drop of vodka?

ASTROV No. I don't drink vodka every day. It's too close anyway. [*pause*] By the way, Nanny, how many years have we known each other?

MARINA [*Pondering*] How many? The Lord help my memory. You came to live around here . . . Well, when was it? Sonechka's mother, Vera Petrovna, was still living then. You came to see us for two winters when she was alive. . . . That means at least eleven years have gone by. [*after a moment's thought*] Maybe more.

ASTROV Have I changed a lot since then?

MARINA Yes, a lot. You were young and handsome then, but you've aged now. And you're not as good-looking as you were. There's another thing too—you take a drop of vodka now and again.

ASTROV Yes. In ten years I've become a different man. And what's the cause of it? I've been working too hard, Nanny. I'm on my feet from morning till night; I never have any peace. At night as I lie under the blankets I feel afraid all the time that I may be dragged out to see a patient. During the whole time you and I have known each other I haven't had a single day free. How could I help aging? Besides, the life itself is tedious, stupid, squalid. This sort of life drags you down. You're surrounded by queer people—they're a queer lot, all of them—and after you've lived with them for a year or two, you gradually become queer yourself, without noticing it. That's inevitable. [*twisting his long mustache*] Ugh, what a huge mustache I've grown. Silly mustache! I've become an eccentric, Nanny. I haven't grown stupid yet, thank God! My brains are still functioning all right, but my feelings are somewhat duller. I don't wish for anything, I don't feel I need anything, I don't love anybody. Except you perhaps; I believe I'm fond of you. [*kisses her on the head*] I had a nanny like you when I was a child.

MARINA Wouldn't you like something to eat?

ASTROV No. You know, in the first week of Lent I went to Malitskoye, because of the epidemic—spotted typhus. In the houses you could hardly move for sick people. Dirt, stench, and smoke everywhere . . . and calves mixed up with the sick on the floor. Young pigs there as well. I struggled with it all day—hadn't a moment to sit down or to swallow a bit of food. But would they let me rest when I got home? No, they brought me a signalman from the railway. I laid him on the table to operate, and he went and died on me under the chloroform. And just when I least wanted it my feelings seemed to wake up again, and my conscience began to worry me as if I had killed him deliberately. I sat down, closed my eyes—just like this—and I started to think. I wondered whether the people who come after us in a hundred years' time, the people for whom we are now blasting a trail—would they remember us and speak kindly of us? No, Nanny, I'll wager they won't!

MARINA   If people won't remember, God will.

ASTROV   Thank you. You've put it well.

VOYNITSKI   [*Comes out of the house. He has had a sleep after lunch and looks disheveled. He sits down on the garden seat and adjusts his smart tie*] Yes. [*pause*] Yes.

ASTROV   Had a good sleep?

VOYNITSKI   Yes . . . very good. [*yawns*] Since the professor and his consort came to live here, our usual routine has been completely upset. Now I sleep at the wrong time, I eat the wrong kinds of food at dinner and lunch, I drink wine; it's all bad for my health! In the past I never had a free moment—Sonya and I used to work like Trojans. But now only Sonya works while I just sleep, eat, and drink. It's a bad business!

MARINA   [*Nods her head disapprovingly*] Such goings-on! The professor gets up at midday, but the samovar is kept boiling the whole morning waiting for him. Before they came we always had dinner soon after twelve, like everybody else, but now they are here we have it after six in the evening. The professor spends the night reading and writing, and then suddenly, past one o'clock, the bell rings. My goodness, what is it? He wants some tea! So you've got to wake people up to heat the samovar. Such goings-on!

ASTROV   Are they going to stay here much longer?

VOYNITSKI   [*Whistles*] A hundred years maybe! The professor's decided to settle here.

MARINA   You see, it's just the same now. The samovar's been on the table for two hours, and they've gone for a walk.

VOYNITSKI   They're coming, they're coming! Don't fuss!

Voices are heard. Serebryakov, Yelena Andreyevna, Sonya, and Telegin approach from the farther part of the garden, returning from their walk

SEREBRYAKOV   It was beautiful, beautiful! Wonderful scenery!

TELEGIN   Yes, Your Excellency, the views are remarkable.

SONYA   Tomorrow we'll go to the plantation, Papa. Would you like to?

VOYNITSKI   Tea's ready, my friends!

225

SEREBRYAKOV My friends, will you be good enough to send my tea to my study? I've something more I must do today.

SONYA I'm sure you will like it at the plantation.

Yelena Andreyevna, Serebryakov, and Sonya go into the house. Telegin goes to the table and sits down beside Marina

VOYNITSKI It's hot and close, but our great man of learning has got his overcoat and galoshes on, and he's carrying his umbrella and gloves.

ASTROV He's obviously taking care of himself.

VOYNITSKI But how lovely *she* is! How lovely! I've never seen a more beautiful woman in all my life.

TELEGIN You know, Marina Timofeevna, whether I'm driving through the fields or taking a walk in a shady garden or even just looking at this table—I feel inexpressibly happy! The weather is marvelous, the birds are singing, and we all live here in peace and harmony. What more do we need? [*taking the glass she hands him*] Thank you kindly.

VOYNITSKI [*Dreamily*] Her eyes . . . a wonderful woman!

ASTROV Tell us something, Ivan Petrovich.

VOYNITSKI [*Listlessly*] What do you want me to tell you?

ASTROV Isn't there anything new?

VOYNITSKI Nothing at all. Everything's old. I'm just the same as I was—perhaps worse, because I've grown lazy. I don't do anything; I just grumble like some old fogey. As for my *maman*, the old magpie still goes on chattering about the emancipation of women. With one eye she looks into her grave and with the other she studies her learned books looking for the dawn of a new life.

ASTROV And the professor?

VOYNITSKI And the professor, as usual, sits in his study writing from morning till dead of night. "With furrowed brows and thought intense, we write and write our odes immense, but no praise ever comes our way for what we are, or what we say." I feel sorry for the paper he writes on! It would be better if he wrote his autobiography! What a superb subject! A retired professor—don't you see?—a dull old stick, a sort of scholarly dried fish. Afflicted with gout, rheumatism, migraine; his liver swollen with jealousy and envy. This dried fish is living on his first wife's country estate, living there against his will, because he can't afford to live in town. He's forever complaining about his misfortunes, though as a matter of fact he's been extraordinarily lucky. [*becoming excited*] Just think how lucky! The son of a common sexton, trained as a priest, he somehow managed to get university qualifications and a professorship. Later he became "Your Excellency" and the son-in-law of a senator, and so on and so forth. However, all that's not the main thing. Just consider this. The man has been lecturing and writing about art for exactly twenty-five years, and yet he understands nothing whatever about art. For twenty-five years he has been chewing over other people's ideas about realism, naturalism, and all that sort of nonsense. For twenty-five years he has been lecturing and writing about things that intelligent people have known all the time and stupid people aren't interested in anyway. In fact, for twenty-five years he's been just wasting time and energy. And yet what an opinion of himself! What pretensions! Now he's retired and not a living soul is aware of him. Today he is completely unknown, and that simply means that for twenty-five years he's been occupying a place to which he wasn't in the least entitled. But just look at him—he struts around like a little tin god!

ASTROV Come now, I believe you envy him.

VOYNITSKI Yes, I do envy him! And what a success with women! No Don Juan ever experienced success as complete as his. My sister, his first wife—a beautiful, gentle creature, as pure as that blue sky, generous and noblehearted, who had more admirers than he has ever had pupils—loved him as only innocenthearted angels can love beings as pure and beautiful as themselves. My mother still adores him; he still inspires her with a feeling of reverent awe. His second wife—you've just seen her; she's intelligent and a beauty—married him when he was already an old man. She gave him her youth, beauty, freedom—her whole brilliant personality. Whatever for? Why?

ASTROV Is she faithful to the professor?

VOYNITSKI I am sorry to say she is.

ASTROV But why should you be sorry?

VOYNITSKI Because that sort of loyalty is false from beginning

227

to end. There's plenty of rhetoric in it, but no logic. To be unfaithful to an old husband whom she couldn't bear would be immoral; but to do her utmost to stifle within her all her youth, her vitality, her capacity to feel—that is not immoral!

TELEGIN [*Tearfully*] Vanya, I don't like it when you say these things. Come, really! Anyone who can betray a wife or a husband is an unreliable person who might betray his own country too!

VOYNITSKI [*With annoyance*] You dry up, Waffles!

TELEGIN Forgive me, Vanya. My wife ran away from me the day after our wedding with a man she loved, because of my unprepossessing appearance. But even after that I never failed in my duty toward her. I still love her, I'm faithful to her, I help her as much as I can, and I've spent all I possessed on educating the children she had by the man she loved. I've lost my happiness, but I've still got my pride. And what about her? Her youth is gone, her beauty has faded, as nature ordains that it must, the man she loved has died. What has she got left?

Enter Sonya and Yelena Andreyevna. Shortly after Marya Vasilievna enters with a book. She sits down and reads. Tea is put before her; she drinks it without looking up

SONYA [*Hurriedly to the nurse*] Nanny, some peasants have come to the door. Please go and talk to them, and I'll see to the tea myself. [*pours out tea*]

The nurse goes out. Yelena Andreyevna takes her tea and drinks it sitting on the swing

ASTROV [*To Yelena Andreyevna*] You know I've come to see your husband. You wrote and told me that he was very ill—rheumatism and something else—but I find that he's perfectly well.

YELENA Last night he was depressed and complained of pains in his legs, but today he seems all right.

ASTROV And I've galloped twenty miles at breakneck speed to get here. Well, never mind, it's not the first time. At least I can

stay with you till tomorrow and get as much sleep as I need
—*quantum satis*.

SONYA   That's splendid. It's so rare for you to stay the night with
us. I don't suppose you've had dinner?

ASTROV   No, I haven't.

SONYA   Then you'll dine with us. We have dinner soon after six
nowadays. [*drinks her tea*] The tea's cold!

TELEGIN   There's been a big fall in the temperature of the samovar.

YELENA   Never mind, Ivan Ivanovich, we will drink it cold.

TELEGIN   Excuse me. My name's not Ivan Ivanovich; it's Ilya
Ilyich . . . Ilya Ilyich Telegin, or as some people call me on
account of my spotty face, Waffles. I'm Sonechka's godfather
and His Excellency, your husband, knows me very well. I'm
now living here on your estate. You may have been so kind as
to notice that I have dinner with you every day.

SONYA   Ilya Ilyich is our helper, our right-hand man. [*tenderly*]
Let me pour you out some tea, Godfather dear.

MARYA   Oh!

SONYA   What's the matter, Grandmamma?

MARYA   I forgot to tell Aleksandr. I'm losing my memory. I had
a letter today from Pavel Alekseevich, from Kharkov. He sent
us his new pamphlet.

ASTROV   Is it interesting?

MARYA   It's interesting, but somehow strange. He disproves the
very thing he was maintaining seven years ago. That's dreadful!

VOYNITSKI   There's nothing dreadful in that. Drink your tea,
Maman.

MARYA   But I want to talk!

VOYNITSKI   But we've been talking and talking and reading
pamphlets for the last fifty years! It's about time to stop.

MARYA   For some reason you don't like listening when I talk.
Forgive my saying so, Jean, but you've changed so much in the
last year or so that I positively don't recognize you. You used
to be a man with definite convictions, an inspiring personality.

VOYNITSKI   Oh, yes! I used to be an inspiring personality who
never inspired anybody! [*pause*] I used to be an inspiring per-

sonality! You could hardly have made a more wounding joke! I'm forty-seven now. Up to a year ago I tried deliberately to pull the wool over my eyes—just as you do yourself with the aid of all your pedantic rubbish—so that I wouldn't see the realities of life. And I thought I was doing the right thing. But now—if you only knew! I lie awake, night after night, in sheer vexation and anger that I let time slip by so stupidly during the years when I could have had all the things from which my age now cuts me off.

SONYA Uncle Vanya, this is boring!

MARYA [*To Voynitski*] You seem to be blaming those former principles of yours for something or other. It isn't they but you who are to blame. You're forgetting that principles are nothing in themselves—just empty phrases. You ought to have done something that mattered.

VOYNITSKI Something that mattered? It isn't everyone who's capable of being a nonstop writer like your *Herr* Professor.

MARYA What do you mean by that?

SONYA [*Imploringly*] Grandmamma! Uncle Vanya! I entreat you!

VOYNITSKI I'll be quiet. I'll hold my tongue . . . and apologize. . . .

YELENA [*After a pause*] What a lovely day! Not too hot either.

VOYNITSKI It would even be pleasant to hang oneself on a day like this.

Telegin tunes the guitar. Marina walks back and forth near the house, calling the chickens

MARINA Here, chick, chick, chick!

SONYA Nanny, what did the peasants come for?

MARINA The same as before—they are still going on about the wasteland. Chick, chick, chick . . .

SONYA Which is it you're calling?

MARINA The speckled one. She's gone off somewhere with her chicks. The crows might get them. [*walks away*]

Telegin plays a polka. All listen in silence. Enter a workman

THE WORKMAN   Is the doctor here? [*to Astrov*] Mikhail Lvovich, they've come for you, please.

ASTROV   Where from?

THE WORKMAN   From the factory.

ASTROV   [*With annoyance*] Many thanks! Well, I'll have to go.
[*looks around for his cap*] Hang it! What a nuisance!

SONYA   It really is annoying. Come back to dinner from the factory.

ASTROV   No, it'll be too late. How could I anyway? How could
I? [*to the workman*] My good fellow, you might get me a glass
of vodka or something.

The workman goes out

How could I anyway? How could I? [*finds his cap*] In a play
by Ostrovski there's a man with a big mustache but very little
brain. That's me. Well, I'll bid you all good-bye. [*to Yelena*] If
you ever cared to look me up—with Sofya Aleksandrovna
here—I'd be so pleased. I've a small estate, about ninety acres
altogether, but if you're interested, there's a model orchard
and nursery such as you won't find for hundreds of miles
around. And next to my place there's a plantation belonging to
the government. The forester there is old and he often gets ill,
so that in fact I'm in charge of everything.

YELENA   Yes, I've been told that you're very fond of forestry. Of
course, you can do a lot of good that way, but doesn't it interfere with your real vocation? You are a doctor, after all.

ASTROV   Only God knows what our real vocation is.

YELENA   Is it interesting?

ASTROV   Yes, it's interesting work.

VOYNITSKI   [*Ironically*] It must be.

YELENA   [*To Astrov*] You're still a young man. You don't look
more than . . . well, thirty-six or thirty-seven. I doubt
whether you find it as interesting as you say. Nothing but trees
and trees. I would think it must be monotonous.

SONYA   No, it's extremely interesting. Mikhail Lvovich puts
down new plantations every year, and he's already been
awarded a bronze medal and a diploma. He does his best to

stop the old forests from being laid waste. If you'd only listen to him, you'd understand what he means and agree with him. He says that forests add beauty to the country, that they teach men to appreciate beauty and induce lofty emotions. Forests make a harsh climate milder. In countries with a mild climate people spend less energy in the struggle with nature, and so man is gentler and more capable of tender feeling. In such countries people are beautiful, sensitive, and flexible in spirit. Their speech is elegant; their movements, graceful. Science and the fine arts flourish among them; their philosophy is cheerful and there is great refinement and courtesy in their attitude toward women.

VOYNITSKI [*Laughing*] Bravo, bravo! This is all very charming, but it isn't convincing. [*to Astrov*] And so, my friend, you must allow me to go on burning logs in my stoves and building my barns of wood!

ASTROV   You can burn turf in your stoves and build your barns out of stone. Well, I would consent to cutting wood when people really need it, but why destroy the forests? The Russian forests are literally groaning under the ax, millions of trees are being destroyed, the homes of animals and birds are being laid waste, the rivers are getting shallow and drying up, wonderful scenery is disappearing forever—and all this is happening just because people are too lazy and stupid to stoop down and pick up the fuel from the ground. [*to Yelena*] Isn't it so, madam? Anyone who can burn up all that beauty in a stove, who can destroy something that we cannot create, must be a barbarian incapable of reason. Man is endowed with reason and creative power so that he can increase what has been given him, but up to the present he's been destroying and not creating. There are fewer and fewer forests, the rivers are drying up, the wild creatures are almost exterminated, the climate is being ruined, and the land is getting poorer and more hideous every day. [*to Voynitski*] I can see your ironic expression, and I believe that what I say doesn't seem at all serious to you, and . . . and maybe it is just crankiness. All the same when I go walking by the woods that belong to the peasants, the woods I saved from being cut down, or when I hear the rustling of the young trees I planted with my own hands, I'm conscious of the fact that the climate is to some extent in my power too, and that if mankind is happy in a thousand years' time, I'll be responsible for it even though only to a very minute extent. When I plant a little birch tree and then see it growing green and swaying in the wind, my heart fills with pride, and I . . . [*sees the workman who has brought a glass of vodka on a tray*] However . . . [*drinks*] It's time for me to go. After all that's probably just my crankiness. Permit me to take my leave! [*goes toward the house*]

SONYA [*Takes his arm and walks with him*] When are you coming to see us then?

ASTROV I don't know.

SONYA Not for another month again?

Astrov and Sonya go into the house. Marya Vasilievna and Telegin remain beside the table. Yelena Andreyevna and Voynitski walk toward the terrace

YELENA And you have been behaving abominably again, Ivan Petrovich. Did you have to irritate Marya Vasilievna with your talk about "nonstop writers"? And at lunch today you argued with Aleksandr again. How petty it all is!

VOYNITSKI But if I detest him?

YELENA There is nothing you can detest Aleksandr for—he's just like anyone else. He's no worse than you are.

VOYNITSKI If only you could see your face, your movements! You give the impression that life is too much of an effort for you. Oh, such an effort!

YELENA Oh, yes, such an effort and such a bore! Everyone blames my husband. Everyone looks at me with compassion: an unfortunate woman—she's got an old husband! This sympathy for me—oh, how well I understand it! As Astrov said just now: you go on destroying the forests senselessly, and soon there won't be anything left on the earth. Just in the same way you senselessly ruin human beings, and soon, thanks to you, there will be no loyalty, no integrity, no capacity for self-sacrifice left. Why can't you look at a woman with indifference unless she's yours? Because—that doctor is right—there's a devil of destruction in every one of you. You spare neither woods nor birds nor women nor one another.

VOYNITSKI   I don't like this sort of philosophy!

YELENA   [*After a pause*] The doctor has a tired, sensitive face. An interesting face. Sonya is obviously attracted by him; she's in love with him, and I understand her feelings. He's visited the house three times since I've been here, but I'm shy and I haven't once had a proper talk with him or been nice to him. He must have thought me bad-tempered. Perhaps, Ivan Petrovich, you and I are such good friends just because we both are such tiresome and boring people. Tiresome! Don't look at me like that; I don't like it!

VOYNITSKI   How else can I look at you if I love you? You are my happiness, my life, my youth! I know the chances of your returning my feelings are negligible, just zero. But I don't want anything—only let me look at you and hear your voice.

YELENA   Hush, they might hear you! [*they go into the house*]

VOYNITSKI   [*Following her*] Let me talk of my love. Don't drive me away; that in itself will be such great happiness to me.

YELENA   This is torture. [*both enter the house*]

Telegin strikes the strings of his guitar and plays a polka. Marya Vasilievna makes notes in the margin of her pamphlet

CURTAIN

ACT TWO

Dining room in Serebryakov's house. Nighttime; a watchman can be heard tapping in the garden. Serebryakov is sitting in an armchair in front of an open window, dozing. Yelena Andreyevna is sitting beside him, also dozing.

SEREBRYAKOV [*Waking up*] Who's that? Sonya, is it you?

YELENA It's me.

SEREBRYAKOV You, Lenochka. This pain's unbearable!

YELENA Your blanket's fallen onto the floor. [*wraps it around his legs*] I'll shut the window, Aleksandr.

SEREBRYAKOV No, I feel suffocated. I dozed off just now and I dreamed that my left leg didn't belong to me. I was woken up by an agonizing pain. No, it's not gout; it's more like rheumatism. What time is it now?

YELENA Twenty minutes past twelve. . . .

SEREBRYAKOV [*After a pause*] You might look up Batyushkov in the library in the morning. I believe we have his works.

YELENA What?

SEREBRYAKOV Look up Batyushkov in the morning. I seem to remember we had him. But why is it so difficult for me to breathe?

YELENA You're tired. This is the second night you haven't slept.

SEREBRYAKOV They say Turgenev got angina pectoris from gout. I'm afraid I might get it. This damnable, disgusting old age! The devil take it! Since I've aged so much I've become revolting even to myself. And you must find it revolting to look at me—all of you!

YELENA You talk of your old age in a tone of voice that suggests we're all to blame for it.

SEREBRYAKOV You are the first to find me repulsive.

Yelena gets up and sits down farther away

You are right, of course. I'm not a fool and I understand. You're young, healthy, good-looking; you want to live . . . whereas I am an old man, almost a corpse. Well. . . . Do you suppose I don't understand? Of course it's stupid of me to go on living. But wait a little while; I'll soon set you all free. I won't have to linger on much longer.

YELENA I'm worn out. For God's sake be quiet.

SEREBRYAKOV It looks as if everyone's worn out, bored, wasting their youth thanks to me—and I am the only one who's content and enjoying life. Yes, yes, of course!

YELENA Oh, do be quiet! You've worn me out!

SEREBRYAKOV I've worn everyone out. Of course!

YELENA [*Tearfully*] It's intolerable! Tell me: what is it you want from me?

SEREBRYAKOV Nothing at all.

YELENA Well, be quiet then. I implore you.

SEREBRYAKOV It's a strange business: when Ivan Petrovich starts talking, or that old idiot Marya Vasilievna, it's all right, and everyone listens. But I only have to say a single word, and everyone begins to feel miserable. Even my voice disgusts them. Well, I suppose I am disgusting—an egoist, a despot. But haven't I a right to be selfish in my old age? Haven't I deserved it? I ask you, haven't I a right to a quiet old age, to a little personal attention?

YELENA No one is disputing your rights.

The window bangs in the wind

The wind's blowing up; I'll shut the window. [*shuts it*] It's going to rain presently. No one disputes your rights.

A pause. In the garden the watchman taps and starts singing

SEREBRYAKOV After devoting all my life to learning; after growing used to my study, to my lecture room, to esteemed colleagues—to find myself suddenly, for no reason at all, in this
crypt; to have to meet stupid people every day, to have to listen to their trivial conversation! I want to live, I love success, I
like being a well-known figure, I like creating a stir—but here
I feel an exile. To spend every minute regretting the past,
watching others succeed, fearing death. I can't! It's more than
I can bear! And they won't even forgive me for getting old!

YELENA Wait a little; have patience! In five or six years I will be
old too.

Enter Sonya

SONYA Papa, you told us to send for Doctor Astrov, and now
that he's come you refuse to see him. It's discourteous. We've
troubled him for nothing.

SEREBRYAKOV What do I need your Astrov for? He knows as
much about medicine as astronomy.

SONYA We can't send for the whole medical faculty to attend to
your gout.

SEREBRYAKOV I won't even speak to that crank.

SONYA Just as you please. [*sits down*] It's all the same to me.

SEREBRYAKOV What time is it now?

YELENA It's after midnight.

SEREBRYAKOV I'm suffocating. Sonya, hand me my drops from
the table.

SONYA Just a moment. [*hands him the drops*]

SEREBRYAKOV [*Irritably*] Oh, not those! It's no use asking for
anything!

SONYA Please don't be peevish. Some people may like it, but do
spare me, for goodness' sake! I don't like it. And I haven't the
time. I must get up early tomorrow; I've got to see to the hay-
making.

Enter Voynitski in a dressing gown with a candle in his hand

VOYNITSKI   There's a storm coming up.

A flash of lightning

There, did you see? Hélène and Sonya, do go to bed; I've come to take your place.

SEREBRYAKOV   [*Alarmed*] No, no! Don't leave me with him! Don't! He'll kill me with his talking!

VOYNITSKI   But they must have some rest! It's the second night they've had no sleep.

SEREBRYAKOV   Let them go to bed, but you go too. I'd be so grateful. I do implore you. For the sake of our past friendship, don't argue. We'll talk later on.

VOYNITSKI   [*With a sneer*] Our past friendship. Past . . .

SONYA   Be quiet, Uncle Vanya.

SEREBRYAKOV   [*To his wife*] My dear, don't leave me alone with him. He'll kill me with his talking!

VOYNITSKI   This is becoming ridiculous.

Enter Marina with a candle

SONYA   You ought to go to bed, Nanny. It's late.

MARINA   The samovar hasn't been cleared away. I can't very well go to bed.

SEREBRYAKOV   Everyone's awake; everyone's worn out. Only I am thoroughly enjoying myself.

MARINA   [*Going up to Serebryakov, tenderly*] What is it, my dear? Your pain again? I've got a grumbling pain in my legs too—such a pain! [*tucks the blanket in*] It's that old trouble of yours. Vera Petrovna, Sonechka's mother, used to get so upset about it—she couldn't sleep nights. Ever so fond of you she was. [*pause*] The old are just the same as the little ones; they like someone to pity them—but nobody pities the old. [*kisses Serebryakov on the shoulder*] Come to bed, my dear. . . . Come, darling. I'll give you some lime-flower tea and warm your feet . . . and say a prayer for you.

SEREBRYAKOV   [*Moved*] Let us go, Marina.

MARINA   I've got such a grumbling pain in my legs myself, such a grumbler! [*she and Sonya lead him off*] Vera Petrovna used to get so upset, she used to cry over you. You were little then, Sonyushka; you didn't understand. . . . Come along, come along, sir.

Serebryakov, Sonya, and Marina go out

YELENA   I'm quite worn out with him. I can hardly keep on my feet.

VOYNITSKI   You with him, and I with myself. It's the third night I've had no sleep.

YELENA   Things have gone to pieces in this household. Your mother hates everything except her pamphlets and the professor. The professor is irritable; he doesn't trust me and is afraid of you. Sonya is bad-tempered with her father and angry with me: she hasn't spoken to me for two weeks. You detest my husband and openly despise your mother. I am on edge; I have been on the point of crying twenty times today. Things have gone wrong in this house.

VOYNITSKI   Let's leave philosophy out of it!

YELENA   You are cultured and intelligent, Ivan Petrovich. Surely you ought to realize that the world is being destroyed not by fire and pillage, but by hatred, enmity, and all this petty quarreling. Your job should be to reconcile people to one another and not to grumble.

VOYNITSKI   Reconcile me to myself first! Dearest. [*bends down impulsively and kisses her hand*]

YELENA   Don't! [*draws away her hand*] Go away!

VOYNITSKI   In a minute or two the rain will be over, and everything in nature will be refreshed and sigh with relief. Only I shall not be refreshed by the storm. Day and night I feel suffocated by the thought that my life has been irretrievably lost. I have no past—it has all been stupidly wasted on trifles—while the present is awful because it's so meaningless. My life, my love—look at them—where do they belong? What am I to do with them? My feeling for you is just wasted like a ray of sunlight falling into a well—and I am wasted too.

YELENA   When you talk to me of your love I feel quite stupid and I don't know what to say. Forgive me, there's nothing I can say to you. [*starting to go out*] Good night.

VOYNITSKI [*Barring her way*] And if you only knew how I suffer when I think that near to me, in the very same house, another life is being wasted—your life! What are you waiting for? What confounded philosophy is holding you back? Understand, do understand.

YELENA [*Looks at him intently*] Ivan Petrovich, you are drunk!

VOYNITSKI Maybe, maybe . . .

YELENA Where's the doctor?

VOYNITSKI He's in there. He's staying the night with me. It may be, it may be. Anything may be!

YELENA So you have been drinking again today! Whatever for?

VOYNITSKI At least it gives the illusion of life. Don't prevent me, Hélène.

YELENA You never used to drink and you never used to talk so much. Do go to bed! You bore me.

VOYNITSKI [*Impulsively kissing her hand*] Dearest. You wonderful woman!

YELENA [*With annoyance*] Leave me alone. This is really hateful! [*goes out*]

VOYNITSKI [*Alone*] She's gone. [*pause*] Ten years ago I used to meet her at my sister's house. She was seventeen then and I was thirty-seven. Why didn't I fall in love with her then and ask her to marry me? It could have been done so easily! She would have been my wife now. Yes . . . and we two might have been awakened by this storm; she would have been frightened by the thunder and I would have held her in my arms and whispered, "Don't be afraid; I'm here." Oh, what a wonderful thought! How enchanting! It actually makes me laugh with happiness. . . . But, oh, God! My thoughts are in a tangle. . . . Why am I so old? Why won't she understand me? Her fine phrases; her easy moralizing; her silly, facile ideas about the ruin of the world—how utterly hateful it all is to me! [*pause*] And how I've been cheated! I adored the professor, the gouty old invalid, and I worked like an ox for him! Sonya and I squeezed all we could out of this estate. Like tight-fisted peasants we traded in linseed oil, dried peas, and curds; we saved on our food so that we could scrape together kopecks and send him thousands of rubles. I was proud of him and his learning; he was the breath of my life! Everything he wrote or uttered seemed to me the work of a genius. . . . And now what, good God? He's retired down here, and now you can see what his life really amounts to. Not a page of his writing will survive him. He's completely unknown, a nonentity! A soap bubble! And I've been cheated. I see it now. . . . Stupidly cheated.

Enter Astrov, wearing a coat but without waistcoat or tie. He is slightly drunk. He is followed by Telegin with a guitar

ASTROV   Play us something!
TELEGIN   Everyone's gone to bed!
ASTROV   Come on! Play!

Telegin plays softly

[*to Voynitski*] Are you alone here? No ladies? [*putting his arms akimbo, sings quietly*] "Dance my hut and dance my fire; the master's nowhere to retire." The thunderstorm woke me up. A nice little rain! What time is it now?
VOYNITSKI   The devil knows!
ASTROV   I thought I heard Yelena Andreyevna's voice.
VOYNITSKI   She was in here a moment ago.
ASTROV   An exceptionally attractive woman! [*examines the medicine bottles on the table*] What a variety of medicines! From Kharkov, from Moscow, from Tula! He must have plagued every town in Russia with his gout. Is he really ill or faking it?
VOYNITSKI   He is ill. . . .
ASTROV   [*After a pause*] Why are you so depressed today? Are you feeling sorry for the professor or what?
VOYNITSKI   Leave me alone.
ASTROV   Or maybe you're in love with the professor's wife?
VOYNITSKI   She's my friend.
ASTROV   Already?
VOYNITSKI   What do you mean by "already"?
ASTROV   A woman can only become a man's friend in three stages: first she's an agreeable acquaintance, then a mistress, and only after that a friend.

VOYNITSKI   That's a crude sort of philosophy.

ASTROV   What? Well, yes. I must confess, I am becoming pretty crude. You see, I'm drunk too. As a rule I get drunk like this once a month. When I'm in this state I get extremely provocative and audacious. Then there's nothing I don't feel equal to! I undertake the most difficult operations and do them beautifully. I draw up the most far-reaching plans for the future! At such times I no longer think of myself as a crank; I believe that I'm doing a tremendous job for the good of mankind—tremendous! On these occasions too I have my own special system of philosophy according to which all of you, my good friends, appear as insignificant as insects or microbes. [*to Telegin*] Waffles, go on playing!

TELEGIN   My dear friend, I'd do anything for you, but do remember—everyone in the house has gone to bed!

ASTROV   Play, I tell you!

Telegin plays quietly

A drink would be nice. Come on, I believe there's still some brandy left. When it's daylight, shall we go to my place? All right with you? I've got an unqualified assistant who never says "all right" but always "aw-right." He's an awful rogue. Aw-right then? [*sees Sonya entering*] Excuse me, I haven't got my tie on. [*goes out quickly; Telegin follows him*]

SONYA   Uncle Vanya, so you got drunk again with the doctor? You're a fine pair! It's not becoming at your age!

VOYNITSKI   Age has nothing to do with it. When people have no real life, they live on their illusions. Anyway it's better than nothing.

SONYA   All the hay has been cut, it rains every day, everything is rotting, and you are living on illusions! You've been utterly neglecting the estate. I've had to work alone; I'm quite worn out. [*alarmed*] Uncle, there are tears in your eyes!

VOYNITSKI   Tears? It's nothing. . . . Nonsense! You looked at me then as your dear mother used to. My dearest girl! [*eagerly kisses her hands and face*] My sister . . . my dear sister. . . . Where is she now? If only she knew! Ah, if she only knew!

SONYA   What, Uncle? Knew what?

VOYNITSKI It's painful, wrong somehow. Never mind. . . . Later on . . . It's nothing. . . . I'll go. [*goes out*]

SONYA [*Knocks at the door*] Mikhail Lvovich! You're not asleep, are you? One minute!

ASTROV [*Through the door*] Coming! [*a moment later he comes out with his tie and waistcoat on*] What can I do for you?

SONYA You can drink yourself if you don't find it disgusting, but don't let my uncle drink, I implore you! It's bad for him.

ASTROV Very well. We won't drink any more. [*pause*] I will go home at once. That's settled and signed. It'll be daylight by the time they've got the horses ready.

SONYA It's still raining. Wait till the morning.

ASTROV The storm is passing us by; we'll only get a few drops. I'll go. And please don't ask me to see your father again. I tell him he has gout, and he tells me it's rheumatism; I ask him to stay in bed, and he sits up in a chair. And today he wouldn't even speak to me.

SONYA [*Looks into the sideboard*] Would you like something to eat?

ASTROV Well, perhaps.

SONYA I like having little snacks at night. I believe there's something in the sideboard. They say he's had great success with the women, and he's been spoiled by them. Here, have some cheese. [*both stand at the sideboard and eat*]

ASTROV I've had nothing to eat today, only drink. Your father is difficult. [*takes a bottle from the sideboard*] May I? [*drinks a glass*] There's no one here, and I can speak frankly. You know I don't believe I could stick it in your house for a month; I would be suffocated in this atmosphere. Your father, completely absorbed in his gout and his books; Uncle Vanya with his depression; your grandmother; and your stepmother too . . .

SONYA What about my stepmother?

ASTROV Everything ought to be beautiful about a human being: face, clothes, soul, and thoughts. She's beautiful, there's no denying that, but . . . she does nothing but eat, sleep, go for walks, charm us all by her beauty . . . nothing else. She has no responsibilities; other people work for her. Isn't that so? And an idle life can't be virtuous. [*pause*] However, perhaps

I'm being too severe. I'm dissatisfied with life, like your Uncle Vanya, and so we're both turning into old grumblers.

SONYA   You're dissatisfied with life then?

ASTROV   I love life as such—but our life, our everyday provincial life in Russia, I just can't endure. I despise it with all my soul. As for my own life, God knows I can find nothing good in it at all. You know when you walk through a forest on a dark night and you see a small light gleaming in the distance, you don't notice your tiredness nor the darkness nor the prickly branches lashing you in the face. I work harder than anyone in the district—you know that. Fate batters me continuously; at times I suffer unbearably—but there's no small light in the distance. I'm not expecting anything for myself any longer. I don't love human beings. I haven't cared for anyone for years.

SONYA   Not for anyone?

ASTROV   No one. I feel a sort of fondness for your old nurse—for old times' sake. The peasants are all too much alike—undeveloped, living in squalor. As for the educated people—it's hard to get on with them. They tire me so. All of them, all our good friends here are shallow in thought, shallow in feeling, unable to see farther than their noses—or to put it quite bluntly—stupid. And the ones who are a bit more intelligent, of a higher mental caliber, are hysterical, positively rotten with introspection and futile cerebration. They whine; they are full of hatreds and are morbidly malicious; they sidle up to a man, look at him out of the corner of their eyes, and pronounce their judgment: "Oh, he's a psychopath!" or "Just a phrasemonger." And when they don't know how to label me, they say, "He's a queer fellow, very queer!" I love forests—that's queer; I don't eat meat—that's queer too. There isn't any direct, objective, unprejudiced attitude to people or nature left. No, there isn't! [*about to drink*]

SONYA   [*Prevents him*] No, I beg you, I implore you, don't drink any more.

ASTROV   Why not?

SONYA   It's so unlike you! You have such poise; your voice is so soft. More than that, you are beautiful as no one else I know is beautiful. So why do you want to be like ordinary men, the kind who drink and play cards? Don't do it, I implore you! You always say that people don't create anything but merely destroy what has been given them from above. Then why, why are you destroying yourself? You mustn't, you mustn't, I beseech you, I implore you!

ASTROV [*Holds out his hand to her*] I won't drink any more!

SONYA Give me your word.

ASTROV My word of honor.

SONYA [*Presses his hand warmly*] Thank you!

ASTROV Enough! My head's clear now. You see I'm quite sober —and I'll stay sober to the end of my days. [*looks at his watch*] Well, to continue. As I said, my time's over; it's too late for me now. I've aged too much, I've worked myself to a standstill, I've grown coarse and insensitive. I believe I could never really become fond of another human being. I don't love anybody and . . . never will now. What still does affect me is beauty. I can't remain indifferent to that. I believe that if Yelena Andreyevna wanted to, for instance, she could turn my head in a day. But that's not love, of course; that's not affection. [*covers his eyes with his hand and shudders*]

SONYA What is it?

ASTROV Nothing. In Lent one of my patients died under chloroform.

SONYA It's time to forget about that. [*pause*] Tell me, Mikhail Lvovich. If I had a girl friend or a young sister and if you got to know that she . . . Well, suppose that she loved you, what would you do?

ASTROV [*Shrugging his shoulders*] I don't know. Probably nothing. I would let her know that I couldn't love her. Besides I've got too many other things on my mind. However, if I'm going, I'd better start now. I'll say good-bye, my dear girl, or we'll not finish till morning. [*shakes hands with her*] I'll go through the drawing room if I may, otherwise I'm afraid your uncle may keep me. [*goes out*]

SONYA [*Alone*] He didn't say anything to me. His soul and his heart are still hidden from me, so why do I feel so happy? [*laughs with happiness*] I told him: you have poise and nobility of mind and such a soft voice. Did it sound out of place? His voice vibrates and caresses. I can almost feel it in the air now. But when I said that to him about a younger sister, he didn't understand. [*wringing her hands*] Oh, how dreadful it is that I'm not good-looking! How dreadful! I know I'm plain, I know, I know! Last Sunday as people were coming out of church I heard them talking about me and a woman said, "She's kind and generous, but what a pity she is so plain." So plain.

Enter Yelena Andreyevna

YELENA [*Opens the windows*] The storm's over. What lovely fresh air! [*pause*] Where's the doctor?

SONYA He's gone. . . .

YELENA [*After a pause*] Sofya!

SONYA What?

YELENA How long are you going to go on being sulky with me? We haven't done each other any harm, so why should we behave like enemies? Come, let us stop it.

SONYA I wanted to myself. [*embraces her*] Yes, let's not be angry anymore.

YELENA That's fine! [*both are moved*]

SONYA Has Papa gone to bed?

YELENA No, he's sitting in the drawing room. We don't speak to each other for weeks on end, but heaven alone knows why. [*seeing that the sideboard is open*] What's this?

SONYA Mikhail Lvovich has been having supper.

YELENA There's wine too. Let's drink to our friendship.

SONYA Yes, let's.

YELENA Out of the same glass. [*fills it*] It's better like that. Now we are real friends?

SONYA Friends. [*they drink and kiss each other*] I've been wanting to make up for ever so long, but I felt so ashamed somehow. [*cries*]

YELENA But why are you crying?

SONYA Never mind. . . . There's no reason.

YELENA Come, there, there. [*cries*] I'm a queer creature—I've started crying too. [*pause*] You're angry with me because you think I married your father for ulterior motives. If you are impressed by oaths, I'll vow to you that I married him for love. I was attracted by him as a learned man, a celebrity. It wasn't real love; it was all artificial—but you see at that time it seemed real to me. I'm not to blame. But from the day of our marriage you've been punishing me with those shrewd, suspicious eyes of yours.

SONYA   Come, peace, peace! Let's forget about it!

YELENA   You mustn't look at people like that—it doesn't suit you. You should believe everyone—or else you just can't live. . . .

SONYA   [*After a pause*] Tell me honestly, as a friend. Are you happy?

YELENA   No.

SONYA   I knew that. One more question. Tell me frankly: wouldn't you have liked your husband to be young?

YELENA   What a little girl you are still! Of course I would. [*laughs*] Well, ask me something else, go ahead.

SONYA   Do you like the doctor?

YELENA   Yes, very much.

SONYA   [*Laughs*] Have I got a stupid face? Yes? He's gone, but I can still hear his voice and his footsteps, and when I glance at that dark window I can see his face in it. Let me tell you about it. But I mustn't speak so loudly; I feel ashamed. Come to my room; we'll talk there. Do I seem stupid to you? Own up. Tell me something about him.

YELENA   Well, what shall I tell you?

SONYA   He's so clever. He knows how to do things; he can do anything. He treats the sick, and he plants forests too.

YELENA   It isn't a question of forests or medicine. My dear, don't you understand? He's got talent! And do you know what that means? Courage, freedom of mind, breadth of outlook. He plants a tree and wonders what will come of it in a thousand years' time and speculates on the future happiness of mankind. Such people are rare, and we must love them. He drinks; sometimes he seems a little coarse—but what does it matter? A talented man can't stay free from blemishes in Russia. Just think what sort of life this doctor leads! Impassable mud on the roads; frost; snowstorms; vast distances; crude, primitive people; poverty and disease all around him—it's hard for a man who works and struggles day after day in such surroundings to keep pure and sober till he's forty. [*kisses her*] I wish you happiness with all my heart; you deserve it. [*gets up*] As for me, I'm just a tiresome person of no importance. In my music studies, in my home life, in my husband's house, in all my romantic affairs—in fact in everything I've just been a person of no importance. Really, Sonya, when you come to think of it, I'm a very, very unfortunate woman. [*walks about in agitation*] There's no happiness for me on this earth. None! Why do you laugh?

SONYA [*Laughs, hiding her face*] I am so happy. . . . So happy!

YELENA I would like to play something. I would like to play something now.

SONYA Do play! [*embraces her*] I can't sleep. Do play!

YELENA In a minute. Your father isn't asleep. When he's unwell, music irritates him. Go and ask him. If he doesn't mind, I'll play. Go.

SONYA I'm going. [*goes out*]

Watchman taps in the garden

YELENA It's a long time since I played the piano. I will play and cry. . . . Cry like a foolish girl. [*calling through the window*] Is it you tapping, Yefim?

WATCHMAN'S VOICE Yes, me.

YELENA Don't tap; the master's not well.

WATCHMAN'S VOICE I'm just going. [*whistles*] Hey there! Good dog! Come, boy! Good dog!

SONYA [*After a pause, returning*] We mustn't!

CURTAIN

ACT THREE

A drawing room in Serebryakov's house. Three doors, right, left, and center. Daytime.

Voynitski and Sonya are seated, and Yelena Andreyevna is walking about the stage, preoccupied.

VOYNITSKI   The *Herr* Professor has graciously expressed a wish that we should assemble in this drawing room at one o'clock. [*looks at his watch*] It is a quarter to. He wishes to make some communication to the world.

YELENA   Probably some business matter.

VOYNITSKI   He does no business of any kind. He just writes nonsense, grumbles, and feels jealous. He does nothing else.

SONYA   [*Reproachfully*] Uncle!

VOYNITSKI   Well, well, I apologize. [*pointing to Yelena*] Just look at her! She walks about staggering with sheer laziness. Wonderful! Wonderful!

YELENA   And you keep on droning away all the time, all day long! Aren't you tired of it? [*miserably*] I'm dying of boredom. I don't know what to do.

SONYA   [*Shrugging her shoulders*] Isn't there plenty to do? If only you wanted to . . .

YELENA   For instance?

SONYA   You could help in running the estate, teach children, help to look after the sick. Isn't there plenty to do? For instance, before you and Papa came to live here, Uncle Vanya and I used to go to the market ourselves and sell the flour.

YELENA I don't know how to. And I'm not interested. It's only in idealistic novels that people teach and doctor the peasants. How am I suddenly to start teaching and doctoring them for no earthly reason?

SONYA Well, I just don't understand how you can help wanting to go and teach them. Wait a little; you'll get accustomed to the idea. [*embraces her*] Don't get bored, dear! [*laughs*] You're bored and you don't know what to do with yourself, but boredom and idleness are infectious. Look: Uncle Vanya isn't doing anything either, just following you like a shadow, and I've left my work and come running to you to have a chat. I've grown quite lazy; I can't help it! The doctor, Mikhail Lvovich, only used to come to see us very rarely, once a month—it was hard to persuade him to come. But now he comes here every day; he's neglecting his forestry and his practice. You must be a witch.

VOYNITSKI Why be miserable? [*with enthusiasm*] Come, my dear, wonderful woman, be sensible! A mermaid's blood flows in your veins; so be a mermaid! Let yourself go for once in your life! Fall head over heels in love with some water sprite— and plunge headfirst into deep water, so that the *Herr* Professor and all of us just throw up our hands in amazement!

YELENA [*Angrily*] Leave me alone! How cruel all this is! [*is about to go out*]

VOYNITSKI [*Prevents her*] Come, come, my treasure, forgive me! I apologize. [*kisses her hand*] Peace!

YELENA Even an angel couldn't hold her patience with you, you know.

VOYNITSKI As a token of peace and harmony I'll bring you a bunch of roses; I've had them ready for you since this morning. Autumn roses; exquisite, mournful roses . . . [*goes out*]

SONYA Autumn roses; exquisite, mournful roses. . . . [*both look through the window*]

YELENA It's September already. How are we going to live through the winter here! [*pause*] Where's the doctor?

SONYA In Uncle Vanya's room. Writing something. I'm glad Uncle Vanya's gone. I must have a talk with you.

YELENA What about?

SONYA   What about! [*lays her head on Yelena's bosom*]

YELENA   Come, there, there. [*strokes her hair*] Don't . . .

SONYA   I'm not good-looking.

YELENA   You have beautiful hair.

SONYA   No! [*turns around to look at herself in a mirror*] No!
When a woman is plain, they always say, "You have beautiful
eyes, you have beautiful hair. . . ." I've loved him now for six
years; I love him more than I did my mother. Every moment I
seem to hear him, to feel his hand in mine; and I look at the
door, waiting, expecting him to come in at any moment. And
you can see how I keep coming to you just to talk about him.
Now he comes here every day, but he doesn't look at me—
doesn't see me. . . . It's such a torment! I have no hope at
all—none, none! [*in despair*] O Lord, give me strength. I've
been praying all night. . . . I often go up to him, start talking
to him, look into his eyes. I have no more pride, no strength
left to control myself. I couldn't help it—yesterday I confessed to Uncle Vanya that I'm in love. And all the servants
know that I love him.

YELENA   And he?

SONYA   He doesn't notice me.

YELENA   [*Musing*] He's a strange man. I've an idea. Let me have
a talk with him. I'll be careful; I'll do it in a roundabout way.
[*pause*] Yes, really. After all how much longer are you to remain in ignorance? Let me!

Sonya nods her head in consent

That's fine. It won't be difficult to find out whether he loves
you or not. You must not feel ashamed, darling. You don't
need to worry—I'll question him so carefully that he won't
notice. All we want is to find out whether it's yes or no. [*pause*]
If not, then he mustn't come here anymore, must he?

Sonya nods in agreement

It's easier to bear when you don't see him. We won't put it off;
I'll speak to him straight away. He was going to show me
some charts. Go and tell him that I want to see him.

SONYA   [*In great agitation*] You will tell me the whole truth?

YELENA   Yes, of course. I think it's better to know the truth whatever it may be. It's not so dreadful as being kept in ignorance. Trust me, dear.

SONYA   Yes, yes. I'll tell him that you want to see his charts. [*is about to go, then stops near the door*] No, ignorance is better. At least there's some hope.

YELENA   What do you say?

SONYA   Nothing. [*goes out*]

YELENA   [*Alone*] There's nothing worse than knowing someone's secret and not being able to help. [*musing*] He's not in love with her, that's obvious. But why shouldn't he marry her? She is not pretty, but she'd make an excellent wife for a country doctor at his time of life. She's intelligent and so kind and pure. No, that's not the point. [*pause*] I understand the poor girl so well. In the middle of all this desperate boredom, with just gray shadows wandering around instead of human beings, with nothing but commonplace gossip to listen to from people who do nothing but eat, drink, and sleep, he appears from time to time—so different from the rest of them, handsome, interesting, attractive, like a bright moon rising in the darkness. To fall under the fascination of a man like that, to forget oneself. I believe I'm a little attracted myself. Yes, I'm bored when he's not around, and here I am smiling when I think of him. Uncle Vanya says I have mermaid's blood in my veins. "Let yourself go for once in your life." Well, perhaps that's what I ought to do. To fly away, free as a bird, away from all of you, from your sleepy faces and talk, to forget that you exist at all—every one of you! . . . But I'm too timid and shy. My conscience would torment me to distraction. He comes here every day. I can guess why he comes and already I feel guilty. I want to fall on my knees before Sonya, to ask her forgiveness and cry.

ASTROV   [*Comes in with a chart*] Good morning to you! [*shakes hands*] You wanted to see my artistic handiwork?

YELENA   Yesterday you promised to show me some of your work. Are you free now?

ASTROV   But of course! [*spreads the chart on a card table and fixes it down with thumbtacks*] Tell me, where were you born?

YELENA   [*Helping him*] In Petersburg.

ASTROV   And where did you study?

YELENA   At the School of Music.

ASTROV   I don't suppose this will interest you.

YELENA   Why not? It's true I don't know the country, but I've read a great deal.

ASTROV   I have a table of my own here. . . . In Ivan Petrovich's room. When I'm completely tired out—to the point of utter stupefaction—I leave everything and escape here to amuse myself for an hour or two with this thing. Ivan Petrovich and Sofya Aleksandrovna click away at their counting beads, and I sit beside them at my table and mess around with my paints— and I'm warm and quiet, and the cricket chirps. But I don't allow myself this pleasure very often, just once a month. [*pointing to the chart*] Now look at this. It's a map of our district as it was fifty years ago. The dark and light green stand for forest; half of the whole area was covered with forest. Where there's a sort of network of red over the green, elk and wild goats were common. I show both the flora and the fauna here. This lake was the home of swans, geese, and ducks. There was "a power" of birds, as the old people say, of all kinds, no end to them: they used to fly around in clouds. Besides the villages and hamlets you can see all sorts of small settlements scattered here and there—little farms, monasteries, watermills. Cattle and horses were numerous—that's shown by the blue color. For instance there's a lot of blue in this part of the region. There was any number of horses here, and every homestead had three on the average. [*pause*] Now let us look lower down. This is how it was twenty-five years ago. Already only a third of the area is under forest. The goats have disappeared, but there are still some elk. The green and the blue colors are paler, and so on. Now look at the third section— the map showing the district as it is now. There's still some green here and there, but it's not continuous—it's in patches. The elk, swans, and woodgrouse have all disappeared. There's not a trace of the small farms and monasteries and mills that were there before. In general it's an unmistakable picture of gradual decay which will obviously be completed in another ten or fifteen years. You may say that it is the influence of civilization, that the old way of life naturally had to give place to the new. Yes and I would agree—if on the site of these ruined forests there were now roads and railways, if there were workshops and factories and schools. Then the people would have been healthier, better off, and better educated. But there's nothing of the sort here! There are still the same swamps and mosquitoes, the same absence of roads and the dire poverty and typhus and diphtheria and fires. Here we have a picture of decay due to an insupportable struggle for existence. It is decay caused by inertia, by ignorance, by utter irresponsibility—as when a sick, hungry, shivering man, simply to save what is left of his life and to protect his children, instinctively, unconsciously clutches at anything that will satisfy his hunger and keep him warm and in doing so destroys everything, without a thought for tomorrow. Already practically everything has been destroyed, but nothing has been created to take its place. [*coldly*] I see from your expression that it doesn't interest you.

YELENA   But I understand so little about all this.

ASTROV   There's nothing to understand. You're just not interested.

YELENA   To be quite frank, my mind was on something else. Forgive me. I want to put you through a little interrogation, and I feel rather embarrassed. I don't know how to begin.

ASTROV   An interrogation?

YELENA   Yes, an interrogation, but . . . a fairly innocent one. Let's sit down! [*they sit down*] It concerns a certain young person. We'll talk frankly, like friends, without beating around the bush. We'll talk it over and forget everything we said. Agreed?

ASTROV   Agreed.

YELENA   The matter concerns my stepdaughter, Sonya. Tell me, do you like her?

ASTROV   Yes, I respect her.

YELENA   Do you like her as a woman?

ASTROV   [*After a brief pause*] No.

YELENA   One thing more—and that'll be the end. Have you noticed anything?

ASTROV   Nothing.

YELENA   [*Taking him by the hand*] You don't love her, I see it from your eyes. She is suffering. Understand that, and . . . stop coming here.

ASTROV [*Rises*] My time's past. Besides I've got too much to do. [*shrugging his shoulders*] When could I find time? [*he is embarrassed*]

YELENA Ough! What an unpleasant conversation! I feel as though I've been carrying a ton weight around. Anyway we've finished now, thank heaven! Let's forget it, as if we hadn't talked at all, and . . . and go away. You're an intelligent man; you will understand. [*pause*] I feel I'm quite flushed.

ASTROV If you'd told me a month or two ago, I might perhaps have considered it, but now . . . [*shrugs his shoulders*] But if she is suffering, then of course . . . There's only one thing I don't understand: why did you have to have this interrogation? [*looks into her eyes and shakes his finger at her*] You're a sly one!

YELENA What does that mean?

ASTROV [*Laughs*] Sly! Suppose Sonya is suffering—I'm prepared to think it probable—but what was the purpose of this cross-examination? [*preventing her from speaking, with animation*] Please don't try to look astonished. You know perfectly well why I come here every day. Why and on whose account—you know very well indeed. You charming bird of prey, don't look at me like that; I'm a wise old sparrow.

YELENA [*Perplexed*] Bird of prey! I don't understand at all!

ASTROV A beautiful, fluffy weasel . . . You must have a victim! Here I've been doing nothing for a whole month. I've dropped everything. I seek you out hungrily—and you are awfully pleased about it, awfully. Well, what am I to say? I'm conquered, but you knew that without an interrogation! [*crossing his arms and bowing his head*] I submit. Here I am; devour me!

YELENA Have you gone out of your mind?

ASTROV [*Laughs sardonically*] You are coy.

YELENA Oh, I'm not so bad or not so mean as you think! On my word of honor! [*tries to go out*]

ASTROV [*Barring her way*] I'll go away today. I won't come here again, but . . . [*takes her by the hand and glances around*] Where shall I see you? Tell me quickly, where? Someone may come in here; tell me quickly. [*passionately*] How wonderful, how glorious you are! One kiss . . . If I could only kiss your fragrant hair . . .

YELENA I swear to you . . .

ASTROV [*Prevents her from speaking*] Why swear anything? There's no need to. No need for unnecessary words. Oh, how beautiful you are! What lovely hands! [*kisses her hands*]

YELENA That's enough. . . . Go away. [*withdraws her hands*] You are forgetting yourself.

ASTROV Speak, speak! Where shall we meet tomorrow? [*puts his arm around her waist*] You see, it's inevitable—we must see each other. [*kisses her*]

At that moment Voynitski comes in with a bunch of roses and stops just inside the door

YELENA [*Not seeing Voynitski*] Spare me. . . . Leave me alone. [*lays her head on Astrov's chest*] No! [*tries to go out*]

ASTROV [*Holding her by the waist*] Come to the plantation tomorrow about two o'clock. Yes? Yes? You will come?

YELENA [*Seeing Voynitski*] Let me go! [*in extreme confusion goes to the window*] This is dreadful!

VOYNITSKI [*Lays the roses on a chair; in agitation wipes his face and neck with a handkerchief*] Never mind . . . no . . . never mind.

ASTROV [*With bravado*] The weather is not too bad today, my dear Ivan Petrovich. It was overcast in the morning as though it were going to rain, but now it's sunny. It must be admitted that the autumn has turned out very fine . . . and the winter corn is quite promising. [*rolls up his chart*] The only thing is— the days are getting short. [*goes out*]

YELENA [*Goes quickly up to Voynitski*] You will try, you will do your utmost to see that my husband and I leave here today for certain? Do you hear? Today for certain!

VOYNITSKI [*Wiping his face*] What? Oh, yes . . . very well. . . .

YELENA [*Nervously*] Do you hear? I must get away from here this very day!

Enter Serebryakov, Sonya, Telegin, and Marina

TELEGIN I'm not feeling too well myself, Your Excellency. I've been doing poorly for the last two days. Something the matter with my head . . .

SEREBRYAKOV   But where are the others? I don't like this house. It's like a sort of labyrinth. Twenty-six enormous rooms, people wander off in all directions, and there's no finding anyone. [*rings*] Ask Marya Vasilievna and Yelena Andreyevna to come here!

YELENA   I'm here.

SEREBRYAKOV   Please sit down, my friends.

SONYA   [*Going up to Yelena, impatiently*] What did he say?

YELENA   I'll tell you later.

SONYA   You're trembling? You're upset? [*looks searchingly into her face*] I understand. He said he wouldn't be coming here anymore . . . yes? [*pause*] Tell me: yes?

Yelena nods her head

SEREBRYAKOV   [*To Telegin*] One can put up with ill health after all. But what I can't stomach is the whole pattern of life in the country. I feel as if I had been cast off the earth on to some strange planet. Do sit down, friends, please! Sonya!

Sonya does not hear him; she stands and hangs her head sadly

Sonya! [*pause*] She doesn't hear. [*to Marina*] You sit down too, Nanny.

The nurse sits down and starts knitting a stocking

I beg you, my friends, lend me your ears, as the saying goes. [*laughs*]

VOYNITSKI   [*Agitated*] Maybe I'm not needed here? Can I go?

SEREBRYAKOV   No, you're needed more than anyone.

VOYNITSKI   What do you require from me?

SEREBRYAKOV   Require from you . . . Why—are you annoyed at something? [*pause*] If I've offended you in any way, please excuse me.

VOYNITSKI   You don't have to adopt that tone. Let's come to business. What is it you want?

Enter Marya Vasilievna

SEREBRYAKOV Here is *Maman*. Let me begin, my friends. [*pause*] I have invited you here, ladies and gentlemen, to inform you that the inspector general is coming to visit us. But, joking apart, this is a serious matter. I have called you together, my friends, to ask your help and advice and, knowing how obliging you always are, I hope to receive it. I'm an academic, bookish man, and I've never had anything to do with practical life. I must have guidance from people better informed than I am, and so I want to ask you, Ivan Petrovich, and also you, Ilya Ilyich, and you, *Maman*. The point is, *manet omnes una nox:* we are all mortal. I'm an old and ailing man, and I think it's high time to settle the matter of my property in so far as it concerns my family. My own life is over now; I'm not thinking of myself. But I have a young wife and an unmarried daughter. [*pause*] It is impossible for me to go on living in the country. We are not made for country life. But to live in town on the income we are receiving from this estate is also impossible. Suppose we sold the forest—that would be an exceptional measure that could not be repeated every year. We must find ways that will guarantee us a permanent, more or less definite income. One such measure has occurred to me, and I would like to submit it for your consideration. Omitting the details, I will describe it in rough outline. Our estate yields on the average not more than two percent on its capital value. I suggest we sell it. If we invest the money in suitable securities, we should get from four to five percent, and I think we might even have a few thousand rubles to spare, which would enable us to buy a small villa in Finland.

VOYNITSKI Wait a moment. Surely I haven't been hearing correctly. Say that again.

SEREBRYAKOV I suggest putting the money in suitable securities and with whatever is left buying a villa in Finland.

VOYNITSKI Not Finland. You said something else.

SEREBRYAKOV I suggested we sell the estate.

VOYNITSKI That's it. You sell the estate—that's a fine idea— magnificent. And where do you propose I should go—with my old mother and Sonya here?

SEREBRYAKOV We will discuss all that in due course. We can't do everything at once.

VOYNITSKI Wait a moment. It looks as though I must have been incredibly stupid all this time. Until now I've been foolish enough to believe that this estate belonged to Sonya. My father bought it as a dowry for my sister. I've been too simple; not interpreting the law like a Turk, I thought that my sister's estate passed to Sonya.

SEREBRYAKOV Yes, the estate belongs to Sonya. Who's disputing it? Without Sonya's consent I will not venture to sell it. Besides I am suggesting that this should be done for Sonya's benefit.

VOYNITSKI Its inconceivable, inconceivable! Either I've gone out of my mind or . . . or . . .

MARYA VASILIEVNA Jean, don't contradict Aleksandr. Believe me, he knows better than we do what's good for us and what isn't.

VOYNITSKI No, give me some water. [*drinks water*] Say what you like, anything!

SEREBRYAKOV I don't understand why you're so upset. I'm not saying that my plan is ideal. If everybody finds it unsuitable, I won't insist on it.

TELEGIN [*Embarrassed*] Toward learning, Your Excellency, I have not merely a feeling of reverence, but a sort of family relationship as well. The brother of my brother's wife, Konstantin Trofimovich Lakedemonov—perhaps you know him? —was an M.A.

VOYNITSKI Stop, Waffles, we're talking business. Wait a little. . . . Later on. [*to Serebryakov*] Here, ask him. This estate was bought from his uncle.

SEREBRYAKOV Indeed! But why should I ask him? Why ever . . . ?

VOYNITSKI The estate was originally bought for ninety-five thousand rubles. My father only paid seventy thousand, and twenty-five thousand remained on mortgage. Now please do listen. This estate would never have been bought if I hadn't given up my share of the inheritance in favor of my sister, whom I loved dearly. What's more, I worked like an ox for ten years and paid off the whole mortgage.

SEREBRYAKOV I regret that I started this discussion.

VOYNITSKI The estate is free from debt and in good condition simply because of my own efforts. And now that I've grown old, I'm to be kicked out!

SEREBRYAKOV   I don't understand what you're driving at!

VOYNITSKI   For twenty-five years I've been managing this estate! I've been working and sending you money like the most conscientious steward you could have, but all this time you've never once thanked me for it. All this time—when I was young, and now just the same—I've been getting a salary of five hundred rubles a year from you—a pittance!—and never once have you thought of adding a single ruble to it!

SEREBRYAKOV   Ivan Petrovich, how was I to know? I'm not a practical man. I don't understand anything about these matters. You could have added as much as you liked.

VOYNITSKI   Yes indeed, why didn't I steal? Why don't you all laugh at me now because I didn't steal? It would have been fair enough, and I wouldn't have been a pauper now!

MARYA VASILIEVNA   [*Sternly*] Jean!

TELEGIN   [*In agitation*] Vanya, my dear, don't, don't. . . . I'm all trembling. Why spoil our good relations? [*embraces him*] You mustn't.

VOYNITSKI   For twenty-five years I sat with my mother here, buried like a mole in these four walls. All our thoughts and feelings belonged to you alone. By day we talked of you and your work. We were proud of you; we uttered your name with reverence. We wasted our nights reading books and magazines, which now fill me with contempt.

TELEGIN   Don't, Vanya, don't. . . . I can't bear it.

SEREBRYAKOV   [*Angrily*] I don't understand what it is you want.

VOYNITSKI   To us you were a being of a higher order, and we knew your articles by heart. But now my eyes are opened! I can see it all! You write about art, but you don't understand anything about art! All your works, those works which I used to love, are not worth a kopeck! You've been deceiving us!

SEREBRYAKOV   Make him stop this! I'll go!

YELENA   Ivan Petrovich, I insist that you stop. Do you hear?

VOYNITSKI   I will not be silent! [*barring Serebryakov's way*] Wait; I haven't finished yet! You've ruined my life! I haven't lived. I have not lived! Thanks to you I've destroyed, I've annihilated, the best years of my life! You've been my worst enemy!

TELEGIN   I can't bear it. . . . I can't. . . . I'm going. [*goes out in great agitation*]

SEREBRYAKOV   What do you want from me? And what right have you to speak to me like this? You nonentity! If the estate is yours, take it! I don't need it!

YELENA   I'm going to get away from this hell this very minute! [*screams*] I can't stand it any longer!

VOYNITSKI   My life is ruined! I have talent, courage, intelligence. If I had had a normal life, I might have been a Schopenhauer, a Dostoevski. . . . Oh, I'm talking rubbish! I'm going out of my mind. Mother, I'm in despair! Mother!

MARYA VASILIEVNA   [*Sternly*] Do as Aleksandr tells you.

SONYA   [*Kneels before the nurse and huddles up against her*] Nanny! Nanny!

VOYNITSKI   Mother! What am I to do? No, you don't have to tell me! I know what I must do. [*to Serebryakov*] You'll remember me! [*goes out through middle door*]

Marya Vasilievna follows him

SEREBRYAKOV   What does he mean by this behavior? Take the madman away! I can't possibly live under the same roof with him. He lives there [*points at the middle door*] almost next door to me. Make him move into the village or into the lodge —or I'll move—but I can't remain in the same house with him.

YELENA   [*To her husband*] We'll leave here today! We must make arrangements immediately.

SEREBRYAKOV   That nonentity!

SONYA   [*On her knees, turns to her father and speaks tearfully and with agitation*] You must have pity, Papa! Uncle Vanya and I are so unhappy! [*restraining her despair*] You must have pity! Remember—when you were younger Uncle Vanya and Grandmamma used to spend whole nights translating books for you, copying your papers. . . . Whole nights on end! Whole nights! Uncle Vanya and I worked incessantly; we were afraid to spend a kopeck on ourselves and sent it all to you. We really did earn our daily bread! I'm saying it all wrong—all wrong—but you must understand us, Papa! You must be charitable!

YELENA [*In agitation, to her husband*] Aleksandr, for heaven's sake, go and talk it over with him. I implore you!

SEREBRYAKOV Very well, I will talk it over with him. I'm not accusing him of anything; I'm not angry. But you must agree with me that his behavior is very strange, to say the least of it. Very well, I'll go and see him. [*goes out through the middle door*]

YELENA Be as gentle as you can with him. Try to reassure him. [*follows him*]

SONYA [*Nestling up to the nurse*] Nanny! Nanny!

MARINA Never mind, child. The ganders will cackle a bit—and then they'll leave off. They'll cackle and leave off.

SONYA Nanny!

MARINA [*Stroking her head*] You're shivering as if you were out in a frost! There, there, my little orphan, God is merciful. A drink of lime-flower tea or hot raspberry, and it'll go away. . . . Don't get so upset, my little orphan. [*looking at the middle door, with annoyance*] What a row they're making, the ganders! Damn them!

A shot is heard offstage, then a shriek from Yelena; Sonya starts

Ough! Damn them!

SEREBRYAKOV [*Runs in, staggering in terror*] Stop him! Stop him! He's gone mad!

Yelena and Voynitski struggle in the doorway

YELENA [*Trying to take a revolver from him*] Give it to me! Give it to me, I tell you!

VOYNITSKI Let me go, Hélène! Let me go! [*freeing himself from her, runs in and looks around for Serebryakov*] Where is he? Ah, there he is! [*fires at him*] Bang! [*pause*] Missed? Missed again! [*furiously*] Damn it! . . . Devil . . . devil take it! [*flings the revolver on the floor and sinks onto a chair, exhausted*]

Serebryakov looks stunned. Yelena leans against the wall, almost fainting

YELENA   Take me away from here! Take me away! Kill me! . . . But I can't stay here, I can't!

VOYNITSKI   [*In despair*] Oh, what have I done? What am I doing?

SONYA   [*Softly*] Nanny, dear! Nanny!

CURTAIN

ACT FOUR

*Voynitski's room, which serves both as his bedroom and his of-
fice. By the window a large table with account books and various
papers; also a bureau, bookcases, and scales. A smaller table is set
apart for Astrov with paints, drawing materials, and a large portfolio. A cage with a starling in it. On the wall a map of Africa,
obviously serving no useful purpose here. A large divan uphol-
stered in American cloth. On the left, a door leading to other
rooms; on the right, a door into the hall. In front of the right-hand
door there is a mat to protect the floor from mud from the peasants' boots. It is an autumn evening and is very quiet.*

*Telegin and Marina, sitting opposite one another, are winding
wool.*

TELEGIN Hurry up, Marina Timofeevna. They'll soon be calling
us to say good-bye. They've ordered the horses to be brought
around.

MARINA [*Tries to wind faster*] There isn't much left.

TELEGIN They're going to Kharkov. Going to live there.

MARINA That will be much better.

TELEGIN They've had a fright. Yelena Andreyevna keeps saying,
"I won't stay here another hour. Let's get away. Let's get
away." "When we've lived in Kharkov for a bit and had a look
around, we'll send for our things," she says. They're traveling
light. It seems they're not ordained to live here, Marina Timofeevna. They're not ordained to. Such is the will of Providence.

MARINA   It's better so. The row they made this morning—and shooting too—a regular disgrace!

TELEGIN   Yes, a subject worthy of the brush of Ayvazovski, one might say.

MARINA   What a sight for my old eyes! [*pause*] We'll be living again as we used to—in the old way. Morning tea soon after seven, dinner at twelve, and in the evening we'll sit down to supper. Everything as it should be, just like other people. . . . Like Christians. [*with a sigh*] It's a long time since I tasted noodles, sinner that I am!

TELEGIN   Yes, it's a long time since they had noodles in this house. [*pause*] A very long time. Marina Timofeevna, as I was walking through the village this morning, the shopkeeper shouted after me, "Hey, you scrounger . . . Living on other people, you are!" I felt so hurt!

MARINA   You shouldn't take any notice, dearie. We all live on God. You and Sonya and Ivan Petrovich are just the same. None of us sits with folded hands; we are all working—all of us! Where's Sonya?

TELEGIN   In the garden. She keeps walking around with the doctor looking for Ivan Petrovich. They're afraid he may do himself harm.

MARINA   Where's his revolver?

TELEGIN   [*In a whisper*] I've hidden it in the cellar.

MARINA   [*With a smile*] What goings-on!

Enter Voynitski and Astrov from outside

VOYNITSKI   Leave me alone. [*to Marina and Telegin*] Please go away from here. Leave me alone—if it's only for an hour! I can't stand this supervision.

TELEGIN   Of course, Vanya. [*goes out on tiptoe*]

MARINA   You old gander! Ga-ga-ga! [*gathers up her wool and goes out*]

VOYNITSKI   Leave me alone!

ASTROV   With the greatest pleasure! I should have left here hours ago, but I must repeat I'm not going away until you give me back what you took from me.

VOYNITSKI   I haven't taken anything from you.

ASTROV I'm speaking seriously—don't keep me waiting. I should have gone long ago.

VOYNITSKI I didn't take anything from you. [*both sit down*]

ASTROV No? Well, I'll wait a little longer; and then, I'm sorry, but I'll have to use force. We'll tie your hands together and search you. I'm speaking absolutely in earnest.

VOYNITSKI As you please. [*pause*] To have made such a fool of myself—firing twice and missing both times! I will never forgive myself for that!

ASTROV If you really felt like shooting someone, you might as well have taken a potshot at yourself.

VOYNITSKI [*Shrugging his shoulders*] It's queer! Here I've tried to commit a murder, and yet no one arrests me, no one charges me with anything. It must mean they think I'm a madman. [*with an angry laugh*] I'm mad—but people who conceal their utter lack of talent, their dullness, their complete heartlessness, under the guise of the professor, the purveyor of learned magic—they aren't mad. Women aren't mad who marry old men and then deceive them for everyone to see. I saw you with your arms around her! I saw it!

ASTROV Yes, I did put my arms around her, and as for you—you can take this. [*thumbs his nose at him*]

VOYNITSKI [*Looking at the door*] The earth must be mad because it still supports you.

ASTROV Now you're being just silly!

VOYNITSKI Well, I'm mad. I'm irresponsible. I have the right to say silly things.

ASTROV That's an old trick. You're not mad; you're simply a crank. A silly old fool. I used to think that every crank was sick or abnormal. But now I believe it's normal for a man to be a crank. You are perfectly normal.

VOYNITSKI [*Covers his face with his hands*] I feel so ashamed. If you only knew how ashamed I feel! This acute sense of shame—it's worse than any pain! [*miserably*] It's unbearable. [*leans over the table*] What am I to do? What am I to do?

ASTROV Nothing.

VOYNITSKI Give me something! Oh, my God! I'm forty-seven. If I live to be sixty, I've got another thirteen years. What a time! How am I to get through those thirteen years? What shall I do? How shall I fill in the time? Ah, don't you see . . . [*squeezing Astrov's hand convulsively*] Don't you see, if only you could live the rest of your life in some new way! To wake up on a clear, calm morning and feel that you're starting your life over again, that all your past is forgotten, blown away like smoke. [*weeps*] To begin a new life . . . Tell me how to begin. . . . What with . . .

ASTROV [*With annoyance*] Oh, get away with you! A new life indeed! Our situation's hopeless—yours and mine!

VOYNITSKI Do you mean that?

ASTROV I'm certain of it.

VOYNITSKI Give me something. [*pointing at his heart*] I've a burning sensation here.

ASTROV [*Shouts angrily*] Shut up! [*softening*] The people who come a hundred years or a couple of hundred years after us and despise us for having lived in so stupid and tasteless a fashion—perhaps they'll find a way to be happy. As for us . . . There's only one hope for you and me. The hope that when we're at rest in our graves we may see visions—perhaps even pleasant ones. [*with a sigh*] Yes, my friend! In the whole of this province there have only been two decent, cultured people—you and I. But ten years of this contemptible routine, this trivial provincial life, has swallowed us up, poisoned our blood with its putrid vapors, until now we've become just as petty as all the rest. [*with a sudden animation*] But don't you try to talk me out of it: give me back what you took from me.

VOYNITSKI I didn't take anything from you.

ASTROV You took a bottle of morphine out of my traveling medicine chest. [*pause*] Look here now: if you really feel you must put an end to yourself, why don't you go to the woods and shoot yourself there? But do give me back the morphine or else there will be talk and suspicion. People might think I'd given it to you. It'll be quite enough to have to do your postmortem. Do you think I will find it interesting?

Enter Sonya

VOYNITSKI Leave me alone.

ASTROV [*To Sonya*] Sofya Aleksandrovna, your uncle has stolen a bottle of morphine from my medicine chest and won't give it back. Tell him that it's . . . well . . . it's not a bit clever of him. Besides I haven't the time to waste. I ought to be going.

SONYA   Uncle Vanya, did you take the morphine?

ASTROV   [*After a pause*] He did. I'm certain of it.

SONYA   Give it back. Why do you frighten us like this? [*with tenderness*] Give it back, Uncle Vanya! I must say I'm just as unhappy as you are, but I don't despair all the same. I bear it, and I will continue to bear it till my life comes to its natural end. You must bear it too. [*pause*] Give it back! [*kisses his hand*] My dear, kind uncle—give it up, dear! [*weeps*] You're so good; I know you'll feel sorry for us and give it back. You'll have to bear it, Uncle! You must bear it!

VOYNITSKI   [*Takes a bottle out of his desk and hands it to Astrov*] Here, take it! [*to Sonya*] But we must start work at once; we must start doing something or else I can't . . . I can't . . .

SONYA   Yes, yes, work. As soon as we've seen the others off, we'll settle down to work. [*nervously turning over the papers on the table*] We've been neglecting everything.

ASTROV   [*Puts the bottle into his case and tightens the straps*] Now I can be on my way.

Enter Yelena

YELENA   Ivan Petrovich, are you here? We're just going. Go and see Aleksandr; he wants to say something to you.

SONYA   Go along, Uncle Vanya. [*takes Voynitski's arm*] Let's go. You and Papa must make it up. It's essential.

Sonya and Voynitski go out

YELENA   I'm going away. [*gives Astrov her hand*]

ASTROV   Already?

YELENA   The horses are waiting.

ASTROV   Good-bye.

YELENA   Today you promised me you'd go away from here.

ASTROV   I haven't forgotten. I'm just going. [*pause*] Did you get frightened? [*takes her hand*] Is it really so frightening?

YELENA   Yes.

ASTROV   Why not stay all the same? Well? Tomorrow, at the
plantation . . .

YELENA   No. It's settled. The reason I'm looking at you so fear-
lessly now is just that our departure has been settled. I only
ask one thing of you: do think better of me. I would like you
to respect me.

ASTROV   Oh! [*makes a gesture of impatience*] Stay, I beg you.
You must admit you have nothing whatever to do, you have
absolutely no object in life, nothing to occupy your mind with;
so that sooner or later you'll be bound to give way to your feelings—it's inevitable. And it will be better if that happens not
in Kharkov or somewhere in Kursk, but down here in the lap
of nature. At least it's poetical here, quite beautiful in fact.
There are forestry plantations, half-ruined country houses in
the Turgenev style. . . .

YELENA   How funny you are. . . . I'm angry with you, and
yet . . . I'll remember you with pleasure. You're an interesting, original man. We will never see each other again, and so
why should I conceal it? You did turn my head a little. Come,
let us shake hands and part friends. Think well of me.

ASTROV   [*Shakes hands with her*] Yes, you'd better go. [*musing*]
You seem to be so good and warmhearted, and yet there's
something strange about your personality. You just happened
to come along with your husband, and all of us here, who'd
been working and running around and trying to create something, we all had to drop everything and occupy ourselves
wholly with you and your husband's gout. You two infected
all of us with your indolence. I was attracted by you and I've
done nothing for a whole month. And in the meantime people
have been ill and the peasants have been using my woods, my
plantations of young trees, as pasture for their cattle. So you
see, wherever you and your husband go, you bring along destruction with you. I'm joking, of course, but still . . . it *is*
strange. I'm convinced that if you'd stayed on here the devas-
tation would have been immense. I would have been
ruined . . . and you wouldn't have fared too well either. Go
away then. *La commedia è finita!*

YELENA   [*Takes a pencil from his table and quickly puts it in her
pocket*] I'm taking this pencil as a keepsake.

ASTROV   It is strange somehow. Here we've known one another, and all at once for some reason . . . we will never see each other again. That's the way with everything in this world. While there's no one here—before Uncle Vanya comes in with a bunch of flowers—allow me . . . to kiss you . . . good-bye. Yes? [*kisses her on the cheek*] There . . . That's fine.

YELENA   I wish you every happiness. [*looks around*] Well, here goes—for once in my life! [*embraces him impulsively, and both at once quickly step back from each other*] I must be off.

ASTROV   Go as soon as you can. If the horses are ready, you'd better be off!

YELENA   I think someone's coming. [*both listen*]

ASTROV   *Finita!*

Enter Serebryakov, Voynitski, Marya Vasilievna carrying a book, Telegin, and Sonya

SEREBRYAKOV   Let us let bygones be bygones. What with everything that's happened, I've thought and lived through so much in the last few hours that I believe I could write a whole treatise on how one should conduct one's life—for the benefit of posterity. I gladly accept your apologies and I ask you to forgive me too. Good-bye! [*he and Voynitski embrace and kiss each other three times*]

VOYNITSKI   You'll be receiving the same amount as before, regularly. Everything will be as it was before.

Yelena embraces Sonya

SEREBRYAKOV   [*Kisses Marya Vasilievna's hand*] Maman . . .

MARYA   [*Kissing him*] Aleksandr, do have your photograph taken again and send it to me. You know how much you mean to me.

TELEGIN   Good-bye, Your Excellency! Don't forget us!

SEREBRYAKOV   [*Kisses his daughter*] Good-bye. Good-bye everyone! [*shakes hands with Astrov*] Thank you for the pleasure of your company. I respect your attitude of mind, your enthusiasms, your spontaneity; but permit an old man to add one thing to his farewell greetings: you must try to do real work, my friends, yes, real work! [*he bows to them all*] I wish you all happiness and good fortune! [*goes out, followed by Marya Vasilievna and Sonya*]

VOYNITSKI [*Warmly kisses Yelena's hand*] Good-bye. Forgive me. We will never see one another again.

YELENA [*Moved*] Good-bye, dear Ivan Petrovich. [*kisses him on the head and goes out*]

ASTROV [*To Telegin*] Waffles, you might tell them to bring my horses around too.

TELEGIN Certainly, my dear friend. [*goes out*]

Astrov and Voynitski remain alone

ASTROV [*Clears the paints from the table and puts them away in his case*] Well, why don't you go and see them off?

VOYNITSKI Let them go. As for me—I . . . I can't. I'm depressed. I must occupy myself with something as soon as I can. Work, work! [*rummages among the papers*]

A pause. The sound of harness bells is heard

ASTROV They've gone. The professor's glad, that's certain. Wild horses won't drag him back.

MARINA [*Enters*] They've gone. [*sits down in an easy chair and knits a stocking*]

SONYA [*Enters*] They've gone. [*wipes her eyes*] God grant them a safe journey. [*to her uncle*] Well, Uncle Vanya, let's start doing something.

VOYNITSKI Work, work . . .

SONYA It's a long, long time since we sat at this table, just the two of us. [*lights the lamp on the table*] There doesn't seem to be any ink. [*takes the inkstand, goes to the cupboard, and fills it with ink*] But I feel sad now they've gone.

MARYA VASILIEVNA [*Comes in slowly*] Gone! [*sits down and becomes absorbed in reading*]

SONYA [*Sits down at the table and turns over the pages of the account book*] First of all, Uncle Vanya, let's write out the bills. We've neglected it all dreadfully. Someone sent for his account again today. You make it out. While you do one, I'll do another.

VOYNITSKI   [*Writes*]   Delivered . . . to . . . Mr. . . . [*both write in silence*]

MARINA   [*Yawns*] I feel like going to sleep. . . .

ASTROV   How quiet it is! The pens scratch, the cricket sings. It's warm and snug. I don't feel like leaving here.

The sound of harness bells is heard

My horses are coming. There's nothing left for me but to say good-bye to you, my friends—to say good-bye to my table and—be off! [*packs up his maps in the portfolio*]

MARINA   Why are you in such a hurry? I'd stay on if I were you.

ASTROV   I can't.

VOYNITSKI   [*Writes*] Remaining to your debit: two rubles, seventy-five kopecks.

A workman comes in

WORKMAN   Mikhail Lvovich, the horses are ready.

ASTROV   I heard them. [*hands him the medicine chest, the bag, and the portfolio*] Here, take these. See that you don't bend the portfolio.

WORKMAN   Very good, sir. [*goes out*]

ASTROV   Well . . . [*approaches them to say good-bye*]

SONYA   When will we see you again?

ASTROV   Not before next summer, I expect. Hardly in the winter. Naturally if anything happens you'll let me know and I'll come. [*shakes hands with them*] Thank you for your hospitality, your kindness—for everything, in fact. [*goes to the nurse and kisses her on the head*] Good-bye, old woman!

MARINA   So you're going before you've had tea?

ASTROV   I don't want any, Nurse.

MARINA   Perhaps you'll have a drop of vodka?

ASTROV   [*Irresolutely*] Perhaps . . .

Marina goes out

[*after a pause*] One of my horses has gone lame for some reason. I noticed it yesterday when Petrushka took it to water.

VOYNITSKI   You must change its shoes.

ASTROV   I'll have to call in at the blacksmith's in Rozhdestven-
noye. It can't be helped. [*walks up to the map of Africa and
looks at it*] I suppose down there in Africa the heat must be
terrific now!

VOYNITSKI   Yes, very likely.

MARINA   [*Returns carrying a tray with a glass of vodka and a
piece of bread*] Here you are.

Astrov drinks vodka

Good health, my dear. [*makes a low bow*] Why don't you eat
some bread with it?

ASTROV   No, that'll do for me. Well, good luck to you all! [*to
Marina*] Don't see me off, Nurse. There's no need to.

*Astrov goes out, Sonya following with a candle to see him off.
Marina sits down in her easy chair*

VOYNITSKI   [*Writing*] February the second, linseed oil, twenty
pounds. . . . February the sixteenth, linseed oil again, twenty
pounds. Buckwheat . . .

A pause. The sound of harness bells is heard

MARINA   He's gone. . . .

SONYA   [*After a pause, comes back and puts the candle on the
table*] He's gone.

VOYNITSKI   [*Counts on the abacus and writes down*] Total
. . . fifteen . . . twenty-five . . .

MARINA   [*Yawns*] Lord forgive us our sins.

*Telegin enters on tiptoe, sits down by the door, and quietly
tunes his guitar*

VOYNITSKI   [*To Sonya, passing his hand over her hair*] My child,
there's such a weight on my heart! Oh, if only you knew how
my heart aches!

SONYA   Well, what can we do? We must go on living! [*pause*] We will go on living, Uncle Vanya. We will live through a long, long succession of days and tedious evenings. We will patiently suffer the trials that fate imposes on us. We will work for others, now and in our old age, and we will have no rest. When our time comes we will die submissively, and over there, beyond the grave, we will say that we've suffered, that we've wept, that we've had a bitter life, and God will take pity on us. And then, Uncle dear, we will both begin to know a life that is bright and beautiful and lovely. We will rejoice and look back at these troubles of ours with tender feelings, with a smile. And we will have rest. I believe it, Uncle, I believe it fervently, passionately. [*kneels before him and lays her head on his hands; then, in a tired voice*] We will have rest!

Telegin plays softly on the guitar

We will rest! We will hear the angels, we will see all the heavens covered with stars like diamonds, we will see all earthly evil, all our sufferings, swept away by the grace that will fill the whole world. And our life will become peaceful, gentle, and sweet as a caress. I believe it, I believe it. . . . [*wipes his eyes with her handkerchief*] Poor, poor Uncle Vanya, you're crying. [*tearfully*] You've had no joy in your life, but wait, Uncle Vanya, wait. . . . We will rest. . . . [*embraces him*] We will rest!

The watchman taps. Marya Vasilievna makes notes on the margin of her pamphlet. Marina knits her stocking

We will rest!

THE CURTAIN DROPS SLOWLY